THE CHIRICAHUA JOURNALS

2014

Sherri:

Enjoy these tales
from the Old Homestead.

Love,
Michael

THE CHIRICAHUA JOURNALS

STORIES OF ARIZONA LAWMEN, COWBOYS, & MINERS IN THE OLD AND NEW WEST

REVISED AND EXPANDED 2ND EDITION

R.W. MORROW

CHIRICAHUA PRESS TUCSON, ARIZONA

This edition was edited and prepared for printing by:
Michael W. Morrow
The Chiricahua Press
4402 E. Presidio Place
Tucson, AZ 85712-1121

Front cover photograph:	Cliff Darnell with Ten-Horse Jerk-Line Team, Early 1900s *Courtesy of Cliff Darnell's daughter, Sally Richards*
Back cover photographs:	R.W. Morrow, Webb Air Force Base, 1953 *Morrow Family Collection*
	Ralph Morrow on horseback, 1965 *Morrow Family Collection*
	Carson Morrow in front of Tucson Border Patrol Headquarters, 1944 *Courtesy of the National Border Patrol Museum, El Paso, Texas*
Cover design by:	Michael W. Morrow

ISBN: 978-0-9824841-1-1

Library of Congress Control Number: 2010908333

Printed in the United States of America

First Printing: September, 2010

10 9 8 7 6 5 4 3 2

Contents

PHOTOGRAPHS AND DOCUMENTS

Acknowledgments and Introduction

Any true and honest dedication for a collection of sometimes rustic stories such as these must be first and foremost to the resilient, resourceful—and colorful—old timers, men and women alike, who really lived them.

Next, I must offer special thanks to my sister, Audrey Morrow Miller, who years ago had the foresight to commit the memories of so many people to audio tape; transcripts of these recordings were invaluable in the writing of much of this book.

Then, of course, I have to single out my uncle, Carson "Chief" Morrow: the lively collection of yarns he included in his *Chiricahua Bull Sheet* brought back the feeling of real life in the old west, and the old times in the Chiricahuas.

Contributions from my wise and patient wife Patricia Morrow, and my well-traveled and knowledgeable daughter Mollie Morrow, were of great value in the writing and revising of the many versions of this manuscript.

Last but not least, the man who took what I now consider a "jumped-up" first edition of the *Journals* and made this second edition into a real book is my son, "the Editor" Michael Morrow. He devoted many hours to historical research, made dozens of text corrections, and added many new photographs and figures to this edition. Moreover, he got the manuscript itself—along with a handsome new cover—ready for "digital printing," a mysterious and somewhat daunting process for someone such as myself who hails from the "hot-lead" era of typesetting. It could never have happened without him.

¡Muchas gracias, compañero y asociado!

R.W. MORROW
AUGUST 2010

The Author (left), and the Editor (right), 1966

For additional copies of *The Chiricahua Journals*, mail a $20.00 check, payable to Michael Morrow, to the following address:

4402 E. Presidio Pl.
Tucson, AZ 85712-1121

Bulk-order discounts from the Chiricahua Press are also available. Please direct pricing inquiries to the address above.

You may also purchase *The Chiricahua Journals* from Amazon.com or BarnesAndNoble.com, or at one of these local vendors:

Rodeo, New Mexico

- *The Chiricahua Desert Museum*
  4 Rattlesnake Canyon Rd
  (NM Highway 80 & Portal Road)
  575-557-5757
  desertmuseum@gmail.com

Silver City, New Mexico

- *High-Lonesome Books*
  P.O. Box 878
  Silver City, NM   88062
  800-380-7323
  Orders@High-LonesomeBooks.com

Willcox, Arizona

- *Western National Parks Bookstore*
  Chiricahua National Monument
  13063 E. Bonita Canyon Rd.
  Willcox, AZ   85643
  520-824-3560

Tucson, Arizona

- *Western National Parks Bookstore*
  12880 N. Vistoso Village Drive
  Tucson, AZ   85755
  520-622-1999
  info@wnpa.org

- *Mostly Books*
  6208 East Speedway
  Tucson, AZ   85712
  520-571-0110
  mostlybooks@cox.net

- *Bob Pugh*
  Trail to Yesterday Books
  P.O. Box 35905
  Tucson, AZ   85740
  520-293-1260
  520-299-8517

THE GREAT WILLCOX BANK ROBBERY

On an early autumn day in 1976, Ralph Morrow was buried in the Paradise Cemetery of the Chiricahua Mountains. Many old-timers remember and reminisce and recount stories and happenings centered around and about him. This is one such story.

A game ranger, then an old head at the game of rangering, got to yarning about being a young recruit, and how he and Ralph Morrow left the Chiricahuas at, as the military oft says, "O Dark 30." They trailered their horses to the Dragoons, and after a hard day of riding and hiking, when the shadows were long, apprehended several violators of the game laws.

Anyway, this saddle-sore, leg-weary, hungry recruit began describing Morrow as looking like and acting like movie actor John Wayne. Well, that is not exactly so. Ralph Morrow was around six foot, three inches in height, and weighed, in fighting trim, 200 pounds.

He came to Arizona at age three from Roswell, New Mexico, where his family was in the ranching business. He was a cowboy, accomplished horseman, miner, and rancher, and even planted a substantial apple orchard in later years.

But, what he is most remembered for are his law-enforcement years, and these began in 1929.

Ralph Morrow said, "When I was in the game department so long ago, the first go-around, I was in the game department from 1929 until 1931. Then the game department suddenly was without funds. The Director, or State Game Warden, as he was called at that time, embezzled all the funds that were in the treasury. At that time, all he had to do was write checks, because it didn't have to go through the auditor's office. So, we were bilked. At the time I was offered a job as deputy sheriff in Cochise County."

After several years in the sheriff's department, Morrow was back in the department as a district ranger, regional supervisor and, until he arrested a member of one of the Game Commissioner's hunting party for violations of the game laws and would not back down, he had even been chief deputy in charge of law enforcement. The then director of the game department and a game commissioner tried to force Morrow to resign. He would not do so and stated, since the violation was of a federal nature, that he would take the case to Washington if he had to do so. He was demoted to district ranger and after retiring in 1963, became a Game Commissioner.

On cold nights around a crackling fire, and when summer evenings were long, beneath the sycamore trees, one was apt to talk of the old days and other times. Fortunately, someone would start a tape recorder, and that is how some stories are yet about. Now, to the Great Willcox Bank Robbery, circa 1931, as told by Ralph Morrow.

§   §   §

"My officer's experience took us into every class of law enforcement, from bank robbery to horse stealing. I'll just take time to tell you about one time. I got a call that a fellow by the name of Browning had lost a horse and saddle at Willcox.[1] I started out, up to Willcox, and when I got there, I got some more information that another horse had been stolen.

"I went ahead and caught this fellow who had stolen the horse that Browning lost. We got him about noon that same day some 30 or 40 miles from there, sent him back to jail in Willcox and I went on down to Animas, New Mexico. The next day I caught another man with two horses he had stolen in Animas. So we took him back, and they both went on and spent six months in jail in Lordsburg. They turned them loose, which was pretty good for that country.

"Bank robbing—that was going on also. I remember one morning in Douglas I received a call that the Willcox Bank had been robbed that morning. The court interpreter, Chino McMann, and I went there right fast, and when we got to Willcox, it was rather comical. All the bank officials were sitting in a back room, smoking cigars, and guessing what might have happened.

---

[1] Morrow operated out of Douglas, but covered the county as a range deputy.

"About that time, along came the railroad officer from Bowie who I had known around the Duncan area. I didn't trust the fellow at all, and in came a fellow by the name of Samuels who had been a cattle buyer in our region here some, with kind of a shady reputation. Right away, this railroad bull introduced me to Samuels and told me that the fella that robbed the bank had forced Samuels to park his car in front of the bank, and at gun point, Samuels was forced to carry the loot out of the bank, and so forth. I became pretty suspicious, because there was no point in telling me that windy story.

Ralph Morrow, Mormon church, Mexico, circa 1934
Holes in wall from Pancho Villa's firing squads

"Anyway, Samuels began telling us about how the robber had made his escape. He had forced everyone from the bank out into the car, and after about a quarter mile, they were dropped off every so often, one at a time. Samuels was driving the car. This fellow Hale, as his name turned out to be, he told Samuels to drive straight ahead, and the last banker he'd let off there noticed he didn't drive straight ahead. He turned and drove straight to the right. That was real odd that Samuels wouldn't take orders from a man sitting in the back with a gun pointed at Samuels' head.

"We went out with Samuels to the site he mentioned, and when we got to this place—in this country there are places where the ground is just slick, with no vegetation—we came to this spot, and I noticed Samuels' automobile had turned around three or four times there. This added to my suspicions.

"All these stories just didn't add up and make much sense. Samuels said, 'Now, right here, this robber, he forced me to stop at the point of a gun and threatened to kill me. If I'd had a gun, I'd have killed him when he walked away from the car. He told me to sit right here in this car until he was out of sight. And, not to move or he would kill me.'

"Samuels went to great pains to tell us this story. Tracks led right out from where the car was parked to about 100 yards across the slick flat, and ended at a big clump of grass, and someone had sat down in that grass. That was the end of the shoe tracks. I noticed there were tracks like bear tracks without any claws, and I surmised that the man had pulled off his shoes and walked back to the car.

"I began observing the shoe print Samuels' shoes were making, and noticed one of the shoes Samuels was wearing had a split in one heel. About then Samuels began telling me how clever this robber was, and had put lye on his tracks so that dogs would not be able to trail him.

"But, I saw that the lye that had been sifted onto the tracks was leached around the lye, which indicated that the lye was placed on the tracks the night before and the night moisture had moistened the lye.

"It was Samuels' tracks beneath the lye. Samuels saw the jig was up, and he got scared and tried to run back to the automobile, but I forced him to stop. I told my partner, Chino McMann, to search Samuels' car. He found a 30-30 with a 15-inch barrel, well-oiled and loaded to the brim. Samuels was trying to get hold of that 30-30.

"We took Samuels back to Willcox, and when we got there, it was really discouraging to see men so foolish as these bank men were, particularly Cummins, who was the bank president. We walked in the door with Samuels, and Samuels was plumb limber and willing to give it up, and he was not going to fight the case or anything. He was the bank robber in fact.

"We walked in and Samuels said, 'Well, I done it fellows. No doubt about it, I done it.' The fellow sitting there with the big cigar, this Cummins said, 'Yes, I know, Samuels, if you hadn't done what you were told to do you wouldn't be alive right now. The robber would have killed you for sure.'

"That put the wind back in Samuels' sails. He got on his feet, and even stood trial, however, he didn't make it. We caught his helper about two weeks later over at Hot Springs, New Mexico. He was a dope head, hophead. He broke down and told the whole story, and they both went up for a stretch.

"Samuels never was in the penitentiary, actually. I took some prisoners to the penitentiary shortly after that, and there was a well dressed man on the steps out front, looking out from under a big white hat, and it was nobody but Lem Samuels. He happened to be a friend of the warden, who hadn't seen fit to lock old Samuels up. That is the story of one of our great bank robberies."

BILLY BEN AND THE CAP ROCK DAM

Years past there was a comic strip by J.R. Williams called *Out Our Way*. Some were set in a ranch in the west, and cowboys working on the ranch. These cowboys had descriptive names such as "Curly" and "Stiffy" and "Cotton," and one sort of husky fellow who came from back east. He was, naturally, called "Wes."

One *Out Our Way* was titled "The Rusty King." In this panel, there was a man sitting on a mule. He was wearing brogan shoes and one spur. His hat was worn out, as was his saddle.

Wes says something like: "You mean to tell me that is so and so, the cattleman who owns thousands of acres of ranch land?" Curly answers: "Yep, that's him. Every time he got enough money to look like a cowboy, he bought another ranch."

Well, Williams could have been describing Birt Roberds.

Birt came out to Arizona from Texas, and began building stock tanks using mules and a scraper—or a "Fresno," as they were called in those days. He started ranching, and as the years passed, whenever an adjoining ranch was up for sale, he bought it. In time he had added probably five or six ranches to his original spread. In his later years, he would visit the Douglas, Arizona, bank on the northeast corner of G Avenue and Tenth Street. As with all banks its name changed throughout the years—from the Bank of Douglas to ultimately The Bank of America. Whatever the name, that is where Birt had much of his money.

The bank visits went like this: Birt would wander in behind the tellers' cages and declare that he wanted to see what they were doing with his money. This caused a bit of distress to the tellers and they complained to the bank manager. The manager told his tellers to try to keep from getting excited and if they wanted to know why it was okay for Birt to act as though he owned the bank, they should look at his bank records. There were no more complaints from the tellers.

After a couple of months in the high country of the Chiricahuas, the summer rains began, and I was out of a job with the Forest Service. Smoke chasing and clearing trails was winding down, and on my way to Fort Huachuca, where my parents were living, and the game department had some buffalo, I stopped off at Sulphur Canyon. Guy and Audrey Morrow Miller lived there and worked for Birt Roberds at the time. In later years they acquired ranch land and some well done-up homes and improvements, becoming downright affluent. Guy was a good cowboy, cattleman, and team roper of some repute. But, in those days he was a cowboy, and in ranch work there is always something more than cowpunching to do.

Birt decided some water was needed up high against the mountain on one of his acquired ranches. Cattle were not using the range as it was too far to water. Guy, Birt, and an Englishman named Smitty—a stone mason by trade, and a western rancher by choice—had constructed a low dam across a draw which was slick cap rock, bottom and sides. This had caught some rain, but sand and cement still had to be packed to the dam site. A cement mixer was already on site when I began helping out on the project. There was a big sorrel horse on the ranch that had been bucking every time Guy rode him, and he had given up trying to stop such behavior. The sorrel—naturally, called "Sorrel"—was being used as a pack animal. The cement mixer had been packed on Sorrel, and a short distance up the trail, he had bucked off the mixer. Guy, Birt, and Smitty gathered up the mixer parts, and took all back for repair to the garage at Rodeo. The mixer was then packed on a different steed.

One morning the four of us were loading sand and cement for the day's work on the dam. Our four saddle horses were tied, bridle reins fastened to small tree limbs. Billy Ben was a small, but muscular burro, and he was on hand, as were our three pack horses. On Billy Ben's pack saddle a wooden box was slung on each side. At the dam site, Billy Ben packed rocks that were being used to construct the dam. On the trip up the mountain, he carried drinking water and lunches, and that morning he was set to go. Billy Ben didn't need to be led, and was standing around observing.

Sorrel had two heavy canvas bags slung on his pack saddle. He was hobbled, and Guy and I were shoveling sand into the pack bags. Close by, next to the sand pile, Birt and Smitty were loading another paint horse with sand. The designated cement pack animal was tied, but not yet packed. I started leading a pack horse over to the stacked bags of cement.

There come times when a disaster is in the offing. It is seen, but too late. Billy Ben had sauntered over and was between Sorrel and Paint. It seemed in retrospect he actually lowered himself, and brought the sharp points up into the sides of Sorrel and Paint. The fuse was lit and the explosion took place. Sorrel gave a great lunge, broke his hobbles and began running and bucking. Paint began a stampede with Smitty hanging onto the halter on one side, and Birt the other. All of the saddle horses broke loose. The horse I was leading broke loose, and all joined the stampede.

After being dragged along by Paint for some yards, both Birt and Smitty gave it up and turned loose. Sorrel bucked one of the heavily-loaded sand bags clean over the pack saddle, and the cinch broke, leaving sand and pack saddle behind.

We all sort of stood there for a minute taking stock as to conditions. No one said a word. We looked around, and there stood Billy Ben in the shade of an oak tree. He may as well have been saying, "That was exciting, wasn't it?! And you people call yourselves cowboys!"

Eventually all the horses were rounded up, re-packed, and the caravan made its way up the trail to the cap rock dam. Billy Ben walked along at the rear of the string of pack and saddle horses.

That is the yarn of Billy Ben and the Cap Rock Dam.

John Dillinger[1] (center, seated), first court appearance, Tucson, Arizona, January 26th, 1934
Dillinger Gang members, seated, from left: Russell Clark, "Fat Charles" Makley,
"Handsome Harry" Pierpont, Dillinger, Opal Long, Mary Kinder
Credit: Associated Press, 1934

---

[1] Following a string of bank robberies, Dillinger and his cohorts had come to Tucson in the winter of 1934 to "lay low." On the night of Monday, January 22nd, 1934, a fire broke out at the Hotel Congress in downtown Tucson, where some of the gang were registered under aliases. Panicked, they escaped down a fire-truck ladder from their third-floor window to the alley below; gang member Makley then offered two Tucson firemen a generous $12 tip to retrieve the luggage they had left behind in the room. Suspicions aroused by both the hotel guests' anxiety and the size of the tip, back at the firehouse the firemen recognized Makley and Clark from their pictures in *True Detective* magazine—which led to the entire gang's subsequent arrest by the Tucson police at a small home on Tucson's North Second Avenue. When captured by what they had derisively called "small-town hick cops," Dillinger simply muttered "Well, I'll be damned!"

RALPH MORROW: DILLINGER, PRETTY BOY FLOYD, INCIDENT AT LIGHT

Ralph Morrow:

"That was when the Great Depression was—and people were unemployed, and the criminal element operating all over the country. They would rob banks and shoot up the town Wild-West fashion, only using automobiles rather than horses.

"Such as Pretty Boy Floyd, Machine Gun Kelly, and those kinds of people were operating at all times. So it made the job of Deputy Sheriff rather risky at times. However, usually, we weren't in any real great danger; although we did put John Dillinger on the plane for his last ride east, when he was here in the West, and was captured in Tucson. That was not really dangerous; we threw out plenty of guards and got him on the plane without any mishap. Some people thought that was real dangerous, but actually it wasn't.

"Another experience about old time gangsters was kind of amusing/comical: One morning I was in the Ford Garage in Douglas and a policeman and my Deputy Sheriff partner came racing down there and told me that Pretty Boy Floyd just went into the bakery. Well, he generally went into banks, and that kind of made me a little bit curious. I said, 'How do you know it was Pretty Boy Floyd?' My partner said, 'Well, it looked just like him, and he's over there.' I said, 'All right, I will find out if he's over there.' The policeman said, 'Why, he'll kill you.' I said, 'Why, he doesn't kill everybody on the street—he doesn't know what or who we are. We don't have any badges or anything out front, and I have my coat on; he doesn't know who I am. I'll just go over to the bakery and find out if it's Pretty Boy Floyd.'

"So, I went over there to the bakery and this man did look like Pretty Boy Floyd quite a bit, all right, but he was talking to the woman by the name of Kaiser who owned the bakery and I was satisfied that she was well acquainted with him. I just stood there and listened to their conversation a little bit. I finally got a good look at this man, and he didn't have a scar over an eye, like Pretty Boy Floyd. So, I went back and told the other officers who were waiting across the street: 'That's not Pretty Boy Floyd; he's talking to Miss Kaiser and he knows her.'

"But, these other officers were scared to death, thinking any minute shots would be fired and I'd be carried out in a box. That was very comical because I never could figure out why they got so scared because Pretty Boy Floyd couldn't have known any of us by looking at us.[2] We looked like ordinary citizens.

Deputy Sheriff Ralph Morrow, with Thompson sub-machine gun; Douglas, AZ, 1934

That same year, Ralph Morrow would be part of the security detail at Douglas Airport, where John Dillinger (captured with his gang in Tucson) changed planes on his way from Tucson to Chicago.

There wasn't any great danger in even approaching Pretty Boy Floyd under such conditions. Walking into a bakery wouldn't have scared anybody."

---

[2] The law officers of that era, when not working the countryside, dressed in expensive three-piece suits—the only concession to western apparel being perhaps a Stetson hat.

Those officers were firm advocates of old Polonius, who advised thus in Will Shakespeare's *Hamlet*:

"Costly thy habit as thy purse can buy.
But not expressed in fancy; rich not gaudy.
For the apparel oft proclaims the man."

Light: A community located west of Turkey Creek, Cochise County, in the Sulphur Springs Valley, now vanished. Settled by homesteaders between 1902 and 1910. John W. Light, a native New Yorker and Civil War veteran, was one of the settlers. Though Light faded with time, there was a building in which dances were held at least into the 1930s, the latter days of Prohibition.

Prohibition: Alcohol, by law, was prohibited in the United States from 12:01 the morning of January 17, 1920 to the rather unusual and puzzling hour of 5:32 in the afternoon of December 5, 1933. During those thirteen years the world of alcoholic beverages and whiskey or whisky, depending on your preference and geographical location, changed forever. Canada and Scotland rushed to the aid of their thirsty and parched brothers and sisters in America, and seized a position of dominance in the world market they enjoy to the present day.

Moonshine: An American term for illegally distilled alcohol, which filled the void often found in the hinterlands. People learned basic tests to avoid blindness or even death. Tests such as igniting some Moonshine, and if the flame burned blue, it was reasonably safe. A yellow flame indicated a low and dangerous grade of rot gut. But the unschooled soon learned Moonshine was highly combustible, and this caused eyebrows to be burned off, noses to be blistered, and an occasional loss of one or two ears. No doubt, Moonshine played a part in the "Incident at Light."

§   §   §

"It was just another country dance, probably sometime around 1932. Well, there was a certain amount of drinking going on, even though it was Prohibition days at the time. There was a gang of would-be toughs that had been disrupting things at the dances. Had even taken some officer's gun away from him at some dance.

"Anyway, there were two of these fellows inside the dance hall, and they were using some pretty bad language. I told them that we couldn't tolerate that sort of talk, and one of these would-be thugs called me an S.O.B. and kind of stuck his chin out.[3] I hit him with an uppercut, and his feet must have come off the floor four or five inches, and he was out cold.

---

[3] What this man as well as others did not know was that Ralph Morrow had been an accomplished pugilist in his younger days, and had gone a number of rounds in the ring.

"This partner of his came rushing at me, and I hit him with a .45 Frontier Model Colt revolver I carried at the time, and he fell across the one I had hit, and he was out for the count also.

"The rest of these rowdies, fired up with a lot of false courage from the Moon-shine they had probably been drinking started in from outside. The door into the dance hall was pretty narrow. I cocked my Colt Revolver and ground it into the belly of the first one at the door. Those behind him were yelling things like 'Let me at him,' and such as that. This one that was under the gun, so to speak, had other thoughts just at that moment, and he said, 'Mr. Morrow, if you will let us take our two friends, there, and leave, why we will not cause any more trouble.'

"I did, and there was no more trouble out of those men anywhere again."

R.W. Morrow, 4 years old; Douglas, AZ, 1934
Deputy Sheriff Ralph Morrow's sub-machine gun

DIGGING UP SKELETONS: CARSON MORROW'S *CHIRICAHUA BULL SHEET*

Explanatory Note

In 1903, Carson Morrow was seven years of age when the William King and Eva Rosetta Morrow family settled in Paradise, Arizona. Carson Morrow's formal education was in the Paradise school. He was fifteen years of age when the family took up a homestead and began ranching once again, on East Turkey Creek, about two miles north of Paradise.

In World War I he saw combat as a field-artillery Sergeant. In the Army, he excelled in track, running the 220-yard dash before shipping out for Europe. When the United States entered World War II, he applied for a commission as a Major in the Army; however, for petty political reasons, this was ultimately blocked.

Carson was also a cowboy, miner, and wagon boss for the Riggs Cattle Company, as well as a distinguished lawman—first as a Border Patrolman, then as assistant Chief Patrol Inspector, Border Patrol, Tucson Sector, and ultimately as Chief Patrol Inspector of the Border Patrol, Tucson Sector. Following his retirement as Chief Patrol Inspector, Carson—or "Chief," as he was afterwards known to many—and his family lived a number of years in the United States Forest Ranger Station near Portal, Arizona.

In 1952, Carson began writing *The Chiricahua Bull Sheet*, a newsletter about local happenings and history in the Chiricahua Mountains. He wrote, typed, mimeographed, and mailed the *Bull Sheet* to local and far-away subscribers, who paid nothing, but occasionally contributed toward the cost of postage.

The American Museum of Natural History's Southwestern Research Station is located up canyon from the Ranger Station—referred to as the "Editorial Office" by Carson—and visitors there often stopped in to swap stories, weather permitting, on his front porch. These stories provided him with much material for the *Bull Sheet*.

Starting in 1957, Carson (aka the "Old Cub Reporter") included a regular column he called "Digging up Skeletons," in which he recounted tales of people and events of bygone days—some of which are excerpted in this chapter. Most, but not all, misspelled words have been corrected here. Some punctuation has been added or corrected. Capitalization of words remains as originally written. Comments on the original text are in footnotes—or italicized and enclosed in brackets.

R.W. Morrow, *Sobrino del Jefe Carson Morrow*

Carson ("Chief") Morrow and wife Leona, circa 1925

Parson Chenoweth and Stephen Reed: Tough Hombres of the Old West

from *The Chiricahua Bull Sheet*, May 7, 1957

We propose to publish in each issue a thumb nail sketch of one or more of the people who resided in or near the Chiricahua Mountains during the period 1903 to 10. Those sketches will be written from memory, and since our memory isn't the best, and since a good many of those people's pasts were more than somewhat sketchy before they came here, we will just tell it the best we can and apologize for any offensive mistakes we might make. That is if we can't lick or outrun the offended.

Many yarns, lies, stories, and songs have been written about the old time Peace Officers, outlaws, and other swashbucklers of the old west, but at least two of the most outstanding characters who ever inhabited Cochise County, Arizona, have been entirely overlooked or ignored.

Parson Chenoweth and Stephen B. Reed—these men were honest, hard working pioneers who came into this country in the late 1870's by ox wagons, established homes, raised families, and started the development of the civilization we now enjoy.

The Parson settled at the San Simon Cienega and Mr. Reed in Cave Creek in the Chiricahua Mountains. Neither of them made any pretense of being Tough Hombres, in fact they were, each in his own way—mild mannered, friendly, and courteous. Yet they had something about them that caused the Tough Boys to tread a little more softly when they were around; certainly they did not command the respect of both the outlaw and marauding Indian on account of their looks or manners but because when the chips were down, they knew that these old boys would play for keeps, and no holds barred

During the 80's and 90's, murder, robbery, horse stealing, and cattle rustling were rampant, and the Apaches were promiscuously killing settlers, burning ranches, and raising hell in general throughout Arizona. The Chenoweth and Reed ranches were never molested although Bands of renegade Indians camped within sight of their houses many times. And, both peace officers—so-called—and outlaws came to put their feet under the table. All were welcome so long as they behaved themselves.

So far as is known, Mr. Reed was never called upon to prove his superiority as a fighting man, and was content to tend to his own business and shoot a bear once in awhile for amusement. But, the Parson was challenged a few times. He had no church or regular congregation, so he preached his sermons in dance halls, saloons, bunkhouses, or out in the open to any and all who cared to attend.

One time when he was in Galeyville for a preaching, one of Curly Bill's henchmen, who was probably somewhat in his cups, decided it would be fun to bait the Parson a little, but he promptly learned a lesson which didn't benefit him much because in answer to one of his jibes, the Parson landed an upper cut on his jaw and killed him deader than a hammer. The Parson then helped make a coffin and dig his grave in the Galeyville Graveyard and preached his funeral.

On another occasion the Parson met one of the Tough Boys on a trail in the Chiricahua Mountains. The Tough Boy drew his pistol and ordered him to dismount and take his saddle off as they were going to trade horses. The Parson stepped off of his horse on the side away from the outlaw, drawing his rifle from the scabbard as he did so. When the Tough Boy glanced down to see how things were going, he found the table turned and he was looking full into the business end of a .50 caliber Buffalo gun pointed from underneath the horse's belly.

The Parson then explained that he wasn't in much of a trading mood that day and didn't want to trade horses at all, but that being as how his old saddle was about to fall to pieces, and that the outlaw had such a nice new one, they would just trade saddles.

There is no record of him having converted anyone to Christian faith, and probably didn't instill much reverence for the scriptures in many of his listeners, but they surely learned to take off their hats and bow their heads in some semblance of reverence when Parson Chenoweth went into action—either with his fists, his Buffalo gun, or his Bible.

El Cuento de Quong Kee

from *The Chiricahua Bull Sheet*, May 13, 1957

Quong Kee came to this country in the late seventies as a coolie and worked on the Southern Pacific Railroad which was building from the west coast to the East. After the RR was completed, he ran restaurants and boarding houses at Tombstone, Gleason, Courtland, Pearce, Willcox, Paradise and Hilltop, and other places in southern Arizona. He was a generous man and any hungry Prospector, Miner, or cowboy was always sure of a meal at Quong's whether he had any money or not. Some of them paid him later on but most of them didn't as a good many of the old timers thought it no wrong to cheat a Chinaman or to play a practical joke on him. Quong had quite a sense of humor and occasionally played a joke in return, but was never known to resort to law to collect a board bill.

One winter, when times were hard, Quong was running a restaurant in Willcox and several cowboys were out of a job and laying around town, eating at Quong's on the cuff. Finally he told them that he was about broke too but if they would shoot some jack rabbits, he would make jack rabbit pie and continue to feed them until they could get work.

They readily agreed and did go out and shoot a few rabbits, but soon tired of it and just left it up to Quong to get his rabbits any way he could. He kept right on feeding them Rabbit Pie for sometime although no one ever saw him go out hunting.

The day finally came when in spite of Quong's thrift and ingenuity he could no longer feed his Star Boarders. So, when they were all assembled at the counter and had begun banging on their plates and yelling for their usual Jack Rabbit Pie, Quong calmly picked up the meat cleaver and announced: "NO MORE JACK RABBIT PIE, LITTLE PUPPY DOG HE ALL GONE."

There was a wild scramble for the back door, and sure enough the gang of mangy dogs which generally hung around Quong's for a hand out wasn't there any more.

Generally the Chinese of Quong's era eventually acquired considerable wealth and returned to China before they died so their bones could rest amongst those of their ancestors, or arranged for their bones to be shipped back to the old country if they died here. No doubt Quong hoped his carcass would be disposed of in the same manner, but he was too busy feeding unappreciative bums and stray dogs to save money to take care of the situation before it arose. After he had passed well beyond the three-score-and-ten mark and was no longer able to work, he drifted back to a little shack he owned on the outskirts of Tombstone and there slowly starved to death. No one knows how long he was without food, but finally someone came along and found him just before he died, and he was sent to the Cochise County Hospital where he lived a short time before he cashed in.

What thoughts Quong had of the hundreds of hungry people he had fed, while he lay in his shack starving, can only be surmised.

Ordinarily after a good horse is ridden to death and the buzzards have picked his bones, he is left in peace, but no such luck for Quong. His spirit escaped whatever kind of Heaven a Chinaman goes to and his body was quietly and economically laid away in a pauper's grave at Bisbee. But, he hadn't gotten good and cold until he was dug up, placed in a coffin, and taken to Tombstone and re-interred with all the pomp and fanfare usually accorded to great or near great. The City of Bisbee threatened to sue the City of Tombstone for stealing Quong and the newspapers ran box car headlines on the affair for several days.

WHAT THE HELL???? Had someone remembered old Quong for all the good he had done while he was alive??? Of course not! The Town Council of Tombstone had decided that Quong would be quite a good attraction for their "Boot Hill Cemetery," which they are using to lure tourists. So the "Melican" people kept right on exploiting poor old Quong in death the same as they did in life.

The School at Paradise

from *The Chiricahua Bull Sheet*, May 31, 1957

This story is about a school that has been out of business so long that very few people even know where the school house was. The town it belonged to has been dead so long that not one building remains standing—the town was Paradise, Arizona. This mining camp once boasted an estimated population of 2,500; had 13 saloons, seven honky-tonks, four general merchandise stores, two hotels and three restaurants, a jail, one meat market, but no church of any kind. That is, until Parson Chenoweth showed up and converted any establishment he may choose into a temporary church. However, the town is another story.

The Paradise School: In the year of 1904, the business men and other influential people of Paradise got together and decided that they should have a school, but learned that the County was too poor or too something else to provide money for a school house. So, they had another meeting and made contributions in the form of money, labor, commodities, etc., to get the job done. The next problem was selection of a site for the school house, which should have been easy as George A. Walker, who owned the townsite, at that time offered to give them any lot in town, and in addition to that, the town was surrounded by public domain, and any part of which they were free to build on. But, there was one merchant by the name of Joseph Slater, who had no children but was willing to make a large contribution provided the school was located on a high, rocky ridge about one-half mile west of town. He made some lame excuse for wanting it there, but stood by his guns and the building was erected where he wanted it. There was considerable speculation as to why Joe was so arbitrary about the site, but when the kids started wearing out about a pair of shoes a month going to school, Joe began to reap his harvest and speculation ceased. His stock consisted largely of children's shoes of assorted sizes.

When finished, the building consisted of one room about forty feet in width and seventy feet in length. Toilet facilities were outside, and water was carried by the pupils in buckets, bottles, or canteens. The entire inside furnishings consisted of the teacher's desk and chair—perched on a small platform in one end of the building—about forty modern, for that time, school desks, several Giant Powder boxes for seats with orange crates for desks, and a large sheet iron wood burner heater set near the front of the room with the stove pipe running along the ceiling to the back.

When the building was finished and furnished, the County provided the necessary $60 per month to pay the teacher for a seven-month term of school, and the stage was set.

Miss Mand McDonald, a scrappy little red head about 30 years of age, and weighing about 90 pounds and hailing from some place back east was employed. Eighty four pupils, consisting of about an equal number of bronco Americans and non-English speaking Mexicans in ages ranging from 6 to 21 years, were mustered from the hills, hollows, and deserts for several miles around. They came mounted on horses, burros, and hob-nailed shoes.

The school got off to a fairly good start, taking everything into consideration. That is, nothing of a very serious nature happened before 9 A.M. the first day. If you can visualize one undersized, half scared little teacher trying to classify and group a mob like that into some semblance of a school organization, all in one room, with the big boys rooster fighting and shoving each other around like a herd of two year old muley bulls. The big girls tittering and whispering and trying to look demure, and all the little kids trying to hide behind the big ones, and keep from being stepped on at the same time, then you have a fairly good picture of the first day.

Group photo, in front of the Paradise School, circa 1905

Back row, left to right: Maggie Bendele, Ola Martyr, Gertrude Chamberlain, Tom Hawkins, Jim Hancock, Laura Hancock, Eva Morrow, Rosaline Morrow, Hollis Sweeney, W.K. Morrow, Harry Chamberlain

Front row, left to right: Bendele baby, Carson "Chief" Morrow, Erle Hancock, an unknown child, Bertha Bendele, Mart Moore, Jerry Chamberlain, Chester "Bally" Morrow, Irene Hancock, Ralph Morrow (holding his cat), Dorothy and Ted Chamberlain

The classification job would have proven entirely impossible but for the fact that about half of the pupils of assorted ages had attended some sort of school somewhere previously, the fourth grade being the highest scholastic rating any of the pre-educated pupils had attained. So, Miss McDonald used these semi-halter broken ones as "Bell Mares," and finally got the whole bunch lined up in four classes.

As an example how the grades stacked up: In the first grade, which was far the largest, you would find Charlie McComas age 21, 6 feet tall along side Ralph Morrow, age 6, and undersized for his age. Then there was Jose Pacheco—age unknown, 5 feet 7 inches, "no speaka the eenglish." In the fourth grade you would see Alejo Bedoya, age 12, alongside Fran Gilpin, age 18. The other grades were smaller in number, but similarly assorted as to individuals.

Public School,

Paradise, Arizona.

1907-8

Delia Sweeten, Teacher.

❦ ❦ ❦

TRUSTEES

Henry Chamberlain.   W. H. Morrow.
James Hancock, Clerk.   John R. Rockfellow, Co. Supt.

Delia Sweeten[1], Mand McDonald's successor as Paradise School Teacher, 1907-1908

Trustee name "W.H. Morrow" should have read "W.K. Morrow"

---

[1] Miss Sweeten's brother Noah Sweeten was a veteran of the Spanish-American war, and in later years was a game trapper for Cochise County. Noah Sweeten also owned at least one saloon in the town of Dos Cabezas. (A 1916 drought spelled the beginning of the end for Dos Cabezas, now largely a ghost town some 14 miles southeast of Willcox, Arizona on Highway 186.)

The term lasted for the full seven months, but finished with considerably less students than when it started. Naturally, Miss Mand found it necessary to wield the long ruler on about all that she was physically able to, and some of the parents took their children out of school on that account. She had to expel some of the ones who wouldn't submit to the ruler, and others just quit. At different times, two young ladies pulled the teacher's hair and slapped her face before they left for good.

Another thing that further weakened the teacher's already shaky hold on discipline was that she fell in love about mid-term with Jim Knowles, who was the superintendent of the Chiricahua Development Company. Jim was so ardent that he came to see her during noon hour nearly every day, so she lengthened the noon period to two hours, and they would go for a stroll. That wasn't so bad in its self, but the adult students took advantage of her absence by throwing all the little kids out and having a dance. That is to say, something more resembling a riot. Lon Gilpin and some others would play harmonica, and the grand romping and stomping would take place, desks being turned over and broken was the usual thing, and the jointed stove pipe, about 60 feet in length, was knocked down occasionally. When the teacher would return, all flushed with love and affection, she would fly into a tantrum which occasionally resulted in an expulsion or two.

Four students of the first term of the Paradise School are presently [*1957*] in the neighborhood—Ralph Morrow at Hilltop, William W. Sanders at Paradise, Mrs. Emma Maloney and yours truly at Portal.

"The Jerk-Line Skinner"

from *The Chiricahua Bull Sheet*, July 24, 1957

If a man should go out looking for a job as a "Jerk-Line Skinner" today, he wouldn't find half a dozen people in a day's ride who knew what he was talking about. By the same token, should you go out to hire a man for that job, you wouldn't find half a dozen men in the State of Arizona who could qualify for it.

A jerk-line skinner was the cream of the crop of horsemen of all time. In fact, he was an artist, but instead of an easel and brush, he used a shot whip, a jerk line, and a morral[2] full of small pebbles to control anywhere from ten to twenty horses in harness, and hauled all kinds of freight from the railroad to towns, mines, and ranches in the back country.

---

[2] From the Spanish word meaning "nosebag" (a feed bag for livestock) or "knapsack."

We have now and always have had plenty of people who can handle one horse in some fashion, ranging from the top cowboys who can ride just about any horse for fun, or the dude boy with all the fancy trappings, who lets his gentle old nag get away from him while out on a Sunday "pasear" with his girl friend. But, there never was a surplus of the kind of horsemen we are trying to tell about.[3]

We have seen horse-drawn artillery in action, cavalry at the charge, 5,000 head of cattle in one round up, and all sorts of rodeos and stampedes, but none of these produced a greater thrill than the one-man show put on by a jerk-line skinner with ten or more horses strung out in pairs in front of a heavily-loaded freight wagon on a crooked mountain road. To his way of thinking, he was only getting the freight over the road, which he did, come hell, high water, or broken axles. When he came to a hair-pin turn, he put on a display of horsemanship that has never been excelled. He had no manual control of any horse except the near leader to which the jerk line—a small cotton cord—was fastened. All others were controlled by voice and signals—the signals emanating from the shot whip and the pebbles.

As a turn was negotiated, this master horseman's voice, together with the pistol-sharp crack of the whip, and the thud of a few pebbles, told each horse just when and where and how much he was supposed to do to keep the wagon in the middle of the road—although the lead horses and those following in turn would be headed in almost the opposite direction in which the wagon was moving.

Those old boys wore no special garb except that they might have been a little more rugged than ordinary, as they didn't have much opportunity to doll up, as they were generally on the road and traveling from sun rise to sun set. And they did all the harnessing, unharnessing, feeding, watering, shoeing, cooking, and sleeping, in the mean time.

---

[3] In John Steinbeck's 1937 novel *Of Mice and Men*, the character named "Slim" is one of these master horsemen. Steinbeck describes him like so:

"He moved with a majesty only achieved by royalty and master craftsman. He was a jerk-line skinner, the prince of the ranch, capable of driving ten, sixteen, even twenty mules with a single line to the leaders. He was capable of killing a fly on the wheeler's butt with a bull whip without touching the mule. … His authority was so great that his word was taken on any subject, be it politics or love. This was Slim, the jerkline skinner."

Cliff Darnell with a ten-horse jerk-line team, outside Silver City, New Mexico, early 1900s

Photograph courtesy of Cliff Darnell's daughter, Sally Richards

So far as we know, there is just one of these real horsemen left in this neck of the woods, and he was one of he best. So, if you would enjoy having a man that really knows all about horses and how to handle them tell about it, drive over to the Old San Simon Headquarters Ranch[4] and present owner, Cliff Darnell is the man. We will publish a story written by Mrs. Darnell in a subsequent issue of the *Bull Sheet*.

Striking it Rich or "Want To Buy Some Mining Stock?"

from *The Chiricahua Bull Sheet*, July 24, 1957

Farming and mining are pretty closely related—in some respects. Some years ago Billy Wright and Fred Bernudy shipped several trunk loads of something pretty heavy from Cripple Creek, Colorado to Paradise, Arizona. There was considerable speculation at the time as to the contents of the trunks. Some guessed it was fertilizer of a specific kind, while others guessed that it was mining equipment, etc. But, Billy and Fred were in the mining business and knew all the angles. After the trunk episode was forgotten, they struck the richest gold and silver ore ever known in these parts, and sold thousands of dollars worth of stock in the mine to the very people who had been wondering about the trunks. The boom only lasted a few days before the mine pinched out, and then the suckers didn't wonder any more.[5]

What brought this to mind was seeing two of our most prominent mining men—John Shad and John Pence—hauling what appeared to be manure out of Rodeo the other day, and so far as we know they aren't farming.

---

[4] About five miles southwest of Rodeo, New Mexico.

[5] Just north of Paradise, if you are headed north, high up on the limestone peak to the east of the road through Galeyville, there is a mine dump with a southern exposure. That is the Wright-Bernudy gold and silver mine. Ralph Morrow was asked what he knew about the property, as it appeared a most unlikely spot for mining anything but limestone. He told about the con game and stock swindle, and added that even he and Chief had invested in the bogus mine. Thus, Carson Morrow—the "Old Cub"—had first-hand knowledge of the venture. He neglected to mention that he himself happened to be one of the "suckers."

A Road to Paradise

from *The Chiricahua Bull Sheet*, September 13, 1957

Back in the days when there were no automobiles in Arizona if we had County Boards of Supervisors, State Highway Commissions, and Federal Bureaus of Roads, etc., no one seemed to know much about them and the old boys of those times—women couldn't vote then—had a way of getting things done without all the Political Fanfare it takes to get the roads improved through the auspices of those more or less stuffed-shirt governmental organizations nowadays.

When Paradise first came into existence if you were travelling from Rodeo to Paradise by wagon, you either went up the canyon through Round Valley or you took the longer route around through the lower Box in Turkey Creek above the old Red Top Ranch, as there was no passable road through Silver Creek. With an automobile the difference in distance would be negligible, but by horse, mule, or burro it wasn't, so the Paradise boys didn't appeal to any organization to build a road through Silver Creek, they elected a fellow by the name of Luke Short—not the famous one—Constable, and an old worn out miner by the name of Big Foot Jim Williams, Justice of the Peace, and informed them that they wanted law enforcement well mixed with building a road through Silver Creek and those two officials proceeded to get the job done.

The old Chiricahua Development Company was going full blast and employing in the neighborhood of five hundred men who worked twelve hours a day seven days a week, except they nearly all laid off on pay day which was the first day of the month. That was the day when Luke and Big Foot recruited most of their Road workers. Luke would arrest all the miners who got too boisterous and handcuff them to a chain stretched between two trees and after they had sobered up a little the next morning he would get on his horse and walk them down to the Court which was in Jim's shack located about 5 miles north of Paradise on the East Bank of Turkey Creek. Occasionally Frank Barfield or the Chamberlain and Hawkins Grocery would donate the use of a wagon to convey the prisoners and some of the thirteen Paradise Saloon Keepers might donate a bottle of rot gut to cheer the boys up on the way to the Bar of Justice.

Big Foot always dished out the Justice impartially, if the prisoner had any money, he fined whatever amount he had. If not, he got ten days on the road, but after being searched at the time of arrest, ten days on the road gang was by far the most popular sentence.

The miners were supplemented occasionally by a cowboy who happened to imbibe too much red eye and tried to do a little round up work inside a saloon on horseback, and several of the old town Bums including Old Dorsey, Jack Buford, and Dutch Arthur, who also made their unwilling contributions to the development of the Country. The old boys who dug the Road over Silver Creek Hill with pick and shovel and those who caused them to do it have all drifted on now, nearly all of them to "Fiddlers' Green," but you can still see the road off to your left as you follow the newer road for a mile or so en route to the Paradise Cemetery from Portal.[6]

We couldn't get our present day Bum Roads improved by that method because we don't have enough population to warrant a Justice of the Peace and Constable. Nor, do we have the drunken miners and cowboys to supply the labor, so the C.B.S. suggests that we all drive a pretty hard bargain on the road question with our Politicos the next time they come around to kiss the babies.

Just in case you might have liked this little skit, we will add a few more or less pertinent paragraphs as a sort of encore.

Judge Williams was defeated by Jim Hancock for the Office of J.P., and Luke Short resigned and left the country sometime before his second term as Constable expired. He was somewhat of a ladies man, among other things, and he was visiting at a miner's home one night while the miner was supposed to be on shift but wasn't.

Luke went out the back door with his boots in his hand fast enough that the miner coming in the front door in the dark couldn't positively identify him, but the next day after having a few drinks, the miner dropped a few remarks around town regarding his strong belief in the sanctity of the home, and the infallibility of a ten gauge shotgun to keep it that way. So, Luke saddled up and drifted to a lower elevation—he evidently didn't want to speed up the change of climate by dropping straight from Paradise to the fiery furnace carrying a few ounces of Buck Shot to accelerate the trip.

---

[6] Evidence of the old road is yet to be seen where it wound up through Silver Creek, at the summit, and north of the Paradise Cemetery.

The 1927 Battle of Bear Valley

from *The Chiricahua Bull Sheet*, September 23, 1957

A few issues back our old compañero Alden Hayes excavated a few ancient Apaches for this column, so we will dig up some more modern Yaquis this time.

In about 1927 the Yaquis were at war with the Mexicans. One battle was fought in Bear Valley west of Nogales. There were only a few shots fired and no one on either side was injured, but the Yaquis decided that they had lost the battle and over a hundred of them crossed the line into the United States where they ran into three Immigration Border Patrolmen.[7]

For some time it was difficult to decide whom was whose prisoners. The Border Patrolmen were quickly and completely surrounded by armed Indians, and while they were not disarmed or molested in any way, they simply could not go any place or do anything but stand there. The Yaquis did not offer to surrender their arms, but told the Patrol boys that they were the Border Patrol's prisoners. The Yaquis were armed with every known make and caliber of gun plus knives and clubs.

It was late in the evening and the Yaquis quickly set up camp, such as that was, and posted sentries in the brush surrounding the camp. They asked one of the Patrol to go to Nogales and bring back the American Army as they were afraid the Mexicans would cross the line and attack them if they started for Nogales. But, they told the Patrolman to also notify the army that they would not be admitted into the Yaqui Camp before day break the following morning.

The commanding Officer of the Post at Nogales was sort of an eager beaver and immediately started for Bear Valley with a detachment of colored troops, arriving about midnight. There he received about the same treatment the Border Patrol had earlier in the evening. The Yaquis surrounded the whole outfit and held them at gun point until daylight when the Indians laid down their arms and surrendered to the troops. They were taken to Nogales and held in the stockade at the army camp for a short time and then taken to Tucson, where they camped on an irrigation ditch bank to the North of Town. This camp became what is known as Pascua Village.

---

[7] The Cub would have been working as a Border Patrolman at the time, and may even have been one of the three Patrolmen.

Carson Morrow (seated, right), Tucson, Arizona, 1932
Photograph (cropped) courtesy of the National Border Patrol Museum, El Paso, Texas

These Yaquis were never admitted to the United States for permanent residence under the Immigration laws but were considered admissible as political refugees and allowed to come and go at will. Many of them sneaked back to Mexico from time to time and no doubt a good many guns and ammunition went with them as they never gave up hope that some day they would whip the Mexicans.

The Mexican Government has made several attempts to exterminate the Yaquis. In about 1910 they rounded up all of them that they could catch and sent them to Yucatan but most of them quickly found their way back to the Yaqui River in Sonora where they resumed their age-old custom of sniping Mexicans when the opportunity presented.

In about 1930, a self-appointed War Chief by the name of Guadalupe Flores, a resident of Pascua Village, decided to start an all-out war on Mexico. He accumulated a lot of rifles and ammunition and hired a barnstorming aviator by the name of Charlie Mays to fly them to the Yaqui Country in Mexico, having first arranged to clear a landing field near Bacatete. Guadalupe flew down with Charlie and the guns, but when they arrived they couldn't land because when the field was cleared of Mezquites the stumps were left sticking up three feet or more.

They flew around awhile and decided that they would drop their cargo and hope for the best. So, Charlie skimmed the top of the stumps and Guadalupe threw the guns out by the arm full. The result was a few busted Mezquite stumps and complete ruination of the cargo. Charlie later said that some of the gun barrels were bent until they rolled away looking like barrel hoops and that some of the wood from the gun stocks actually bounced back into the plane.

La Leyenda de Ignacio Flores

from *The Chiricahua Bull Sheet*, October 16, 1957

The old Z Bar T Ranch over on Whitetail Canyon has a lot of green grass and fat cattle on it this year and the present owner, Herman Kollmar, is just about as happy as he should be. It seems the biggest worry he and his little frau has is whether old Ignacio Flores is going to freeze or starve to death before he gets to be two hundred years old. Old Nacho is an Opata Indian[8] who originated down in Sonora and drifted into the San Simon Valley shortly after 1900 or so, and he has chopped several million fence posts and about as many cords of wood since that time and finally got on the old age pension. However, accepting the pension is about the only concession he has made to the Pale Face's civilization and mode of living. Of course, he will drink beer out of a can instead of Pulque out of a goat skin bag, but in about every other way he lives pretty much the same as he would if he still lived down in Opata. He has his patched-up tent stretched up under a tree and builds a camp fire three times a day to warm up the frijoles con chili, make a few tortillas, and boil the coffee. All those commodities are more easily obtained here among the gringos than in Sonora because down there he wouldn't have a patron y patrona como el señor y la señora de Kollmar, who have given him lots of good warm clothing, blankets, cold cerveza, and most of his grub plus

---

[8] See the chapter "The Silver Creek Wreck" for more about Nacho Flores.

a lot of Pension money for which he has little use, but keeps cached away just in case those good Samaritans should come to their senses some day.

To say Nacho is living high on the hog is to state the case mildly, the Kollmars have finally persuaded him to accept a brand new tent as a Christmas gift instead of the lumber house they wanted to build especially for him there on the ranch. When first approached as to whether he wanted a house, he stated flatly that he did not want it because houses are unhealthy, and to the argument that he would get cold in his old tent this coming winter, he said that if he got cold he would only have to shiver a little to get warm, that all his tent needed was a few patches to make it almost as good as new. He didn't want a new tent because they cost a lot of money, but after it was carefully explained to him by la Señora—through an interpreter—that the new tent was a Christmas gift, and he fully understood that he wouldn't have to pony up any of his treasured gringo pesos to pay for it, he enthusiastically accepted and selected about the highest priced tent in the Monkey Ward Catalogue.

The one thing that still had Nacho bewildered is the importance the gringos attach to the passage of time. Invariably, they look at their watches to see if it is time to eat or to go to bed, and all such things as that. They look at the calendar to see whether it is winter or summer, and above all they want to know how old he is. All the while he goes on eating when he is hungry and sleeping when he feels like it and not knowing or caring anything about his age.

But, don't get the idea he is just a dumb old Indian who doesn't know the score. Mr. John Foster Dulles could learn a lot about diplomacy from him if he would just take note of how Nacho has become famous and well-off financially by using only two words at a time: "Quien Sabe" and "Si, Señor." He never goes to the trouble of saying "No, Señor" because if he don't want to do anything he just don't. His two expressions are made to answer all the foolish questions the gringos care to ask, and that is the way he started to become famous. A few years ago, he was camped up on Cave Creek cutting wood, and some half-baked journalist came along looking for something to write about and Nacho being an odd looking, weather beaten, old Character, he proceeded to write quite a sensational story for the New York papers about an Indian who was over one hundred years old fighting and whipping a bear. And, of course, from that Nacho's age has ever since been over a hundred years and he is actually at the point of becoming a living myth.

All of this occurred simply because when the journalist asked him how old he was, he probably answered: "Quien Sabe," and when the journalist said you must be over a hundred, he answered: "Si, Señor." And, in answer to the question about his arm which he had scratched on a snag while cutting wood, he answered with the inevitable, "Quien Sabe," and when the writer asked if a bear did it right in his camp, the answer couldn't have been anything but, "Si, Señor."

In conclusion, *The Chiricahua Bull Sheet* will bet a paid-up subscription against anything of value that by using the same line of questioning we can fix Nacho's age at either one year or one thousand years and have him whipping a Bengal Tiger instead of a bear. And, it is a cinch we will win if we happen to jingle a few coins in our pocket while interrogating Nacho.

The Mysterious Vanishing of Jim Artle

from *The Chiricahua Bull Sheet*, November 9, 1957

Awhile back we mentioned Jim Artle's name in connection with some scientists who got lost up near the Research Station, and since then several of the old boys who were in circulation at the time Artle disappeared—the last part of March 1905—have given us the benefit of their knowledge and surmises which we will pass on to you. Artle and another old German fellow by the name of Chris Grauer were partners in some mining claims up in the head of Whitetail Canyon. Their camp was just over the divide in the North Fork of Pinery Canyon. The Hands brothers—John and Frank—owned adjoining claims and were living at the old Hilltop Camp which is about a mile from the Artle and Grauer camp.

The Hands brothers were hard-headed Britishers from the old country, and the others were still harder headed if that is possible and also from the old country so naturally they were not getting along very well. It seems the bickering had reached the point that each of the four wanted to get rid of the other three by just about any means—fair or foul. There is little doubt that some of the three did put Artle away so well that he has not been found to this day and very likely never will be as the others are gone to the happy hunting ground too.

The day Artle vanished he came into Paradise and bought a new pair of shoes, and said that he was going back to his camp, pick up a few personal effects and go on to the ZZ Ranch at Apache Pass for a visit. He stopped at Ulrich Rieder's place in Whitetail Canyon en route to his camp that same day and started up the trail from there to oblivion. That is about all the known facts. A big snow storm came and obliterated all tracks before Artle was missed so tracking him was out of the question. If anyone makes a search for him now, the chances of finding him are just about as good as they were then. So go right ahead and solve one of the great mysteries of the Chiricahuas.

Frank Noland is pretty sure that one of the Hands brothers did the foul deed, and old Joe Schaefer is just as certain that old Chris Grauer did it. Conjecture and opinions were divided in about the same proportion at the time it happened. At any rate Artle more than likely had things pretty well warmed up for all three of the suspects when they arrived at the fiery furnace. At the time Whitetail Canyon was the liveliest part of the Chiricahuas. There was old Oatmeal Sam Dale, Bull Hill Duncan McDonald, Doctor Hitchins, and Cal Dewey each holding and developing groups of claims up the Indian Creek Fork of Whitetail. Over on the south side Charley Lavery, Dick Larue, Headburg, Kessler, and several others were doing likewise. Further down the canyon George Gardner, Ulrich Rieder, Perry Smith and old man John Sullivan had cabins at the Rieder Orchard where the Dixons are now living. Steve McComas and Jim Gould were squatting on the Z–T Ranch which was then called the Rockhouse. Charlie Gallagher and Dave Doran were holding what is now known as the Ajax Mine which is just across the draw to the north of the Oliver Richardson place. Oliver and his brother, Doctor Richardson, together with the Doctor's family, lived in the old lumber shack which is still standing on the left hand side of the road going west on Whitetail Flat.

Each and every one of the aforementioned gents were real characters and no doubt an interesting book could have been written about any one of them. But, they generally revealed very little of their past lives, or if they did, the ones they told it to have either passed away or forgotten. As time goes along, we will dig up one or more of their skeletons—that is, with a pencil—and try to tell you what little is remembered of them. With the help of Frank Noland, Jack and Emma Maloney, Joe and Mrs. Schaefer, Tom Stafford, Bill Sanders, Ralph Morrow, and any of the other boys and girls who survived the droughts and starvation through-out those so called "good old days," and are still walking around. We will tell you some short stories from time to time that may be of some interest.

Doctor Flower and the Old Terrible Mine

by Stanley Good, Alamogordo, NM
from *The Chiricahua Bull Sheet*, November 26, 1957

Around 1900, Arizona Territory hadn't progressed very much beyond what it was when the Apaches ran it. The Southern Pacific and Santa Fe had each managed to snake railroads from east to west, across the Territory, so people could go from the Atlantic to the Pacific without going around Cape Horn. Very few travelers left the trains, en route across the Territory because of alleged danger from wild Indians and wilder whites. Those that stopped, did so because they were afraid of Vigilantes in California and couldn't go back to Texas until the Sheriff died. Anyway, those early settlers in Cochise County, especially, were a hardy bunch. They took hold of some mighty rough country and tamed it. It was tough, but the country didn't scare those pioneers who paved the way for investors with outside capital.

One easterner, who awakened the world to the mineral wealth in Cochise County is probably unknown in the area today. He arrived just after the Spanish-American War. Mining was slow and the cattlemen in the Southwest were "broke" due to a protracted drought. He was known as "Doctor" Flower. He was a Canadian promoter who sold gilt-edged mining stock—mostly to rich widows as he was quite a ladies' man—and to anyone else who had money. Doc acquired worked-out and "lost" Spanish Mines. He developed them and managed to find ore where none existed, shipped the ore to the smelter, and declared dividends. He provided jobs for local people, building roads and developing mines. Local citizens looked upon Doc as a genius. He had to be, to make the mines that he operated, pay off. He even brought a Pullman Car load of Easterners to Willcox and took them in carryalls, over "their" roads to see "their" mines. He showed them certified assays and smelter returns; and even let them examine the books. They scurried back home and sold other securities to buy more stock in the Dos Cabezas Mining Company.

My father hadn't been doing very well since he returned from the war. He was mighty glad when a friend got him a hoisting job at the mine, but it didn't last very long after the visiting easterners had made their trip. There was a "temporary" shut down because of falling silver and lead prices. Doctor Flower assured the investing public that things would pickup again, as soon as Teddy Roosevelt got things in hand. He assured them that gold was pegged and always in demand.

He let a few of them know that he had acquired a gold mine, close by Dos Cabezas that would take care of them until lead and silver came back.

The Old Terrible Mine had been worked out years before, but Doctor Flower's experts had determined that by following a fault line, there was a bonanza in sight. The mine was in the Dragoon Mountains, about six miles from Cochise City. The Old Terrible Mining Company was organized and people started clamoring for stock. My father landed the hoisting job, and although he was hoisting nothing but waste rock, he took part of his wages in stock. My father didn't know anything about mining, but he learned quickly.

Doctor Flower did things up right, once he got started. His Superintendent had a well dug out in the flat—good water at 350 feet. He started building a twenty stamp mill and a lot of frame houses to make the place look like a mining camp. The population consisted of about forty Mexicans, two Texans, a Mormon, a New Yorker, a Chinaman, and a "few white men." A fellow named Johnson who had a store north of Texas Canyon, put in a branch store and divided his time between both places. The Mormon was the millwright, the Chinaman ran the "Mulligan" (boarding house) and the New Yorker had been brought all the way from New York to keep the books. The "Super" also doubled as mine foreman. He and the Mexicans were the only persons that worked in the mine.

One day, the General Manager showed up in camp, with his wife and son. I had lots of fun with that boy, but that's another story. The General Manager and the Super went underground for an inspection. Then they exhibited a few flakes of gold, mixed with talc, that they said they had scraped off the "slick and slide" of the fault. The next few days resulted in a second shift being put to work. Excitement was at a fever pitch. It wasn't long before they hoisted the first skip load of ore. The bosses asked everybody to keep it quiet until there was a payday so that those that wanted to buy stock could get it before it got higher. But, the news leaked out and stock skyrocketed and sold like hot cakes. The next thing that happened was a strike. The Mexicans struck for higher wages. The big boss sent his family to Tucson by way of the Dragoon Summit station. I went along in the hack to tell the boy adios. I heard his mother whisper "El Paso" when she bought her ticket. That puzzled me, but I kept my mouth shut and my eyes open. When the agent put the tags on her baggage, they said "El Paso." The hack driver picked up the mail and we returned to camp. I hunted up my father and gave him the news. He looked puzzled and told me not to tell anyone else.

Soon the strikers tried to negotiate but the Boss wouldn't deal with them so they demanded their pay. The Boss told them that he would have to go to Willcox to get the money to pay them. In those days pay day came once a month. He explained that they never kept such large amounts of money in camp. So, the General Manager and the Superintendent saddled up and left camp. I don't know who started the suspicions that things looked bad, but the Mexicans got together with the rest and they went over the ridge. There they saw a road and a ventilation raise that had been used recently to pour ore into the mine. They took one look and left for the horse corral on the run. Dad and another fellow rode to Dragoon Summit, so they could check the west bound train which arrived there first. Then if they hadn't found their quarry they would ride the east bound through Cochise in case the Bosses boarded the train there. The bosses boarded the east bound train at Cochise, but they didn't see Dad. When the train reached Willcox, the bosses made no move to get off the train, until they saw my father and his partner approaching them, and then they got off. There was no money at the store that doubled as a bank, so the bosses decided to go back to camp—voluntarily, of course. Mr. Johnson, the store owner, had an unpaid bill for groceries delivered to the cook house, in addition to wages owed. It was arranged to draw a draft on Doctor Flower's New York Bank. The bosses were real cooperative. They stayed right there until the money showed up. They paid everybody and even redeemed all the Old Terrible stock in camp. In one way or another, men like these contributed much to the early development of Cochise County.

Galeyville Days, 1880 to 1908

from *The Chiricahua Bull Sheet*, December 23, 1957

We have had a number of requests for a story about Galeyville and we would love to oblige, but Father Time and Mother Nature have just about wiped out all the evidence. The town took its name from John H. Galey. He discovered some silver ore just west of the old townsite and entered into several agreements of sale and operations with a man by the name of Wessels. Whether all conditions and stipulations incorporated in the agreements were met is unknown. It appears from the original sales agreements that Galey would ultimately receive ten thousand dollars for each of two mines—The Texas and The Dunn.

Texas & Dunn Mining Claims Sales Agreement, October 8th, 1880
Seller: John H. Galey (President, Galeyville Townsite Co.)
Purchaser: S.M. Wessels (owner of the Galeyville Hotel &
Galey's Texas Consolidated Mining and Smelting partner)

in prospecting and developing either one or both of said mines, building and operating said Smelter or Furnace, as well as and together with the original cost and consideration money so paid for one or both of said mines by said party of the second part. And that until such indebtedness so specified herein shall have been fully paid and liquidated the said party of the first part, is not to draw or receive any part or portion of such profits or proceeds. on account of his said One quarter interest: But when the same shall have been fully paid and satisfied then the said part and thereafter the said party of the first part is to draw and receive one quarter of all such nett profits and proceeds. as they may from time to time accrued.

In Witness Thereof the parties hereto have hereunto set their hands and seals the day and year first above written.

Signed Sealed and Delivered in presence of.

Jos. C. Perry

S. M. Wessels [L.S.]

John H. Galey [L.S.]

Texas & Dunn Mining Claims Sales Agreement, Galey's & Wessels' signatures

Galey named the one mine the "Texas," which indicated that he was either a Texan or felt it wouldn't amount to much.[9] When Paradise was on the boom in 1903 to 1907, there were still a few old fellows around who had resided in Galeyville. From their tales, which are not too well remembered, and from the physical aspects at the site, we will try to give you some idea of what it was like.

Ruben Hadden, Albert Hoch, and Jim Hancock were the old residenters referred to, together with Old Man John Sullivan on Whitetail Canyon; Albert Fink on Silver Creek; Lew Scanlon down at the big bend in Turkey Creek; and, Baldy George Walker, with residence just about wherever night happened to overtake him.

No doubt Steven B. Reed also visited Galeyville on occasion as he settled in Cave Creek on what is now the Southwestern Research Station at about the time mining and smelting operations in Galeyville were at the peak. The town was located on a mesa a short distance west of Turkey Creek, and a bit over a mile north of Paradise. The slag dump is visible from the present road. There are no houses or even any walls standing. The only indication of past habitations are graded-out places where the wooden structures stood and mounds of dirt where the adobe ones tumbled down.

The old dance hall was still in pretty good condition until about 1908, when it caught fire and burned all the wood work, the adobe walls have completely weathered away. An old fellow by the name of Mills was living in it at the time it burned. He was the last resident but he had moved in quite a time after the town had been abandoned. No census was ever taken, but judging from old stories and from the building sites, there were probably about one hundred fifty regular residents, supplemented from time to time by hundreds of visitors—good and bad, but mostly bad.

---

[9] John H. Galey was not a Texan; he was in fact an oil man from Titusville, Pennsylvania. He and his partners organized the short-lived Texas Consolidated Mining and Smelting Company in 1881 for the purpose of mining and smelting lead and silver ore in the Chiricahuas. See the chapter "Galeyville" for more background on Galey and his town.

Billy the Kid[10], Big Foot Wallace, Curly Bill Brosius, and his numerous followers were frequently there. Big Foot Wallace shot Curly Bill through the neck one night in a saloon brawl. Bill did not die from the gunshot, but Big Foot might have. There is no record of him ever being seen again after he hurriedly left town the night Curly Bill was shot. Many years later Bill Sanders found the skeleton of a man in a crevice of rock on a little hill just north of Grapevine Spring. An old rotted saddle was on top of the skeleton and Bill thinks this might have been the remains of Big Foot. He probably had been Dry-Gulched by some of Curly's henchmen. There have been many stories told and written about Galeyville, but if they are true, you can come to one of two conclusions: either those people were cannibals, or they were the poorest shots in the world, as the graveyard had exactly three graves after the smoke had cleared and the population had departed in its entirety. One grave was reportedly occupied by one of Curly Bill's men who Parson Chenoweth killed with a blow from his fist. Another was a stranger found dead on the street one morning with his head bashed in by a pick handle in the hands of a party or parties unknown; the third died of pneumonia.

There is no one alive today that was in Galeyville at that time. The chances of verifying any of this are nil, but the fact that there are a total of five graves is indisputable, and several of we old Paradise residents know for sure that two of the people died in Paradise. That was before the present day Paradise Cemetery was established. One of the two was a little boy about ten years of age by the name of Willie Shipman, and the other was a miner whose name is not remembered.

Jim Hancock in later years until his death was Justice of the Peace and Postmaster at Paradise, was inclined somewhat to the Blood and Thunder with his Galeyville tales. Baldy George Walker was generally drunk from the time he hit town until he ran out of money, so he knew only the saloon where he had bought his first drink, and the last place he bummed a meal. He then headed back to work on some ranch. He sometimes worked for Old Man Shanahan who was the origi-

---

[10] This "Billy the Kid" mentioned by Carson Morrow was probably not the infamous William H. Bonney who fought in New Mexico's Lincoln County War, and was gunned down by Sheriff Pat Garrett in 1881. This name was also given to a "William H. Claiborne," who drifted into southern Arizona territory as a teenager and hired on as a ranch hand at the John Slaughter Ranch—where he earned the nickname "The Kid" for his reputed diminutive stature. He later was rumored to be involved with the notorious Clanton-McLaury Gang (aka "The Cow-boys"), and in 1882 was killed in a Tombstone gunfight with Buckskin Frank Leslie when the latter refused to refer to him as "Billy the Kid."

nal owner of the Red Top Ranch which now belongs to Sam Mosely. Albert Hock was a taciturn old German blacksmith who seldom talked of the past, or the future either, for that matter.

Ruben Hadden had a better memory and was the most conservative and interesting story teller of the lot. He claimed to be a Utah born Mormon, and that he had quit the Church because of the Mountain Meadow Massacre, which occurred in September of 1857.[11] Haddon said he was about nine years of age at the time, and helped drive away the stock after the older Mormons had murdered the immigrants. As soon as he was big enough to shift for himself, he came to Arizona and was at Galeyville throughout its active existence. He never mentioned his activities during that time, but whatever they were they must have been lucrative for throughout the ensuing years of his life, he seldom if ever engaged in any gainful occupation. He always lived well and paid for everything he bought either in gold coin or with gold certificates. Hadden said Galey never could make ends meet on his mining and smelting venture until after Curly Bill robbed the Mexican smugglers in Skeleton Canyon and took their loot to Galeyville and blew it on wine, women, and song. Galey acquired over two hundred thousand of the Mexican Silver Pesos at reduced rates and ran them through his smelter to sweeten up the values of the low grade ore. In that manner he not only recovered the silver in the form of bullion, but boosted up the figures on his smelter certificates, which perhaps enabled him to sell out to Wessels. If any good neighbors can supplement, correct, or enlarge on this story, we will appreciate it if they will do so.

Portal: The Early Years

from *The Chiricahua Bull Sheet*, January 16, 1958

A while back we published a little story predicting that Portal would move away from the present location to a site further up the creek, and everybody

---

[11] This is in reference to Mormons murdering approximately two hundred men, women, and children in southern Utah. The presumed motive for the Mormons' treachery and murder was to rob the wealthiest wagon train and livestock herds to pass through Utah Territory. Two books—of many—pertaining to the murders and theft are: *The Mountain Meadows Massacre*, by the Mormon apologist Juanita Brooks; and *Massacre At Mountain Meadows*, by William Wise. Wise's book is possibly the truest portrayal of the monumental crime; not until September 2001 were more civilian lives lost in an act of terrorism on American soil. (In a chilling coincidence, the 1857 massacre's date was also September 11th.)

thought we were joking. Maybe we were, but Portal has moved one time before. When it first came in to existence circa 1905, it was named Portal because it was considered a gateway to Paradise, which at that time was a thriving mining camp. And, Portal was at the entrance to Cave Creek Canyon.

Not one of the present buildings were any part of the original town, nor were there any buildings on the present site. All that is left of the original town is the name, and the only original residents still living in this part of the country are Mr. and Mrs. Ed Epley, who now reside at Paradise. The founders of the town thought they had good reason to build up on the Mesa to the west of what is now Newman's Store, rather than down along the creek in the shady spots. About that time a flood came down Cave Creek which covered all the bottom land to a depth of several feet, and left drift wood high up in the trees as a reminder.

Old Portal had a considerably larger population than at present. Ed Epley was the first Postmaster and ran a grocery store and meat market in conjunction with the Post Office. He soon sold out to Emmett Powers and Fitch McCord. They built a large General Merchandise store stocked with all kinds of supplies and implements for ranching and mining. They also erected and put into operation a small hotel which was nice but not modern by present day standards. Neither of these ventures ever did very well financially. After a few years the hotel was torn down and moved away, and the store either burned down or was torn down and moved away. There were two saloons, one in a walled up tent was operated by a man by the name of McManus, who had a wife and daughter. The daughter, Minnie, married a fellow named Frank Hunter.

The other saloon was housed in a lumber building and was owned and operated by a man by the name of Boswell. He was a nice appearing quiet spoken man, but he nevertheless shot and killed two men in his saloon. The first was a fellow by the name of Reed—no relation to Stephen B. Reed—and the other man was named Jewell. Reed is buried across the creek to the east of Newman's Store. Jewell was buried in a prospect hole near the old Virtue Mine Tunnel, but some time later his brother, who was here with him, went back to Texas on the train, and came back with a wagon and team, disinterred the body and hauled it back to Texas for re-burial.

Reed and several others had been on an all night binge at Boswell's, and when the party broke up about day break, he went home and got his rifle, forced his way into the saloon and attempted to shoot Boswell, who pulled his pistol from under the bar and shot Reed in apparent self defense.

The second killing also occurred after a night of drinking and gambling, and before daybreak. Jewell came back to Boswell's and demanded another drink. Boswell had gone to bed in his living quarters which were adjoining the bar, and refused to get up and let Jewell in, so Jewell—armed with a heavy caliber rifle—shot off the lock and part of the door facing and came into the bar. Boswell got up, went into the bar room to pour Jewell a drink. While he was doing that, Jewell shot out the light, and Boswell ran back into his bedroom, picked up his double barrel shotgun and mowed Jewell down.

Two old-time residents—Jim Coachman and Hugh Rowe—went insane and were committed to the Insane Asylum in Phoenix. Some time before this happened, Coachman told Ed Epley that Rowe was going crazy, that he could tell from the look of Rowe's eyes. It happened that Coachman went off the beam first and was sent to the bug house a few months before Rowe. When the officers arrived there with Rowe, Coachman came up, shook hands with him, and said: "Hello, Hugh, I knew damned well you would be here before long. I told them fellows down there that you was going crazy a long time ago."

Several different things contributed to the short lived prosperity of the original town of Portal. The Savage Mine in Round Valley, of which Jim Reay was superintendent, was employing several miners and some men were building a small smelter, which was never in operation as it was built before the mine was developed, or should we say over-developed? Anyway, when all was said and done, there was no ore to smelt so the whole works was shut down, the machinery sold and moved away. Jim Reay moved onto his homestead down at the mouth of Cave Creek and started farming and raising horses and cattle.

The Virtue Mining Company, with Ed Epley as superintendent, was employing several miners driving the long tunnel into the limestone mountain Northwest of Portal. That work was done without benefit of machinery. They used single and double jacks—four and eight pound hammers—with hand-turned steel drills and bits. The operation lasted longer than the Savage, but with the same results—no ore.

Filing Homesteads on Government land was just getting under way in this part of the country at that time. Fred Finnicum homesteaded the place which now belongs to the Toles Sisters; Hugh Rowe's claim was on the north side of the lane to the west of town; Powers and McCord filed claims on most of the land laying between the Ranger Station and the Post Office; and, a widow whose name is not remembered homesteaded the land covering the little seep spring on the mountain side about two miles directly west of Portal. She married Walt Finnicum while proving up on her claim, but they didn't stay hitched very long. The main part of the AVA Ranch was homesteaded several years later by an ex Forest Ranger by the name of Billy Stewart. There were a good many Nesters or other homesteaders located further down in the valley who did most of their trading in Portal. Considerable trade came from people travelling between Paradise and Rodeo up to the time when Paradise went on the rocks for the same reason the aforementioned two mines failed—no pay dirt.

A lot of wood was being cut and shipped to Douglas, Bisbee, and Tucson. Frank Kelsey had a big bunch of Mexican wood cutters camped about where the John Hands Dam is now located. Powers and McCord and some others were also in the wood business. The wood was hauled to Rodeo on wagons, and shipped from there on the railroad.

The Spectacular Paradise Jail Break

from *The Chiricahua Bull Sheet*, January 28, 1958

Now that Ingwold Isaacson has acquired the old Paradise Jail and remodeled it into a dwelling, some of our readers have requested that we tell them the history of it. Well, right at the beginning, it is not the original jail. The first one was an open air establishment consisting of a log chain stretched between two oak trees, one of which is still standing. For a time, it did the job as most, if not all the customers were in durance vile for the crime—being drunk and disturbing the peace. Speaking in plain English, the culprit had spent all their money for booze and were trying to mooch a free drink. Few women were arrested, but once in awhile one of the girls from across the creek, as the Red Light District was called, would go on a binge and carve up her man a little, or throw a few whiskey bottles through the big mirror behind some bar. Instead of shackling them to the log chain, they were shackled to an old style iron bedstead in the back room of one of the honky-tonks. Hiram Fisher owned a saloon in Paradise, and used to relate some pretty lively tales about that, but in this pure and gentle publication, we can't re-tell them.

Paradise began to boom when Cap Burns sold his mining claims located at the head of what is now called Hospital Canyon to the Chiricahua Development Company in 1903. The boom ended with the Money Panic of 1907. The present jail was built at about the time of the Bust, or a short time thereafter, so probably never housed over a half dozen prisoners all together. However, it was the scene of the most spectacular jail break on record anywhere. It was effected by an hombre named Pablo Zuniga, who was ordinarily a most un-spectacular fellow to have ever come up from Old Mexico. Pablo, in his own opinion, was a man of considerable consequence, and by Chiricahua Standards of that day he was somewhat wealthy. He owned ten burros and pack saddles, and had a big fat wife and seven or eight kids ranging in age from ten downward. He could cut and pack into town a cord of wood every day, which he sold for two good round silver American dollars. Flour for tortillas and Frijoles were cheap, and he frequently got enough ahead financially to buy a few bottles of vino, and go on a spree. At such time he invariably wore out a few doubles of pack rope on Maria and the kids. There was nothing wrong with that in his way of thinking, nor in the family's way of thinking either. How were they to know that he still truly loved them if he didn't beat hell out of them once in awhile?

They all lived in a tent, and had some pretty fair clothing, and led a happy life until a nosey gringo neighbor happened to go by while the Zuniga family was being set to rights and being assured of Pablo's undying love as their lord and master. That was the beginning of the end. The neighbor, not knowing that class of Mexicans and their way of life, rushed to town and told Mart Moore, who had succeeded Luke Short as Constable, that Pablo was beating his wife. Mart couldn't see anything wrong with that as he had a Mexican wife and three half breed kids himself. He had lived among them all his life and knew their idiosyncrasies—boy, ain't that a dandy word? In fact Mart had shot and killed three wood cutters in a brawl in Ben Hilam's saloon not long before. But, the complainant was so insistent that he went out and collared Pablo and threw him in the clink. Now Maria didn't understand the gringos and their strange ways any better than the nosey neighbor understood Mexicans. Who ever heard of throwing the head of a family in jail for exercising his rights and attending to his duty? Maria took a big monkey wrench down to the jail and proceeded to twist the bars out of the window before Mart Moore hardly got the door in front locked. That occurred in the middle of the afternoon.[12]

Anyone but Pablo would have waited until nightfall to escape, but he was still full of vino and feeling Muy Bravo, so he started climbing straight up the mountain side east of the jail. The further up the mountain he climbed, the more bravo

---

[12] A man by the name of Henry Paulhemus laid the stone walls of the jail.

he felt. When he got about half way to the top, he stopped and began yelling and cursing all the gringos at large, and Mart Moore in particular. He invited Mart to come and get him if he was man enough and not just a damned coward. Pablo was in plain view of practically everybody in town, and his yelling soon afforded him a large audience. In the annals of jail breaking it is doubtful that an escapee ever had that many eye witnesses. Although he was in a position to see everything in town, he failed to see Mart saddling his horse and riding across the creek toward him. When Pablo finally did see Mart, it was much too late. He climbed as he had never climbed before, but a belly full of vino slowed him up and Mart overtook him just before he topped out, so he lay down on his back and defied anyone in the world to take him back to jail. Mart whipped out his pistol, apparently with the full intention of putting Pablo out of business for keeps. Before he "lowered the Boom" on Pablo, he realized he was in plain view of practically the entire population of Paradise. Pablo was still "playing to the audience," shouting and daring Mart to shoot him, but under the circumstances, Mart decided against that. Mart knew his Mexicans, so instead of shooting the escapee, he put his pistol back in the holster, pitched a loop of his rope around Pablo's feet, and started dragging him down the mountain toward the Calaboose, a distance of several hundred yards.

Just like Mart knew he would, Pablo soon changed his tune, and began begging: "Please shoot me like a man." The physical punishment of being dragged through the boulders wasn't what did it. He would actually have preferred being killed to the humiliation of being treated like anything less than the "Hombre Valiente" he felt himself to be at the moment. So, Mart let him get up and walk back to the jail where he was shackled to the "bull ring" embedded in the floor until he sobered up and promised to leave town. Prosecuting him for wife beating was out of the question as Maria refused to testify against him.

DRUNK AS A SKUNK

When Carson Morrow was yet a patrolman along the border, on one sortie he apprehended two bandidos. He fired a shot to alert his partner, who was off a distance, and then he reached around one of the men to search for weapons. The thug grabbed his hands, and his fellow illegal alien stabbed Morrow. The knife cut through to the outer layer of his heart. He fell back, one alien fleeing the scene, and Morrow's assailant coming at him to finish him off. Carson drew his revolver—a favorite .44 caliber—and shot the bandido.

The bullet hit the thug square in the belly button, but did not immediately kill him. Morrow finished the job, hitting his attacker on the head with the butt of his revolver. In the heat of the moment, Carson apparently exerted considerable force, as he bent the frame of the revolver. Some of the advice he gave new recruits was: "If you are going to hit someone with a revolver, hit them with the barrel. Otherwise, you may bend the frame."

There was a different atmosphere in the realm of law enforcement in those days. If you broke the law—were a criminal—you were treated as such. There were no grey areas; it was pure black and white. In a hurry, Carson jumped out of his vehicle chasing an illegal alien—they were, just as today, breaking the laws of the United States, and were not called "undocumented aliens" or "emigrants" as they are now. In haste, Carson left his firearm in his car. Going through a barbed wire fence he became entangled in the wire. The wetback—"mojado," or more appropriately in the desert, an "alambre" or "wireback"—saw the situation. He threw some good-sized rocks at Carson, hitting him in the head. When he lost consciousness, the illegal thought Morrow was dead and ran away.

Carson Morrow, Tucson, Arizona, 1944
Photograph courtesy of the National Border Patrol Museum, El Paso, Texas

I stayed with my Aunt and Uncle Carson at their Tucson home on River Road the first years I attended the University of Arizona. On winter afternoons, sometimes he and I would sit around, backs to the concrete southern side of the barn, where the sun had warmed the wall. On occasion he would point to a spot in the corral and say: "That is where I buried that wetback's skull—the one who tried to kill me. My men caught up to him, and brought me his skull." That is all he would say. His property was directly in line with Stone Avenue in those days. When the area was cleared of his house, barn, and corrals, and Stone Avenue was extended to River Road, maybe a skull was found. If so, the excavators probably thought it was a long-dead Indian's skull.

Carson always had a cabin in the Chiricahua Mountains, which he and his family would visit from time to time. Nearing retirement, he owned a home in East Whitetail Canyon in the Chiricahuas. There was a small apple orchard on the property, planted many decades before Carson acquired the place. Apples were harvested, and apple cider made. Some of the cider became hard—had a bit of alcohol. On one junket to the mountains, when winter had come, Carson got an idea of putting some hard cider in an open pan.

The cider froze, to some extent, with an alcoholic slush coming to the surface—a version of applejack. Carson—or "Chief" as he was known—and some others gathered around the kitchen table began skimming spoons of the applejack. It was sweet and tasty, and the more they consumed, the better it tasted, until everyone had a fine glow on. After a few days at the cabin everyone left bound for Tucson. Since there was a good supply of hard cider on hand, it was decided that they would leave some in open pans for nature to process into applejack.

There was a screened-in porch attached to the house and in it was a chest type deep freeze. Nothing was stored in the freezer. A perfect place for the pans of hard cider. With the lid open, the winter weather could work its magic, and the elixir would be ready when next the cabin was visited. A perfect plan. All was in place, and Chief and associates vacated the premises. Only, someone—none confessed—left the screen door to the outside unlatched.

Another trip to the mountains was made in a week or so. The days were brisk and the nights cold, and there was no concern that the applejack experiment had been anything but successful. Maybe, the Morrows allowed, they would not partake of the fine drink in quite the amount consumed on the previous trip—at least at one sitting. Supplies carried, and a fire burning in the wood burner stove, it was suggested that the applejack be checked for content and taste. One of Chief's daughters went to the screened porch. She noticed that the screen door was open, and seemed to have been for a time as sycamore leaves had blown in and scattered across the floor. She hoped none were in the cider pans. She looked into the freezer, gasped, and fled the room.

"What is the matter?" Carson asked. "Is something wrong?" She answered: "Someone left the screen door unlatched and the wind blew it open. Not only that, there is a large striped-backed skunk in there and it is *in* the freezer." This caused a bit of alarm. Not only was the applejack ruined, but what to do about the skunk?

Carson ventured a quick look into the freezer. He looked at the skunk and the skunk looked at him. The animal appeared calm. What to do? A board was slowly lowered into the freezer. The cider pans had been overturned, applejack all over the bottom of the freezer. The skunk investigated the board, climbed to the rim of the freezer, hesitated, and then fell to the floor. It lay on its side for awhile, got up and staggered out the door. Applejack had kept it alive and happy, and it left—drunk as a skunk.

"Stuttering" Harry Lipstrew & his dog, Ruby
At Harry's Cabin in Jhus Canyon, circa 1921

STUTTERING HARRY, BILLY BOWLEGS, BULL HILL, AND BARFIELD

"Lordy, my Lord," Blumberg said. "If Harry only knew who he is." Blumberg, said to be of German descent, was a prospector and miner in Paradise days, which began in the early 1900s. Blumberg's cabin was located at the mouth of the canyon which joins East Whitetail Canyon near the junction of Indian Creek, and today bears his name.

Blumberg referred to Harry Lipstrew, who was called "Stuttering Harry." Blumberg said Harry was from a noble European family, either German or possibly of Romanian origin. Harry and Blumberg spoke fluent German, but Harry stuttered when he conversed in English, and in those early days it seemed practically everyone had a nickname. It was certain that Harry had sustained a severe head injury resulting in a degree of amnesia.

Stuttering Harry was a merchant seaman. When his ship docked at Brownsville, Texas, he was on shore leave when he heard about the mining boom at Paradise, in the Chiricahua Mountains of Arizona. He jumped ship and purchased two burros, which he named Jenny and Monkey. He packed his possessions on Monkey, and riding Jenny, headed for Paradise. It was 1904. Harry did not find a vacant spot that suited him when he arrived in Paradise, but he found an old abandoned log cabin in Jhus Canyon.[1] He moved in, fixed up the cabin to some extent, and began searching for "pay dirt." His efforts, as with many, failed to

---

[1] Named for the Apache Indian Chief "Jhu" or "Juh," Geronimo's brother-in-law and a fierce fighter against both Mexican and American military forces in the late 1800s.

strike it rich. Between prospecting, Harry grew vegetables and fruit, packed his burros, and sold his produce to a ready market in Paradise.

Harry worked as a hired hand on nearby ranches and often as a miner in the Paradise diggings, when the growing seasons ended. Harry's burros and his dog Ruby kept company with Harry, and visitors to his cabin oft heard his long monologues directed to his animals, in broken English. Occasionally he sang to his companions in German. Harry and his companions seemed content with their lives, but one cold winter in the early 1920s, his feet were frostbitten and gangrene set in. He struggled over to the Morrow home in Whitetail Canyon. They loaded Harry into their automobile and struck out for the Douglas Hospital. When Harry learned his destination, he said he needed new clothes to replace his worn clothing. After a stop for clothes, Harry was taken to the hospital. Unfortunately, his condition was treated too late, and Harry died a few days later.

In later years, the Duval Mining Company took over Harry's claims. They diamond-drilled the area, and found nothing of commercial value. Stuttering Harry could have told them there was small chance of finding any quantity of lead, silver, gold, or copper where they drilled.

§   §   §

Billy Bowlegs' real name was William Bradshaw. He had been an old-time railroader, and while working in Colorado was injured in a train wreck. The accident resulted in his extremely bowed legs. Leaving the railroad life, Billy Bowlegs acquired some burros, and headed south, searching for gold. His travels took him to Guatemala, where he met another prospector who said there was a big strike on the Yaqui River in the State of Sonora, Mexico. The Yaqui River strike did not pan out for Billy, but he heard talk of vast deposits of silver ore in the Chiricahua Mountains of southeastern Arizona. Billy and his two burros arrived in the Chiricahuas and he staked a claim at Iron Springs near the head of Pinery Canyon. Billy had been grubstaked by a man named Stamps, and he named his cabin after his friend. The cabin was little more than a lean-to with a chimney and fireplace. There were no windows and when the door was closed the cabin was pitch dark, unless a fire or candle was flickering.

One winter Billy nearly died of pneumonia. It was reckoned Billy pulled through by having developed an iron constitution from eating food he had cooked.

At last Billy gave up his claim, moved to Paradise and took up residence in a shack. Occasionally he invited a friend or two over for a meal. Upon arrival, guests were handed a frying pan, and told to help themselves to the bacon and eggs. If they took but a strip or two of bacon and several eggs, Billy would tell them that if he had not thought they were hungry, he would not have invited them over. Billy would cook a number of eggs and a pound or more of bacon, and while standing, eat everything straight out of the frying pan.

One evening in a Paradise cafe, Billy finished off a large meal. Another diner remarked that he supposed Billy was still hungry after eating such a large amount of food. Billy allowed as how he probably could eat a bit more, and the other man said he doubted that. The two wrangled back and forth and Billy said he could eat a few eggs. So Billy was asked, how many are a few? Billy said, well, maybe fifty or so would just about fill the bill. A wager was made in the amount of fifty dollars, which was a substantial amount of money in those days. There was a variation as to the cooking of the eggs: Some said the eggs were fried, others said they were hard-boiled. Fried or boiled, Billy ate fifty eggs, then two more—just rubbing it in a bit. The fifty dollars was paid over, and the loser, somewhat chagrined, said now he supposed Billy must have reached his limit. Billy replied that he had in actuality not reached any limit and could eat a few more eggs provided they were accompanied by several nice thick ham steaks. The food was prepared and Billy once again cleaned his plate. It is not known whether he ate standing or sitting down, when faced with a challenge.

Billy packed up and left Paradise one day, and settled down on the outskirts of Tucson. There he raised chickens and sold eggs. One of Billy's miner friends remarked that Billy's hens must be good producers to lay eggs faster than Billy consumed them. Billy sort of faded away, and no one knew what became of him. The great eating contest at Paradise lived on long after Billy was gone.

§   §   §

"Bull Hill" (Duncan) McDonald came down to the Chiricahuas from Canada. On his way to Paradise he stopped off at a mining camp in Colorado called Bull Hill, and McDonald talked about his time at Bull Hill to such an extent that he became known as Bull Hill McDonald. McDonald worked some claims he held in the northern reaches of the Chiricahua Mountains, located in Indian Creek and Wood Canyon near Jack Dunn's 1870s silver strike.

Upon returning from a trip, Bull Hill discovered that a neighbor prospector named Claire had jumped one claim. McDonald had kept up annual assessment work as required by mining law on the claims, and had monuments and claim notices posted on the claims. Bull Hill McDonald met Claire on the Indian Creek Trail and politely asked Claire what the hell did he think he was doing on Bull Hill's claims. Claire whipped a hand behind his back. Bull Hill, thinking Claire was going for his gun, swung his rifle around and fired, killing Claire on the spot.

McDonald was arrested and tried for manslaughter in a Tombstone court. Prospectors and miners testified on Bull Hill's behalf. They said he was a steady, honest, kind-hearted man, and it appeared that Bull Hill would win free of the charge. And he would have, but when asked by the presiding judge if he would do the same again, Bull Hill looked the judge in the eye, and said he would probably do the same again. Bull Hill was sentenced to ten years in the Territorial Prison at Yuma, but through the efforts of his friends the governor pardoned Bull Hill McDonald.

§   §   §

Frank Barfield came west from Texas and settled around Paradise, Arizona just as the town began to boom about 1903. Frank made his living driving freight wagons from San Simon and Rodeo, hauling goods and machinery of all kinds. There were few wells and no piped-in water, with the town residents relying on Frank to supply them with barrels of water. Frank used "retired" whisky barrels, well sterilized and often with a hint of flavor from previous contents. Frank also freighted in barrels of whisky for the saloons. In those days most saloons did their own bottling and labeling.

Frank Barfield was a drinking man and an enterprising one. On any haul from the railroad town to Paradise, Frank would tap a barrel or two for a jug full of its alcoholic elixir. This he accomplished by driving up one of the barrel hoops, boring a small hole with a brace and bit in the exposed area, and draining a small jug from the barrel. Each hole was then plugged with a wooden pin Frank had shaped to fit the drilled hole. The plug was trimmed flush and the hoop driven down to its original position, covering the plugged hole.

Barfield hid his jugs along his route where he could pause for refreshment and further fortification. He avoided sobriety while never being seen carrying a bottle or buying a drink in a saloon. When the barrels were opened for use as water containers, some of their insides were said to have resembled a porcupine as a result of Frank's numerous tappings.

RALPH MORROW: THE RUSTLERS OF MONTEZUMA PASS

"There is always some cattle rustling going on, even in these modern days. A few years past [*circa 1950*], I noticed some buzzards circling in the head of the North Fork of Cave Creek, here in the Chiricahuas. It turned out someone had butchered one of Jack Maloney's yearlings. Jack first came to this area as a cowboy for the San Simon Cattle Company. He had a little ranch, ran about a hundred head of cattle. He later sold the outfit and cattle to me when he got too old to run cattle in the mountains.

"There was dried blood on beer cans, with good fingerprints around where this beef had been killed, but what put me onto the rustlers was a handkerchief they had left. This had a laundry mark, this handkerchief, and through that we were able to round up everyone involved in the cow stealing.

"The only time I ever came under anything that was really what I considered dangerous, was when I was patrolling one day in the Huachuca Mountains around Montezuma Pass. I happened to see three men apparently hunting out of season. I settled down in one of these bear grasses, they are called. If you sit down in one of those large grass bunches, it is pretty hard for anyone to see you at a distance. I began watching these fellows, and after awhile, they went down the mountain there and killed a big, fat, yearling that belonged to the rancher there, a man named D'Albini. Why, I had to take action some way, and they were about half a mile from me on the face of the mountain. I figured that these men must have come up the road from the lower Montezuma Canyon, on the south end of the Huachuca Mountains, and that all I had to do was get down below their automobile and wait and catch them on a roadblock, because the road to the west side had a locked gate, and they couldn't go that way.

"Nevertheless, I finally decided to go over the hill, get my car, and race down the mountain, which would indicate that I wasn't concerned with them or hadn't seen them at all. They would stand pat. After they killed this yearling, two of them started butchering it and one of them took a rifle and sat down on a little mine dump in the edge of some brush watching. He was the guard against people picking them up—arresting them. Anyway, I raced down the other side, and got out of sight of these men, and they didn't know but what I had gone on, for sure. I left the car and walked back up the mountain and went in on top of a ridge and down through some brush. When I got to where the guard had been sitting, why, he wasn't sitting there. However, I was close enough that I could hear these men chopping on the beef with a hatchet. They were not too far from me. I worked my way down into where I could see the two men operating, and they were very close to me, but I wasn't afraid of them. But I was afraid of the man with the gun, because I realized if he saw me, he was going to take a shot at me.

"I was really uneasy. I decided on a plan of action, which I thought was best at the time. On one side of the canyon there was a cliff parallel to the bottom where they were working and it wasn't too far from them. I went in behind this cliff; worked my way around to the end of it, and I was going to throw down on the guard with a shotgun I had. That morning I had set out a .401 automatic rifle to carry along, this was a gun made specially for shooting bank robbers, but I had taken a shotgun loaded with bird shot instead. Just as I came to the end of the cliff, I saw the guard sitting there close to me with a gun on his lap, but he hadn't heard me at all. So, when I gave them the command to throw up their hands, and for the men butchering the beef to come up there, why, this fellow—the guard—pushed the gun off into the dirt and just turned around with his hands up and started walking up slowly toward me.

"The other two fellows got so excited, they were just jumping up and down—I have never seen men quite as excited as they were. They left the hatchet, butcher knives, and one of them left his glasses there at this beef they were butchering. Coming up toward me, this head outlaw, he was right behind the guard who had dropped the gun, and he just reached down and grabbed the gun. He started trying to get a shot at me, and I was holding my fire because at that distance a shotgun loaded with bird shot wouldn't do much damage. I was figuring to shoot this outlaw in the head. Anyway, he dogged back and forth there for a few passes, and then he jumped toward some bushes. But, just as he jumped, I let this gun go off and it did hit him in the side of the head and one hand which he had thrown up. He let out a big yell, threw the rifle back over his head, and ran on all fours into the brush, and got away—for a time. I got the guard and got everything shaped up, and we caught the other two men. The ringleader got five years in the penitentiary for cow stealing. That was, I consider, one of the more dangerous situations I encountered."[1]

---

[1] The audio tapes from which these transcripts were made were short on dates. Best estimate for when the "Rustlers at Montezuma Pass" happened was around 1936—a year or two after Ralph broke his leg riding a big Harley-Davidson or Indian motorcycle while out patrolling for other lawbreakers. See the chapter "Ralph Morrow: For Whom The Laws Hold" for more description of this accident.

Paint Rock Mining Company Stock Certificate issued to William King Morrow, 1917

THE STRIKER AND THE SHAKER

The Hilltop Mine in the Chiricahua Mountains was first located by Jack Dunn. Jack was a packer and scout for the army, operating out of Fort Bowie. Much of his time afield was spent prospecting. He located claims in the 1880s. Frank and John Hands acquired the property and sold it to the Hilltop Metals Mining Company in 1913. A small town was established on the west side of the ridge separating North Pinery and East Whitetail Canyon. A tunnel was driven through the mountain, and a second larger town was developed on the east side of the ridge, which included a power house for generating electricity and compressed air.

Blast-hole drilling had for years been done with drills powered by compressed air; however, prospectors and small mines, in most cases, drilled by hand methods altogether. For example, circa 1910, one of William King ("W.K.") Morrow's mining ventures in the Paradise area—dubbed the "Malachite"—was entirely hand-drilled. After geological studies, the prospect was eventually shut down—but first, the miners sank a shaft straight down, to a depth of 300 feet. They would drill their blast holes using hammers and hand steel, then load and tamp-cap dynamite into the holes, spit the fuses, and climb the three-hundred-foot ladder back to the surface.

Blasted rock was at first hoisted to the surface using a mine bucket, pulley wheel, and work horse. As the shaft was sunk to greater depths, a steam hoist was installed. Ralph Morrow, then twelve years of age, operated the hoist. Some of the miners complained about him operating the hoist, but he had no accidents.

When Ralph's younger brother John was six years old, he and their father W.K. Morrow rode the mine bucket to the shaft bottom. He said he was scared to death at the time, in spite of Ralph's safety record.

John Morrow said there were two single-jack miners at the Malachite. One was named Housely and the other "Black Joe" Nilsged.

As the name implies, single-jack drilling was a one-man operation: in one hand, the miner held a drill steel with an end sharpened by a blacksmith, or tipped with a star bit; he then struck the steel with his other hand, using a four- or five-pound hammer. After each blow, the steel and bit were rotated a few degrees, and the steel struck again. When drill cuttings began to accumulate in the hole, a powder spoon—a long metal rod with a small cup shaped on one end—was used to remove the broken rock.

When drilling a perpendicular face in an adit or tunnel, a burn hole was drilled, with relievers, trimmers, and lifters completing the pattern. A burn hole was usually centered in the blast-hole pattern, and holes drilled around it.

John A. Morrow, Nicosia, Cyprus, circa 1938

A variation of hand drilling was double-jack drilling. One man held the steel and rotated it after each blow. A second man struck the end of the drill steel with a ten- or twelve-pound hammer. This miner was called the Striker. The holder was, and often for good reason, called the Shaker.

Brothers Carson and Ralph Morrow decided they would develop and mine a property known as the Gardner in Whitetail Canyon. Carson elected to be the Shaker, leaving Ralph the Striker.

Carson lined up the steel for the first hole.

Ralph drew back for a mighty blow …

… and hit Carson on the knee.

End of mining venture.

Malachite Mine prior to installation of steam hoist, 1910
Ralph Morrow at left, W. K. Morrow at right

W.K. Morrow (2nd from right, in bowler hat), Douglas Fairgrounds, circa 1910

The men are posing with what is possibly a Pearse Monoplane, designed by Richard Pearse, a New Zealand farmer, inventor, and early aviation pioneer.

RALPH MORROW, THE EARLY YEARS: WAGON, HORSE, & AUTOMOBILE

"I was around four years of age when the family left Roswell area and ended up on Eagle Creek north of Clifton, where my father established a ranch. My dad [*William King "W.K." Morrow*] sold out and we moved to Douglas where we stayed until November of 1903, when we came to the Chiricahuas—Paradise.

"We loaded up everything in a covered wagon [*leaving Eagle Creek, and later Douglas*], and started toward Douglas. We reached the Frisco River by Clifton, and it was in high flood stage. There were several camps of people traveling the same direction as us, that had to camp; they couldn't cross the river. There was one thing they were doing—I always will remember: The river water was all we had to use and they would get a bucket of water and cut prickly pear leaves and drop in the water to settle the mud, and some way or another, it did. That's one of the things that stand out in a small boy's memory that ordinarily wouldn't be remembered by even older people.

"The trek we made after we left Duncan, here we were alone that time, generally there would be a half dozen wagons, one behind the other, you know. Usually you started early, and stopped for awhile mid-day, then along about 1:00 or 2:00 you would drive along until it began to get sundown. But, no travel was done after sundown. There was a big campfire and we'd eat, and by the time it began to get dark, we'd have our beds rolled out on the ground and we'd go to bed.

"The last thing though, before bedding down, we'd look after the horses and see that everything was straight. One of the things you had to keep in mind all the time was the good health of those horses. Darned sure not cripple any. Water was always one you had to remember. If you didn't make it to water, you had a wagon, you carry barrels of water so you could water those horses, because if there wasn't water for anything else, you had to water those horses.

"People today wouldn't enjoy that because they would be in a hurry and want to get on their way. But, really we enjoyed ourselves. We knew that we were not going to get there any quicker than we'd planned on; we could figure how many days it was going to take us, and so help me it would take that many days; sometimes a little more. When we hit a rainstorm, we pulled up and stopped. If it was near time to camp, we went ahead and camped for the night, and stayed in the wagon, which was waterproof. We always pulled out on high ground. If you stopped on low ground, you were liable to find your wagon bogged down when the ground got wet.

"Train travel, it was here at the time that we showed up. It was built right after the turn of the century through here, built by the Phelps-Dodge Corporation through this part. A different railroad, Southern Pacific, went through San Simon.[1]

"Horses—they certainly were the means of transportation at the time. I remember one time, and this would be typical of the times, that I rode with my father from here in the Chiricahua Mountains to Roosevelt Dam on horseback.[2] I had an uncle up near Roosevelt Lake, and I stayed to work for this uncle. My father went on back, so a few months or so later, I went home by myself. I was around fifteen or so at the time. It was getting pretty cold, I remember that, and I had one of these old Navajo Blankets and they all hump up like a cow hide and I'd get cold at night and have to build a fire and hobble my horse where he could graze. Coming round down there by the Coolidge Dam, wasn't any dam there then, why, a bunch of Indians overtook me. There was five or six of these Indians and one old Indian had his nose cut off I remember. I could speak Spanish, and he found that out, and got to talking and he told me he was born in the Chiricahuas.

---

[1] Southern Pacific's engine No. 31 crossed the Colorado River bridge at Yuma, Arizona on the morning of September 30, 1877. Not until March 20, 1880 did the rails reach Tucson. With two miles of track laid each day, the rails extended east to the Dragoon Summit by the end of July, then on to Willcox on August 26, 1880. Finally, on September 22, 1880, the Southern Pacific line crossed into New Mexico at Stein's Pass. Another line, constructed by The Arizona Eastern Railroad, reached from Bowie to Globe in December 1898. In late 1900, Phelps-Dodge formed the Southwestern Railroad of Arizona to link Bisbee with the Douglas Smelter. By the summer of 1902, this line—and others—became a part of the El Paso and Southwestern Railroad, whose tracks then ran from Douglas, Arizona to Deming, New Mexico.

[2] A distance of nearly 200 miles traveling on modern-day roads.

He was one of the little children when they moved the Chiricahua Apaches out of here. He asked me if I didn't get cold at night, and I told him, yeah, I got cold at night, darned near froze. He said, 'Well, I'll tell you what to do. Tonight when you camp, and you camp where there is sand, and better where a little wash is. You dig out two to three inches of that sand and you build fire with sticks all over it, build a good fire. Let that burn an hour or two and then cover it over with sand. Then you lay down there and put your blanket over you, never get cold.'

"So, that night I did that, and it was about daylight before I began to get cold, and it was time to get up and go anyway. That was the way we traveled. You ride along; you see a mountain way ahead of you. Today it's blue over there, after two or three days, the mountain gets blue on the other side, you've gone past it. That trip took seven days. Of course, my dad was a real horseman and he traveled all over and he drove cattle, he was on the great trail drives from Texas to the Dakotas, you know, delivering those Texas steers. He knew how to ride a horse and get a lot out of a horse. I learned from him. He said, 'If you are going to ride a horse hard, always wait till the last day you're gonna go on that trip, don't do it first.' The last day I rode from north of Bowie plumb into the Chiricahuas here right below Paradise that day, right across rough country, no road. And, that horse just went through with his ears sticking up; course he knew he was going home like I did.

"Speaking of things that impressed me most, one of them was the automobile. When we lived in Douglas in 1903, there was one automobile showed up there. It looked pretty much like a bunch of boxes nailed together; didn't look much like an automobile, but anyway, there were two fellows drove this automobile; wore derby hats, and they were quite something. Another little boy and I were over near what is now called Pirtleville one day, and all the roads wound around through the mesquites the way the wagons traveled. This thing came chugging along about like a good buggy team could trot. It had a sort of rack on the back, so we just ran and jumped on this rack. These fellows told us to get off and we wouldn't do it. We just hung on froze, and they had to stop this thing and pull us off to get rid of us. That was my first automobile ride.

"About 1905, the first automobile showed up in Paradise. It was a Cadillac owned by Doctor Adamson from Douglas. I don't think another car showed up in that town until 1909, then it wasn't much of an automobile. It was what you call a 'push car.' Three fellows were in it; when you came to a hill, two got out and pushed while the other one drove. Later on, I remember the first time I ever drove an automobile, and it was an old Model T and this fellow was drunk and he wanted me to drive him home, which was about a mile away. It was pretty good country or the car and me would have been badly wrecked by the time we got there, but I finally made it. It being an old Ford, every time I'd step down on the pedal that put it into low gear, I'd step too hard and kill the engine. Then I'd have to crank it. By the time we'd gone a mile or so, I'd done more work than if I'd been walking a long ways. By 1917 I even had a car, a Studebaker, and hired it out for trips from Hilltop to Rodeo and sometimes to Douglas or Silver City. We thought it was a pretty good automobile. It certainly wouldn't be now. In those days, if you had a car that ran 5,000 miles, we made history. Most would run maybe 1,000-1,500 miles and blow all to pieces. Early 1920s, wagons and teams began to disappear. You seldom saw a man riding a horse any more than rounding up cattle or some such. The Automobile changed our mode of travel to where it was nothing like it used to be.

"I know there's lots of things about the 'good old days' that were good, all right, and there were lots of things about the 'good old days' that were bad. Just like today."

Juanita (Kuykendall) Morrow, Whitetail Canyon, November 1936.
Her first whitetail buck, taken with "The Black Gun"

THE LAST HUNT

The Winchester Repeating Arms Company of New Haven, Connecticut, began production of the Model 54 rifle in 1925. Rifles were chambered in various calibers, but the .30 GOVT '06 was the most popular rifle produced throughout the years—until production of the Model 54, for all practical considerations, ended in 1937. The Model 54 was manufactured in limited numbers until 1941.

Ralph Morrow purchased a new Model 54 in 1931. It had a nickel steel 20-inch barrel, open sights, and a steel butt plate. Morrow removed the stock and, using heated stain, dyed the stock an ebony black. Thereafter it was always referred to as "The Black Gun." In the 1940s, a master gunsmith replaced the barrel with a longer blued barrel. A recoil pad, scope mounts, and a scope were added. This rifle, chambered in caliber .30-06, was a favorite of Patricia Morrow's.

Patricia was an expert rifle shot and a skilled horsewoman, although she made many hunts on foot. She began hunting whitetail, and some seasons, desert mule deer, in 1955. I had the privilege to go along at first as guide and game carrier, and then as the hunts grew in number, as a subservient guide, game transporter, and at times gun bearer.

Her first hunt was in Whitetail Canyon on Sugar Bill Hill, which is just south of the Morrow Orchard. We rimmed around the basin, and on an opposite hillside there were two whitetail bucks. After her guide declared that one of the bucks was older and larger than the other, the deer was dispatched by a single shot from the Black Gun fired by the beginning big-game hunter, Patricia. A year later, after I had decided to leave the Air Force, in which I was an officer, jet fighter pilot, flight leader, alert team captain, etc., we were again hunting deer.

Patricia Morrow: Target practice with Model 54 Winchester .30-06 ("The Black Gun"), 1954.
Father P.E. Mooney observing.

A buck jumped, a running shot, and, again, only a single shot was required. The same for the following year.

A whitetail buck in Lost Cabin Canyon of the Chiricahuas was dispatched with a single shot. Then the Black Gun was rested and a newly acquired .308 feather-weight Winchester was used. We were driving to Whitetail Canyon, where we would hunt on horseback. As we drove along the road, we stopped to glass the area. On George Hall Mountain—three miles east of Whitetail—we sighted three large mule deer bucks. "Well, Patricia, let's cross the open country on foot and see if you can get one of those bucks." The mule bucks climbed higher on George Hall, and disappeared from sight. We hastened across the flat, and suddenly one of the bucks appeared, looking straight at us. I suggested that we lay down in the grass, which we did, and the buck again disappeared. We continued on.

"When we climb out, those bucks are going to be just to west of us on top. They aren't alarmed, and you will have a good shot. They are all about the same size, so take your pick and shoot."

Up we climbed, and there the bucks were. We saw them, they saw us and ran. Three shots were fired and the bucks ran on unscathed. Now, who is under the gun when things go wrong? The hunter? No, the guide, game carrier and at times gun bearer. "Missed! And all because of this blanky-blank rifle you bought. I am not hunting anymore today. You march me across the flat. We lay down in the sticker grass, and what for? That's it. No more." The guide's job now is to soothe the hunter and offer empty words of encouragement.

"I think you may have hit one of them. We ought to at least see." The hunter agrees, knowing full well, as does the guide, that nothing was wounded. "Okay, suppose we go on a bit. We are up here on George Hall Mountain, might as well take a quick look." Patricia, the hunter, reluctantly agrees. A short while later a large whitetail buck is jumped. He runs far across the basin. "That is a pretty fair buck, Patricia." The response, and no shooting as yet: "I don't know, he doesn't look so large to me." The guide: "He is a pretty good buck."

The buck stops some three hundred yards away. Patricia fires, and the buck falls. "The way that buck acts, I'd say you hit him in the head or neck, and he is dead." The hunter replies: "That is where I was aiming." Once the buck is field dressed, and is being carried by the guide—me—Patricia says she does not think he is so very large after all. The guide says maybe you would like to carry him. Weighed back at the ranch house, he weighs 105 pounds, which is large for a Chiricahua whitetail.

Years go by, and a time comes when Patricia says she will hunt only for trophy deer. She is strong and agile, and could have been a large-bore rifle-shooting champion. She stands five feet and four inches, and weighs 110 pounds—slightly more than the trophy whitetail buck she proposes to hunt.

Early morning came to East Whitetail Canyon. Mollie Morrow, ten years of age, decided she would accompany Patricia, and me. Beyond the junction of Indian Creek and Whitetail a low ridge trends westward crossing the greater basin. We three began climbing the ridge. Some low-growing catclaw bushes thrived on the sunny slope. Thorns caught on Mollie's clothing. More thorns seemed to attack as she resisted the catclaw onslaught. She began to voice loud protestations. Patricia freed her from the diabolical bushes, and cautioned her, since we were hunting, to cease yelling and talking in a loud voice.

On a hillside three whitetail bucks grazed peacefully. One was of trophy size and with large antlers. "That buck on the right is probably as good a buck as you will find, Patricia."

After a moment she replied: "I don't know. I think we should go on hunting. Why don't you shoot him?"

More time lapsed. "I am going to hunt mule deer. Go ahead and shoot him."

More time passes. "No, I am not going to do it."

"Do you really want to hunt any type game—large or small—anymore?"

"No, I do not. I am not hunting again."

And so ended the hunting career of Patricia Morrow.

§　　§　　§

Your scribe hunted a last time with Ralph Morrow—the season of 1974. Leading our horses back to the ranch house, Ralph Morrow endured a rant declaring game would soon be almost gone. No control of predatory animals, such as lion and coyote, sporadic law enforcement of game laws, and too many hunts would probably wipe out the deer, javelina, and wild turkey of the Chiricahua Mountains. The rant ended with a rather theatrical declaration: "I will hunt no more!"

In 1976, our branch of the Morrow family moved back to the Chiricahuas, settling on a part of the Morrow ranch holdings. On an open space just east of our residence, one evening we counted forty mule deer, and two whitetail bucks. Often we would see six or eight bucks grazing near our home. Now, in this year of 2010, we see no mule deer, few javelina, no turkey, and rarely one or two whitetail. In broad daylight lion are sometimes seen.

For Patricia, hunting ended that day on a ridge in East Whitetail Canyon. For me, it was over in 1974. Patricia sometimes says, and on occasion with misty eyes, that she wishes she had never hunted.

Tech. Sgt. Mollie Morrow, Retirement Day, 2004: 21 years active duty.
Wearing a well-deserved Air Force Meritorious Service Medal

Mollie ultimately served with distinction for over twenty years active duty in the United States Air Force, and with the 162nd Fighter Group, Arizona Air Guard—a number of years in the security forces. She never hunted, and never again challenged catclaw bushes.

THE THANKSGIVING GUEST

Sir Skip Em first set foot upon Earth the third day of April in the year of 1975; that was in the State of Kansas, and before he began his journey southward. He was and is to this year of 2010 a sorrel Quarter Horse. His mother was named Penny Jo, and his father's name was Trixie's Skip Bar. The girl who owned him said he was related to the great Quarter Horse Stallion Skipper W. Most every horse person, particularly in the north States knows about Skipper W. Be that as it may, it seemed to make no difference to Sir Skip Em.

A Tucson girl named Jenny Lou Ingram had been given the fine steed by an uncle who raises Quarter Horses up in Kansas. She and her sister Jo called her horse by the name of Duke, which somehow did not quite seem to fit him. For whatever reason—the expense of boarding, other interests, or maybe Duke perhaps throwing off some of the family members—Jenny decided to sell Duke. Patricia Morrow was shopping around for a horse. A trip to Tucson was made; Duke was ridden a bit; a deal was made; and, Jenny and Jo delivered Sir Skip Em to the Chiricahua Mountains of southeastern Arizona. He was sort of a take-charge horse, but soon settled in to mountain living, and picking on some of the horses in his new home. That was in November of 1980. (Incidentally, he is still fat, enjoying life, eating substantial amounts of expensive feed, and appears to be about half his almost thirty-five years.)

Before selling her horse, Jenny and Jo would take him to ranches owned by relatives, some as far away as northern Utah. There they punched cows and matched races with anyone thinking they had a fast horse. The girls said they had only been outrun once. Because of this sort of activity, Sir Skip Em was not sure whether he was a cowhorse, saddle horse, race horse, or all of the above. One thing we mountain dwellers learned soon after his arrival was this: he had even considered a career as a bucking horse.

Patricia said Duke was the wrong name for her horse, and she changed that to Skip, which was, after all, part of his registered name. Skip had a few bad habits, but with some patient work, most were completely cured. Bad habit number one was trying to run over you when you opened a corral gate. Number two was trying to, or at least considering, throwing off the saddle when he was being saddled. Curing bad habit number three took a bit more work. When Skip was ridden down and across a creek or Arroyo, he usually tried to buck, particularly if he had to make a little jump to cross, which sometimes turned into more than a little jump. We began to realize that may have been the reason Jenny and Skip had parted company. Skip was not allowed to buck, if possible.

Ralph Morrow told about a horse he had when he was a youngster that liked to pitch. He thought it was fun and good practice for riding bucking horses. He soon realized that while he was learning, so was the horse. We made efforts to keep Skip from pitching.

When he tried to buck as he crossed a creek or Arroyo, he was ridden back and forth until he finally gave up, and was then allowed to travel onward. This seemed to be working until one day he made four good, high jumps before Patricia circled him around. "Darn!" Patricia said. "That sort of wrenched my back." Her philosophical riding partner opined: "Look at it this way, if you had been bucked off, you may have got skinned up a little." This enlightened observation was met by a cold stare.

Skip finally gave up on his little irregularities and settled down to being a fine cow and saddle horse. For some time after he arrived in the Chiricahuas, when he was loose in the pasture, he was always busy investigating something or other. If he saw some deer, he immediately trotted toward them. A recently-purchased vehicle—or a visitor's—was carefully inspected; it was Skip's mission to check all.

Skip was soon to have things happening of great interest to him: In the northeast area of the pasture that Skip called home, there was a dense growth of mesquite. A bulldozer outfitted for mesquite grubbing arrived, and required investigation by Skip. He soon lost interest, and began looking for other items of concern.

The dozer operator and his wife set up their camp trailer near some corrals. Skip was apparently not interested in the trailer or the pickup parked nearby. Thanksgiving was drawing near, and some relatives were driving out, and perhaps bringing a guest. In true Thanksgiving tradition, the operator's wife baked several pumpkin pies the evening before Thanksgiving. The nights were cold, the trailer heated, and she covered the pies and placed them in the bed of the pickup to cool. Operator and spouse looked forward to Thanksgiving in the country, and retired for the night.

Thanksgiving morning I drove over to check on the work in progress. "There has been some mischief," the wife said. "Last evening I baked my Thanksgiving pies." That did not seem such a bad thing. "I put the pies in the bed of the pickup to cool. So, when I went to get the pies this morning, why, there were no pies, and the tins were scattered all around. I think Patricia's horse, the one she calls Skip, ate the pies. His tracks are all around the truck."

There were many shod horse tracks the size of shoes worn by Skip. The pie tins were empty, licked clean. Skip was grazing nearby and wandered over to check the situation. "See there, he even has pumpkin on his nose." A visitor had indeed come in the night: Sir Skip Em, "The Thanksgiving Guest."

Mollie Morrow on Patricia's horse, Skip*, with Pancho, 1988
*aka "The Thanksgiving Guest"

BUFFALO AT FORT HUACHUCA

When the Fort Huachuca Military Reservation was turned over to the State of Arizona in the late 1940s, buffalo were brought in an initial herd of some one hundred fourteen buffalo cows, heifers, and young bulls. There were over 45,000 acres in the military reservation at that time and no cross fences. The buffalo had a pretty open range in those days. The original idea was to build the herd to six hundred, and then begin controlled hunts or killing of the surplus; however, in the early fifties the government reclaimed the Fort and all of the buffalo were slaughtered.

I went to work at the Fort the middle of July of 1949. (The winters I was staying with my uncle Carson Morrow in Tucson and attending the University of Arizona.) My introduction to roping buffalo was the next day after I started work. My Dad, Ralph Morrow, a fellow by the name of Long who was at the Fort, and I went off toward the east end of the reservation to doctor buffalo for screw worms. The herd had been skinned up transporting them, and screw worms were a real problem. At that time there were no good corrals available and we had to rope buffalo on the range. I sort of hung back observing activities this first go around. Ralph Morrow headed a buffalo, probably a long yearling heifer, and Long heeled the animal. After doctoring the critter, Morrow removed the head rope, mounted up, and Long just jumped his horse up, giving the heifer some slack to kick off his heel rope. The heifer did just that, and promptly charged Long's horse. Right then it seemed roping buffalo might just be a different story than roping domestic cattle. There are plenty of people that have worked buffalo, roped buffalo, and know a great deal about them. We began to learn about the buffalo business. We rode good horses that were fast and strong, and carried 36-foot nylon ropes. Cows with calves, bulls alone or on the edge of the herd always needed to be watched closely.

Buffalo at Fort Huachuca, 1950

On one expedition, Nig Lutz, who was dusky complected, and so named, was riding a big paint horse we called Fred. A buffalo cow with a calf took exception to Nig and Fred and charged them. Fred, being properly motivated, began to make tracks. She managed a couple of brushes to Fred's tail before he shifted into high gear. After about a quarter mile she gave it up.

That was in the summer of 1950.

Back to the summer of 1949. Clell Lee was helping out that summer at the Fort, and he and I did most of the buffalo doctoring, and riding from one end of the reservation to the other. Sometimes Ralph Morrow helped us out. There was one old buffalo cow that had a big calf, and she had one horn broken off and the other grew straight up. Ralph Morrow got to calling her Peg. When she was with a bunch of buffalo that you started moving, she just left at a run, and we would see her way off in the distance still going. I don't think we ever had her corralled. If they didn't kill her when they slaughtered the herd, maybe she and her calf ran off to Mexico. Buffalo are faster than domestic critters, and run at a steady pace for long distances.

Ralph Morrow said we needed more and larger bulls, so he, Clell, and I set out for House Rock Valley that summer of '49 to bring some back to the Fort. Ralph had contracted with a trucking outfit in Flagstaff to haul back some bulls, but when we got to House Rock, the director of the game department, a fellow named Kimble, had apparently had a revelation and talked to God or an even higher authority, and determined that one of the brethren could do the job with a little old bob-tailed truck. The morning we loaded out there were three big bulls in the crowding pen, and in with them was a monster of a bull. We are all standing around trying to figure out how we are going to get the bulls up the ramp and into this truck when this monster takes to the other three bulls and ran them into the truck. We left the monster right there and closed up the other three bulls, and they were sure into a fight with what room they had. This truck driver says he sure hopes they don't hook the racks off his truck as he doesn't have them fastened down. Ralph Morrow in rather strong terms tells him to get on the road.

Down through Arizona we come, Ralph Morrow, Clell, and I following along behind this truck, and this outfit goes forty-five miles an hour cross country, through town, it don't matter. Forty-five an hour, and that takes considerable time to get clear across Arizona at that rate. The highway went right through downtown Phoenix in those days, and Clell got to laughing about what a wreck that is going to be if these bulls can break out in the middle of downtown Phoenix in the middle of the night. He and I had got so fed up with this trucker, we sort of hoped it would happen. We finally got to the Fort, doctored up these bulls as best we could and turned them out.

One of the bulls got screw worms and left the herd. We didn't have any corrals, but there was a fenced area of sorts that had been the dairy for the Fort. Ralph Morrow and I headed out horseback for what is called Garden Canyon on the Fort. Clell hadn't shown up that morning so we went on without him. We found this bull, and our experience was that you couldn't drive a buffalo bull by himself. When we rode up to the bull he charged us. We simply ran our horses in the direction we wanted him to travel. After a bit he would give up trying to hook our horses, and we would ride back toward him and get him to run us again. Finally we got him into a small herd of maybe twenty or so buffalo and headed for the Dairy. Clell showed up about then. He was riding a young horse that had got to bucking with him and fell down and got away back to his corral.

We pushed these buffalo up in a corner where a long shed met the fence, and here they wouldn't go through the gate. It was pretty wild there for a bit with the three of us doing all we could to hold these buffalo which were running around and around in a circle. Finally they went in the gate, and Clell says that is the wildest bit of cowboying he has ever been in on. Ralph Morrow cinched up and heeled this bull; I roped him by the head, and Clell roped his front feet; and, we got him down, doctored him, and he recovered to be slaughtered when the government took over the Fort in the early fifties.

Clell used to come up to the Old Fort where the Morrows had taken up residence in the evenings and my Dad would play the fiddle and Clell the guitar. He sometimes got to yarning about hunting jaguars, and some of the tales set down in Dale's book, *Life Of The Greatest Guide*, he told first hand. There was a movie theatre on the post that had three different films each week, and Clell and I hit that pretty regular. One evening when my folks and I and some neighbors were walking down the street to the theatre, lightning hit a tree about thirty feet across the street and knocked a limb maybe six or eight inches out of the tree. If you ever hear a sizzling sound like something frying, that's the sound right before the big bang, and it is too late, you have been just barely missed, or soon hit dead center. The next summer Clell was gone, and my doctoring partner was Nig Lutz. Before the summer was out we had some really good corrals and quit range roping the bison. Just about the last time I remember going out with Lutz, we were off on the southeast part of the reservation, and this was Nig's undoing, because people would sometimes drive out and watch us running the buffalo. Anyway we had doctored a couple of buffalo, and Lutz always was very polite about allowing someone else to head the buffalo, then he would come in and heel them. He was a fairly good roper at that. I'd run down and roped two head and my horse was getting tired. We came upon a cow that had worms and I set after her. My horse was too tired and he was just plain getting outrun. In desperation I threw my loop, and I had a thirty-eight foot rope. The loop just went clear to the end and closed down, and darned if it didn't barely settle on this cow's horns, and I had her.

After a bit, my horse got his wind back, and we went on, and here is where old Nig got himself into trouble. One of the Game Commissioners was visiting the Fort, and he and Ralph Morrow and a few other people had driven out maybe to see some buffalo work first hand. Nig now has an audience, and we found another buffalo in need of doctoring. Thinking Nig is going to be his usual considerate self and allow me to rope this critter, I give it a run. Well, as I said, my horse was getting tired and to my surprise, here comes Nig right along side giving out with some real wild west yipping and hollering and swinging his loop. So, I think, have at it, Nig. This horse of Nig's, Fred, the one the cow ran so far one time, was a star gazer, and just when Nig's big moment is at hand and he is going to rope this buffalo in front of this distinguished audience, Fred trips up and goes end over end. When Fred got up, I roped him, thinking maybe old wild west Nig might be hung up. He wasn't, and he didn't get hurt much. After that Nig quit and went to work drilling blast holes in the Lavender Pit over at Bisbee.

That was about the last range roping that summer that I remember, and we began using the corrals.

When school let out in the spring of 1951, I went back to the Fort. Ralph Morrow was demoted to District Ranger when he arrested one of the Arizona

Game Commissioner's cronies.[1] After a short time he and my Mother, Juanita Morrow, moved back to the Chiricahuas. I stayed on for awhile, working for a kind of dude wrangler type by the name of Andersen. There was another man working there at the time name of Farrell. Andersen wanted to tell everyone how he roped buffalo, and during the time I worked after he arrived, I don't remember him roping any other than by the heels.

What follows is the story of my last day at Fort Huachuca.

Andersen, insisting on roping a buffalo, kept refusing to use the corrals, and he being the boss, well. . . That morning, the morning of my last day, I remember roping three buffalo. Andersen and Farrell would take to these bison and run the heck out of them and pretty soon the buffalo would get away from them and come back to the herd, and all I had to do was make a short run and rope them. I'd done that twice when we came upon two small bunches of buffalo. One bunch was up on a hill and I loped up there to see if any needed doctoring. None did, and I was sitting there on my horse and I see Andersen running a buffalo down below. He was riding a big sorrel horse that was a pretty fair horse, but this Andersen who was pretty big, was afraid of his horse on account the horse would buck. Andersen disappeared behind trees, and when his horse came out he is sans rider. Andersen is running along behind the horse holding onto his rope, or rather as it turns out, his rope is holding onto him.

What happened was this: There were fox holes left over from the military days, and his horse saw one and jumped it and came down in another one and fell down. Andersen managed to get his rope around under his arms, and he is all set for a "Nantucket Sleigh Ride,"[2] Arizona style. I loped on down and roped his horse, and he lay there on the ground for awhile groaning and moaning and saying please don't let his horse get away. Turns out he wasn't badly hurt, and I sort of in reflection wished I'd let his horse drag him further as I did not particularly like this Andersen character. But, spur-of-the-moment decisions and all that.

What was sort of odd was that Farrell was a lot closer to Andersen and he made no move to do anything. Later he said he had seen one man dragged to death and he thought here was another.

---

[1] See the chapter "Ralph Morrow: For Whom The Laws Hold" for this story.

[2] A term used by Nantucket whalers to describe what happened immediately after a whale was harpooned: the whale would attempt to get away; however, tethered by the harpoon line, it would drag the small whaling boat behind at high speed until it exhausted itself.

Andersen pulled himself together and dusted himself off, and just to show us how tough he was I suppose, we went on looking for buffalo, and pretty soon we found a wormy cow. I had played my usual game and let these other two run the wind out of this cow, and I roped her. No one came to heel her. I didn't want to lose my rope or have a critter running around with a rope tied to it, so I finally dragged the cow over to a small oak tree and got her wound round that. After a bit Andersen and Farrell showed up and supposedly Farrell's horse had fallen down and Andersen had been administering first aid. Well, I thought, to hell with these dudes, and when I got back to the housing area, I packed up and left.

That was the end of buffalo days as I knew them. It was a shame that they were wiped out, but then that seems to be the nature of the human animal to do such.

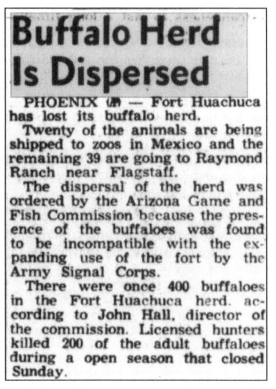

Buffalo Herd Is Dispersed

PHOENIX (P) — Fort Huachuca has lost its buffalo herd.

Twenty of the animals are being shipped to zoos in Mexico and the remaining 39 are going to Raymond Ranch near Flagstaff.

The dispersal of the herd was ordered by the Arizona Game and Fish Commission because the presence of the buffaloes was found to be incompatible with the expanding use of the fort by the Army Signal Corps.

There were once 400 buffaloes in the Fort Huachuca herd, according to John Hall, director of the commission. Licensed hunters killed 200 of the adult buffaloes during a open season that closed Sunday.

The last of the Fort Huachuca buffalo herd
Prescott Evening Courier, Jan. 26th, 1955

THE DISAPPEARANCE OF KOLLEY

While World War II yet raged, there appeared in the Chiricahua Mountain area a man named Herman Kollmar. He was a German. He supposedly was a wizard in international finance. He shuttled from London to Berlin by way of Portugal.

In 1971, Ladislas Farago published a book titled *The Game of the Foxes*. The subject matter centered on the field of espionage, especially German spies. In this book, a "Herman B. Kolmar [*sic*]" was listed as a spy for German military intelligence, operating out of Lisbon, Portugal. Farago wrote that Kollmar "claimed to have entry even into 10 Downing Street while Neville Chamberlain was Prime Minister." That may be true, but—again according to Farago—"shortly after the fall of France, Kolmar vanished from the scene, probably because the British had become wise to him." Apparently, Neville did not put in a good word for Herman.

Herman bought the Z–T cattle ranch, which ranged from Cochise's Head to the San Simon Cienega. Perhaps not unlike his claim about access to 10 Downing Street, the stories of his vast wealth were somewhat inflated: most of his purchases were, as the Old Timers said, "Bought on Jaw Bone." Herman hired a half dozen cowboys of varying degrees of expertise. All met at the ranch headquarters near the mouth of East Whitetail Canyon every Friday night for dinner and Herman's orders of operation for the following week.

On one occasion a "cowboy" from New York City was detailed to keep some cattle pushed onto the forest lease land. In Indian Creek, branching off from Whitetail, there is a natural amphitheater. A shallow cave is on one side, reached after passing "The Narrows," where the canyon closes down to a few feet in width. The vaquero set up camp in the cave, turned his horse loose, and cooked supper over an open camp fire. The cowboy failed to put up a barrier across the Narrows, and during the night, his horse left for the ranch headquarters which was several miles away. The next day the vaquero was seen hoofing it down the canyon dressed in full cowboy garb, including heavy leather chaps and large rowel Chihuahua spurs.

Kollmar bought a stake bed truck, and he was often seen riding in back with several of his cowhands. He would not wear a shirt on such excursions, and the summer sun burned him to a shade of almost black. After a time, the running of the ranch was given over to a series of managers.

Herman had a strong inclination for the drink. So much so that he bought the Rodeo Tavern, and set up a fellow by the name of Byron Miller as bartender and manager. About that time he also hired Alden Ray (A.R.) Mooney to run the Z–T.

A.R. was a good cowboy and cattleman, and did not let his old war wounds slow him down. He had been in the Army Special Forces in World War II, and again in Korea when the UN forces were overwhelmed at the Chosin Reservoir.

Before the Hilltop-Paradise-Portal telephone system modernized, most of the lines were party lines. Telephones were activated by a hand crank, which rang all up and down any branch line. Each telephone had its own code or series of long and short rings. It also led to the favorite pastime of listening in on other callers' conversations. One night the series of rings signaled that a call was being placed to the "hello girl" or switchboard operator at Portal. This meant that another branch line or a long distance call was in the offing. Receivers were carefully lifted, and the conversation was laughed about and discussed by the locals for days. It was somewhat risqué, bordering on indelicacy.

The switchboard operator connected Herman to the Rodeo Tavern and to his managing bartender, Byron Miller. In loud and excited terms, Herman told the bartender to come to his ranch headquarters post haste, and to come armed and dangerous. Herman further elaborated on the need for this: He had hired a painter from one of the distant towns to paint his residence, and furnished the worker with food and a bed. That evening Herman and the painter had taken copious amounts of Jack Daniels bourbon, and both had become somewhat inebriated. Herman, wearing a housecoat, had fallen asleep face down on a couch. He suddenly awoke to find the painter attempting certain—this described on the telephone in explicit terms by Herman—"improprieties" upon the person of the unconscious Herman.

Byron Miller's son and A.R. were also enjoying a few drinks at the Tavern that evening when Herman called. Miller, his son, and A.R. all raced from Rodeo to

Whitetail Canyon. They were met at the cattleguard by Herman, yet garbed in his housecoat. In excited terms, Herman repeated the story of the evening's events. On the walk back to the ranch house, A.R. said Kollmar told Miller that he wanted him to shoot the painter. Miller said that might not be a good idea, but that he and his compadres would see that the painter vacated the premises. Miller, wielding an old .45 single-action revolver, soon put the painter to flight. For years afterward, A.R. would break out laughing whenever he saw someone wearing a bathrobe or house-coat. He told the story of that night at Z–T Headquarters many times.

§   §   §

One night, Herman had been socializing at the bar in San Simon. He called home to tell his wife that he was on the way home. Time went by, and his wife became worried. She called the Arizona Bar at San Simon. Yes, the bartender said, Herman left many hours ago. Morning came, but with it, Herman did not come. A search was mounted. The road from the interstate highway into the Chiricahua Mountains was well maintained, but a gravel road. There had been a few fatal accidents along the road from time to time. The searchers checked arroyos, and for vehicle tracks leaving the road. They found none. If Kollmar had driven the road south, where was he?

Several miles south of the interstate, the Portal Road—as it was named—curved to line up with a bridge crossing the San Simon River. The bridge was constructed of wood, with wooden railings. One of the searchers noticed that the railing along the west side of the bridge was loose, even though it rested on its post. A closer observation was made, and definitely the railing had been disturbed, but not broken. The searcher looked beneath the bridge, and found Kollmar. He was uninjured but passed out, inside his Chrysler automobile, which rested on its top. Kollmar had slowed to a crawl as he negotiated the curve in the road. He failed to straighten the wheels, and the car had gently pushed the wooden rail up and over the vehicle, which then came down on top of the post. The Chrysler had nosed in and rolled back completely out of sight beneath the bridge. That was the disappearance of "Kolley"—as the locals referred to Kollmar.

Herman lived and operated the Z–T Ranch until his death, and his widow sold out and moved away.[1]

---

[1] For more about Mrs. Kollmar in her post-Herman years, see the chapter "Galeyville."

Ralph Morrow, Game and Fish Department Commissioner's License, 1964

RALPH MORROW: FOR WHOM THE LAWS HOLD

Ralph Morrow, after more than a decade as a district Game Warden—or Game Ranger, as they were termed in later years—patrolling the entire County of Cochise, was called to Phoenix and promoted to Chief Deputy in Charge of Law Enforcement. That was in early 1944. The then State Game Warden—later changed to Director—in effect turned the running of the Game Department over to the newly named Chief Deputy. Phoenix and the desert were not to Morrow's liking, and he resigned the position, returning to the Chiricahuas and the District Game Warden job in the fall of 1944.

Jim Burnett used to write an article for the *Brewery Gulch Gazette*, the Bisbee newspaper. Jim called himself the "Barnyard Philosopher." One of his articles was about "The Game Ranger." Burnett told how "Mutt" Morrow (dubbed such after the "Mutt & Jeff" comic-strip character, because of his height) had made a believer of Jim and many other would-be game law criminals. The article recited how Morrow patrolled the entire County of Cochise, sometimes on horseback or by automobile or the Harley Davidson or Indian motorcycle he sometimes rode. Morrow's motorcycle days ended when, as he put it: "I was lollygagging along up in Sulphur Canyon and hit a sandy area. My motorcycle turned over, catching my leg and breaking it in three places. After I got the leg straightened out, and the machine started again, there were a number of wire gates to go through before I rode into Rodeo. The store keeper there, a fellow named Wiley, said there was no way anyone could come out of Sulphur Canyon in the shape I was in, but he would drive me into Douglas anyway."

Jim Burnett's article said Morrow gave real meaning to that old expression, "Enforce the law without fear or favor." Jim allowed as how the people of Cochise County got Morrow's unspoken message: "If you violate the game laws I will catch you and the judge will fine you or put you in jail."

Some transgressors of the laws, once arrested and tried, became lifelong friends of Morrow. An example was Spec Williamson. Spec Williamson worked as a fireman for engineer Jack Bailey on the Southern Pacific. They were hunting deer when Spec announced he was going to shoot a whitetail doe for camp meat. Bailey told him if he did Morrow was sure to arrest him. "Why," says Williamson, "Morrow can't be everywhere, and I have never even seen Morrow." Bailey says okay go ahead, but remember I warned you. It happened that Ralph Morrow was watching Spec with the Bausch and Lomb 10x50 binoculars he carried. Spec shot the doe, was duly arrested and fined and was a friend and believer for life.

In an article titled "Two Hearts Are Better Than One," which he wrote for the Arizona Game & Fish Department's *Wildlife Views*, W.R. Hernbrode recounted a tale of some of these many surprised game-law violators. As evening came, Morrow and a new recruit approached a miner's shack in the Dragoon Mountains. The prospectors were at home and preparing the evening meal. Just as Morrow raised a hand to knock, voices were heard coming from within: "By God, wouldn't ol' Ralph Morrow [*scatological reference*] if he could see this!" The laughter inside was interrupted by a quiet voice from the doorway, "I'm looking right down your neck, Bill." The speaker was still frozen, open-mouthed, with both arms bent at the elbow, and on each index finger was impaled a fresh deer heart.

Back to the true story of "For Whom The Laws Hold." Tom Kimball was appointed Director of the department in 1948. Three supervisory areas were designated covering the State of Arizona. Ralph Morrow was made Ranger Supervisor for the southern part of the state. During an elk hunt near Hannigan Meadow in the White Mountains, Morrow arrested a man named Paul Buss for a violation of the game laws. Buss was camped with the then Chairman of the Arizona Game and Fish Commission, Fred Faver. Faver declared that there had been no violation of the law, but the evidence and Buss's confession said otherwise. Buss was instructed to appear before Justice of the Peace Reed in Safford. Buss appeared with his counsel, Max Layton, and pled guilty to taking wildlife in a closed area— the San Carlos Indian Reservation.

Director Kimball and Buss came to Safford the following day and asked Ralph Morrow to dismiss his complaint against Buss. Morrow said he would not do so and would take the case to Washington, D.C. if necessary. This option was open as the reservation fell under federal jurisdiction. Morrow added he would do so even though he may be fired from his job, but Kimball said there was no chance of that happening.

Kimball and Commission Chairman Faver then met with the Graham County Attorney on behalf of the defendant Buss. It was decided by the conspirators that Buss's plea of guilty would stand, and he was fined one hundred dollars. In March of 1950, Charles Beach, a member of the Game Commission since 1939, told Ralph Morrow that Commissioner Faver and Director Kimball intended to fire him over the Buss case. Beach was a strong supporter of Morrow and stated that there would be a public hearing of the case, which would backfire in the face of the conspirators. Faver and Kimball traveled to Fort Huachuca, where Morrow lived at the time. They said they had come for Morrow's resignation. Morrow, in definitive terms, told them exactly what the result of their unlawful campaign would be. When confronted with the reality of an impending legal and devastating—to them—political storm they were stirring, the two retreated to plan another strategy.

On the eighth day of May, Kimball sent a stooge to inform Morrow that he was now demoted to ranger, his pay reduced, and he was to vacate his premises at Fort Huachuca forthwith. Morrow returned to his home in the Chiricahuas to carry on the work he had so diligently pursued for decades as an officer of the law. Governor Dan Garvey called Director Kimball on the carpet for the embarrassment the administration had endured by Kimball's unethical and illegal conduct in the Buss matter. Congressional leaders, influential people, and many members of the public expressed their displeasure of the entire matter. Greenlee County Game Protective Association requested an investigation into the Buss case.

Even to Kimball and Faver, it became evident that they could not coerce Morrow into violating the very laws they were all sworn to uphold. They could though exact a petty revenge. Suddenly, as Ralph Morrow neared his sixty-fifth birthday, a previously unheard-of department policy appeared on the horizon. Employees of the department would have to retire on or before their sixty-fifth birthday.

So it would seem that a distinguished career had come to the place it had begun—a retired district ranger. However, though rabidly opposed by the President of Tucson-based Wildlife Unlimited, one Lester Stewart—who claimed Morrow had on many occasions attacked the policies of the Game Department—Morrow was appointed to the Arizona State Game and Fish Commission in 1964. He served as a commissioner for three years, during which time the wildlife resources of Arizona improved and flourished. As Morrow's term limit neared, the Director of the Game Department, W. Swank, busily formulated criteria for prospective commissioners to use in blocking Morrow's reappointment as a commissioner. Time and other interests saw Morrow not seeking another term as commissioner.

One Score and a Hundred Years before Game Commissioner Faver, Director Tom Kimball, et al, set forth to unethically and illegally circumvent the laws they were sworn to and professed to uphold—the Buss Case—a new religion appeared in the United States. Most, if not all of the conspirators in the Buss fiasco, from 1949 through the subsequent two decades, were devout members of that Church.

A great and revered leader of Kimball's Church declared that common law and the laws of the United States of America were false. God's laws, as revealed to him, were the only true laws, the Church ruler said. He declared, in referring to his congregation, that "These people are above the law." Apparently, there was not after all a separation of Church and State.

Years past there were many deer and turkey and javelina, and other game. Now, where one would see herds of deer, there is but an occasional track. A few javelina are sometimes seen. The desert mule deer, once in abundance, are almost wiped out. There is no control of predators. Lion, bobcat, and coyote continue to stalk and kill the few surviving game.

Game Warden Morrow with orphan cub "Maggie," near Cave Creek Canyon, 1936
Maggie was raised by the Morrows until she was old enough to be returned the wild.

THE COWDOGS

There is sorrow enough in the natural way
From men and women to fill our day;
But when we are certain of sorrow in store,
Why do we always arrange for more?
Brothers and Sisters, I bid you beware
Of giving your heart to a dog to tear.

Rudyard Kipling, *The Power Of The Dog*

One balmy late summer afternoon, when there was just a faint hint of the autumn to come, Rancher Morrow watched as Bum stretched in the shade of the sycamores. In a rare expression of sentiment Morrow said: "I sure will miss Bum when he is no longer around." Bum was a large, classic Black and Tan Hound. When Bum and one of his companions were not riding the mountain range with Morrow, they lived in a fenced few acres cross creek from the ranch house, where oak and sycamore trees shaded them as they ranged about or rested. That is, Bum ranged about, never worrying the field fence until it broke and an escape made, or climbing the six-foot wooden gate. Bum knew this was his home when not doing the work he and his companions enjoyed and lived for.

Fiddler, a chocolate-colored hound, Bugle, a large crossbred American Fox hound, and Red, another large hound cross, lived with Bum. All, except Bum, had broken out and gone hunting in the mountains. Of necessity they were collared and chained by their houses, and did not enjoy their leisure time to the extent Bum did.

Cowboys of the San Simon Cattle & Canal Co., San Simon Valley, New Mexico, early 1900s

The H ⏚ H (H, "Lazy H," H) brand was one of three brands still registered
to James Parramore's San Simon Cattle & Canal Company in 1908
(*Brands and Marks of Cattle, Horses, Sheep, Goats, and Hogs*
Live Stock Sanitary Board of Arizona, 1908)

In the late nineteenth and early twentieth century large herds of cattle were grazed in the valleys and mountains of southeastern Arizona. The owners of the cattle lived far away and had no love of the land, and thought only to profit from and exploit the rangelands.[1]

Cowboys came and worked for the large companies, and some, when the work was done and the big companies gone, stayed. Jack Maloney was one who stayed. He planted an orchard and distilled a bit of moonshine, and had a ranch with a hundred or so head of cattle in what is known as Cave Creek in the Chiricahua Mountains of southeast Arizona. Some of it is rugged country where cattle can run wild. As Jack grew older, the cattle became wilder. He fashioned "trigger traps" on salt corrals where cows and calves could be caught and branded or sold. Long clear water creeks ran through the eighteen thousand acres and the bovines could not be trapped when they went to water.

Jack and his wife Emma were at the breakfast table one morning and Jack said he thought it was time they sold out. Their good friend Ralph Morrow came to mind. Morrow was a legendary lawman in those parts, and a good cowboy and exceptional horseman. Emma concurred, and they drove to the Morrow home. When Jack and Emma said what they wanted to do, a deal was struck, and Morrow bought out their holdings.

A friend of the Morrows said he had a young dog that he wanted to give them. He said the dog was a black and tan hound, and had been trained by a border collie to trail up cattle and hold them until a cowboy arrived. And, he said, if the cattle tried to run off, this dog would first try to stop them, and then take a bite of a cow's nose in order to communicate what was expected of them. The dog had

---

[1] Although his intentions were probably not deliberate exploitation of Arizona's border ranchlands, a prime example of the largely absentee, big ranch owner of this era would have to be James Harrison Parramore (1840–1917), former Confederate Army Captain, and later a prominent rancher in Texas, New Mexico, and Arizona. (Parramore also played an important role in the founding of Abilene, Texas.)

In 1883, Parramore—together with his brother-in-law Hugh Lewis and their business partner, Claiborne Merchant—organized the San Simon Cattle and Canal Company, which eventually acquired extensive water rights in the San Simon Valley of southeastern Arizona and southwestern New Mexico. Some 15,000 calves were branded on this range in one year, and in 1892 a sale to the Standard Cattle Company of Nebraska earned Parramore and his partners nearly $60,000. In 1902, Parramore and Lewis bought out Merchant's share of the Arizona ranch; the company was dissolved after Parramore's death in 1917.

been named Bum. The name did not fit the dog, but it was what he had been called, and he knew the name.

There were a dozen and a half of Jack's cows that were reasonably gentle. The rest, when they saw a man and horse, were as wild as the whitetail deer that shared their range. Ride over a ridge top and the cattle—young and old—were running away over a distant ridge, or rimming the side of a steep sided mountain peak. Bum's work was cut out for him, and at first—until his helpers Fiddler, Bugle, and Red were added—it was just him and Ralph Morrow against the wild bunch.

Contrary to a hound's inclination to hunt and chase about anything, Bum had only one thing in mind, cattle. There was no chasing off after deer or other animals. Downwind of a cow or cows, Bum would strike straight for the quarry. A fresh track no more than a day old was followed until the bovines were found. Once there, Bum made his presence known while convincing the cows they should stay put and rest until the man on horseback arrived. In later years other breeds were tried, but none worked as well as Bum and the dogs he trained. Bum worked alone until first Fiddler arrived and was trained by him, and then Bugle, and finally Red. Usually Bum and another dog worked together. Sometimes, when Bum needed rest, two of his trainees went out together.

A small bunch of the tame cows were being driven down a creek in the mountains—all of Bum's territory was mountain range. Two men were moving the cows along. From off the hillside, down the creek bank, through the driven cows, there came a two-year-old maverick heifer. Being an unbranded bovine who had never been properly introduced to any humans qualified the wildly careening critter for the designation. Back to the mountain side, trees and brush the heifer ran. Not far behind was Morrow, and he called for Bum. The older and wiser of the cowpunchers opined: "That is the last we will see of that heifer."

Minutes later the errant critter streaked off the creek bank and once again through the cow herd. Around the herd Bum ran. When the heifer emerged, ready for another escape—perhaps a final one for that day—a surprise awaited. This called for sterner measures, and Bum politely grabbed the heifer by the nose. After a few moments of constructive discussion, the heifer was freed to join the other cows, and left her wild life forever behind. Another of many to be gentled by the mighty dog Bum, and in time, by his helper dogs.

There was never a doubt who stood above all in Bum's mind. No amount of pleading, calling, cajoling could entice Bum away from Ralph Morrow. There was a bond of respect, consideration, loyalty, and affection. Though all was not strict business with Bum. When a small or large bunch of cattle were being driven, he would sometimes slip by, take up a position at the leaders, begin barking, and hold up the procession. This invariably led to Morrow voicing his disapproval. Bum continued until his human partner swung out of the saddle and lobbed rocks in the general direction of Bum—always landing well away from him and in no danger of a strike. This went on for a minute or so until Bum decided to return to his place at the rear.

A rancher who liked to hunt mountain lion was riding with Bum, Bugle, and Morrow. For some reason or other Bum and Bugle were to be temporarily left behind. All cattlemen and cowboys carry piggin strings which are short ropes used to tie down calves and large bovines. Morrow loosely looped a piggin string around each dog's neck and tied the ends to bushes. The rancher/lion hunter was amazed, and he allowed as his hounds would chew one of the piggin strings into in a matter of minutes. Bum and his partner of the day, Bugle, knew they were supposed to stay until Morrow returned, which they did.

Bum's first trainee was Fiddler. He was a pure bred hound, and but a pup when he arrived and began his schooling, taught by the maestro Bum. Soon he had learned the tricks of the trade and went out each time Morrow rode the range. It was impractical in that mountainous country to round up and brand as the flatland ranches did. A short branding iron and cinch rings were tied behind saddle cantles. Bum and Fiddler found and held the cattle. If an unbranded calf was at hand, it was a simple matter to drop a loop on calf, tie it down, build a small fire, heat the iron or rings, and brand. Two short sticks were scissored to handle the cinch rings. Calf branded and freed, the trio went on searching for other bovines.

It was soon evident that Fiddler would not stay in the large enclosure set about with giant oaks and sycamores where Bum lived. The six-foot-high fence was easily climbed by Fiddler, and as a last resort, Rancher Morrow had to put him on a long chain.

The next addition to Bum's practical school of cow punching was Bugle. In the town of Bisbee, Arizona, there was a well-shaded park for mobile homes. From someplace, and no one knew where, a hound appeared and began to live. He appeared to be a large American Foxhound, with a little something else thrown in. First one resident of the park and then another fed him and saw that he had water, and he seemed to adapt to park life. The owner of the park knew Morrow, and knew that he used hounds and would give this hound a good and useful home.

Morrow came to the park, opened his car door, called to the hound, who readily jumped in the car, and the two rode away for a long and happy association.

Bugle was on the range with Rancher Morrow, and a cowboy who was helping round up and ship some cattle. This cowboy had a dog that went along, and when the two men and two dogs stopped by one of the mountain streams to eat lunch, the cowboy got to yarning about what a tough dog he had. He said there were no dogs that could best him. Anyone who has ever owned hounds knows what tenacious dogs they are—almost always mild-mannered and friendly toward humans, and rarely looking for trouble from other dogs. Such was Bugle.

A bone or scrap of meat was thrown to Bugle, and the much-touted cowboy's dog decided he would take possession of the offering. That was a mistake. Bugle had soon chastised the impolite dog, in the process taking a firm grip on said dog's nose, which was causing some serious breathing problems. With a great deal of yelling, pulling, and prying the hold was finally broken. Following lunch, Bugle went back to his job of finding and holding up cattle. And his companion of the day experienced a newly-found polite and respectful demeanor. No further disciplining was required of Bugle.

Bugle lived a long and happy life there in the mountains, and as he aged, Morrow gave him more and more freedom. He was no longer chained, but roamed the acres enjoyed by Bum.

One day Bugle's hound blood overwhelmed him and there was an escape—gone hunting in the mountains. The Morrows—Juanita and Ralph—began a search. On the west slopes of the Chiricahuas they found Bugle. He was in the care of a family with several dog-loving children who were feeding, grooming, pampering, and loving the cow dog grown old. The Morrows had not the heart to take away the family's adopted dog, and they left Bugle there to live out his senior years. Maybe he sometimes dreamed of the old days of chasing cattle with his cowdog partners.

Red was the last of Morrow's four cowdogs, joining Bum, Fiddler, and Bugle. Out driving one day, Morrow's daughter, Audrey Morrow Miller, and her daughter, Dixie Louise ("Priss"), saw a large, smooth-haired, red dog alongside their country road. At Priss's insistence, they stopped and tried to get him to jump into the automobile. He would not. The next day they saw the dog again, and still he would not approach. On the third morning when they stopped, Red, as he was to be known, jumped into the car and laid his head on Priss's shoulder for the ride back to the ranch house. He joined the Morrow cowdogs, and went with the ranch when it was sold to Audrey and her husband, Guy Miller. By that time, Priss was married and away from home. Fiddler also stayed with the ranch. How long they lived and nothing more is known. They must have joined Morrow when they all got together to ride and hunt the mountains forever.

Many years ago a United States Government agency reached, as is oft the case, a devastating decision: Prairie dogs should be eradicated. A program of poisoning was carried out. The prairie dogs, residents of the valleys and plains, were destroyed. Many other birds and mammals were also destroyed, some to the point of near extinction. The poison was not selective in dealing death. Rainwater that had flowed into the holes of the prairie-dog towns now flooded across the range. Grasses dried up and died out. The carrying capacity of the range decreased dramatically, and mesquite and catclaw blanketed the land. Predators such as the coyote, whose primary source of food was the prairie dog, left the barren valleys and drifted into the mountains seeking other prey. The coyote joined the mountain lion and bobcat as the principal predators of the mountains.

The coyote now became pack hunters. They followed, harassed, and ran whitetail and mule deer until the animal was exhausted, and could run no further. The unfortunate deer was then torn to pieces and eaten by the predator coyote.

On an afternoon, in the fall of the year, a disturbance at Bum's several-acre off-duty home was heard. A whitetail buck careened off the hillside and dashed to the boundary of Bum and his companions' residence. The exhausted animal threw itself against the fence and collapsed. Bum's associates—Fiddler, Bugle, and Red—all chained, began barking. Bum, separated from the deer by open-squared field fencing, went to the whitetail buck, who pressed firmly against the fence as it lay panting. First Bum put his nose on the deer as though reassuring it that he was now safe. He told the deer that he and the others were cowdogs. They did not hunt or kill deer. The deer listened and lay still.

At the sound and smell of the canines, the coyotes had given up the chase. Next Bum nuzzled and licked the deer along its back and the side pressed to the fence. The buck did not move. Over an hour passed, and Bum did not leave the deer. The deer rested, it could breathe again, its strength returned, and it stood. It took a step, stopped, and looked back at Bum. It cannot be said what communication passed between them. The buck lifted its white tail and trotted away. The scent of Bum went with it. Perhaps it was enough that the handsome buck lived another day, another year.

Across the creek there had arrived another dog that lived in the yard surrounding the ranch house. This was Doodles. He was a cross-bred Dachshund. His legs were longer than a Dachshund's and in all respects his color was exactly like Bum's—a black and tan hound. Doodles on occasion went along on short rides after the mountain cattle. On one such occasion Doodles had a showdown with a "cattalo"—a cattle/buffalo crossbreed—that Rancher Morrow owned.

In the northern reaches of Old Mexico there was at one time a vast ranch of 2,270,000 acres. A friend of Morrow's, Ben Williams, was one of the owners. In addition to thousands of head of cattle on the range, there was a herd of buffalo, or American bison. Williams gave Morrow a cross-bred, year-old heifer cattalo. She was transported to the Chiricahuas and turned out on some of the range land Morrow owned at that time. The cattalo ranged at will over Morrow's land and that of several neighboring ranches, going and coming as she pleased. At around age four the cattalo began to produce offspring at the rate of about one each year. Years later some of the Morrow cattle still had traces of buffalo blood.

On a late fall afternoon, Morrow and two other riders set out from the ranch house. The cattalo and her latest calf—a heifer then of some ten or so months of age—had been running in the mouth of Jhus Canyon (named after an Apache Indian Chief). With the three on horseback, there was Bum and his small duplicate copy, Doodles. Narrow sloping finger ridges ran down from the west to the creek. On one of these Bum and Doodles began to bay. They had trailed up and were holding some cattle, perhaps the cattalo. Soon Morrow and his companions arrived, and it was the cattalo and her calf. Bum was making sure that the critters stayed put and Doodles was assisting. At one point the cattalo heifer calf decided to make a break for freedom, and Bum was busy holding up and taming the calf.

That left Doodles with the task of holding the cattalo. The cattalo weighed over fifteen hundred pounds. Doodles—brave cowdog that he was—weighed less than thirty pounds and stood a foot high.

Head to head they faced off, scarcely fifteen feet separating them, the cattalo poised to charge, and Doodles prepared to turn back the charging animal, as resolute as the

Descendants of the Cattalo, circa 1980

Three Hundred Spartans awaiting the massed millions of Xerxes' army at Thermopylae. There they stood, a picture forever etched in the riders' minds: the cattalo, tail raised; and Doodles, giving no ground, his black body and tan rump patches twins of his large companion, Bum. There was no doubt that Doodles intended to hold the angry critter at all costs, perhaps jumping aside at the last moment.

The calf disciplined, Bum returned to the assistance of his stalwart companion. The cattalo charged, but she was turned back by Bum and Doodles, neither giving quarter. The cattalo calf was separated for weaning and branding, then hauled away in a stock trailer situated nearby. The cattalo was left to ponder the abrupt separation from her offspring, for a day or two. Did she remember the brave adversary Doodles? Perhaps.

Town friends of the Morrows visited, and their young children fell in love with Doodles, and he with them. They took him to live with them, to be fed, and coddled, and loved, and to lie beneath the refrigeration vents on the carpet on hot summer afternoons, and to sleep there on cold winter nights. Sometimes he dreamed, and his dreams were of the mountains and of Bum.

§   §   §

There was a time before Bum and his fellow cowdogs. Ralph Morrow's brother Carson Morrow was the Chief Patrol Inspector for the Border Patrol, Tucson Sector. Carson and his family lived in Tucson. An acquaintance gave him two puppies that were Dachshund and probably English Springer Spaniel. One of the puppies—the female—resembled a full-blooded Dachshund. A niece of Carson and her family adopted the female, which they named Duchess, and she lived a long life with her humans on the ranch home. The only potentially disastrous happening in the life of Duchess occurred when she had gone along with her people who were digging around where they thought some Indian artifacts were to be found. Duchess, joining in on the excavations, stuck her nose in a rat hole and was bitten by a rattlesnake. Her owners promptly rendered first aid, making incisions and using their mouths to suck out the venom—all against medical recommendations, but effective in that Duchess recovered with no effect from the rattlesnake poison.

The second puppy was left at the Morrow ranch home. He was named Dutch. Unlike his sister, Dutch did not resemble a Dachshund. He appeared to be a black-colored, quarter-sized hound.

Everyone loved Dutch, and he returned their affection. He was often picked up and carried while he lay cradled on his back. He was so agreeable and ready to please that none could refrain from succumbing to his charm.

The Morrows were away from the ranch house when Carson Morrow left Dutch. There had been no communication that a puppy was on the way. In the yard, in front of the house there was a large chair with an oval lattice work support. Dutch was placed beneath the chair, and a heavy rock weighed on the chair seat completed his temporary prison.

It happened that there was a pet shepherd dog, named "Tip," in the yard also; once Carson departed, Tip answered Dutch's cries for help. Soon a suitable escape tunnel had been dug and Dutch's freedom gained. He promptly repaid his savior by executing that time-honored display of puppyhood affection—mauling and hanging onto the scruff of any older dog at hand. The Morrows upon return soon were under the spell of the fine dog Dutch.

Ralph Morrow was a genuine horseman, and he had a great affection and respect for those noble beasts. Throughout the years he kept a band of brood mares, and raised, trained, and rode their offspring. Young horses, just under saddle, were taken on a ride of a few miles up Whitetail Creek, where the ranch house was located. Dutch and the shepherd Tip went along on the rides. On a first outing, when Dutch was but a puppy, he disappeared. Tip was with the horses, but Dutch was not. Then a great high-pitched barking began up out of the creek bottom on a steep hillside. Horses were rimmed out to the commotion, and there was Dutch. He had trailed up a small bunch of cattle and was holding them as best he could. He had not had the benefit of training by such as Bum, who was several years away in the future. Dutch the natural cowdog had further won the heart of Ralph Morrow.

Dutch had lived at his home there in the Chiricahua Mountains for about three years. A primitive road ran near the Morrow home, and deer hunters often stopped to fill their canteens and five-gallon water jugs. The Morrows were often away as Ralph Morrow was a law officer, who truly was "a legend in his own time." Returning from a trip afield, Juanita and Ralph were shocked. The dog Tip was in the fenced yard, but there was no sign of Dutch. They called, and they looked and drove up and down Whitetail Creek, and to neighboring ranch houses, some a dozen miles away. No, no one had seen Dutch.

Ralph Morrow, 1965

Heartbroken, the Morrows returned home to resume the search the following morning. Dutch was not to be found. At last they knew what had happened. Someone had taken him, had stolen the beloved Dutch.

Days were spent driving the streets and alleys of cities and towns within a large radius of the ranch. If Dutch was inside a home, they would not see him, but perhaps fortune would smile upon the Morrows and he would be in some yard in some town as they drove by. Days turned to weeks, and though hope was not lost, Dutch was lost to the Morrows forever. He was never seen again. They could only hope that the person or persons who had stolen him cared for him and treated him well.

Then came Bum, and while he would never take the place of Dutch, he found a place in the hearts of the Morrows just as Dutch had.

§ § §

As Bum grew older, Morrow took Bum's companions more often when there was cow work to be done. Many times, Bum still went along, and the rides into the mountains were shortened and tailored to him. He was not to be left out, not to remain behind when Bugle or Fiddler or Red went with horse and rider.

On one such ride, Morrow and another rider paused on a ridge line, looking off across the great Cave Creek Basin. Bum and Red rested nearby in the shade of an oak.

Morrow turned to his companion. "Wouldn't it be something," he asked, "if this was all we had to do?"

How could life have been better?

Often on warm autumn days, before winter came, Bum napped in the shade of a sycamore in his off-duty home. Though he was still active and able to hunt cattle, and rim the mountain hillsides, his naps grew longer. One afternoon, Bum lay down in a favorite spot and went to sleep. Later that afternoon, without awakening, Bum died. When Morrow went to feed and water the cowdogs that evening, he found Bum.

Bum was buried beneath a large sycamore tree. It was as Ralph Morrow had said: "I sure am going to miss Bum when he is no longer around."

Maybe they are all together again, riding in the mountains, doing things they loved so well.

DUNNY'S WILD RUN

Jim Hathaway's ranch was on the southwestern slopes of the Huachuca Mountains, sharing a part of the border between Old Mexico and the United States. He is not to be confused with Federal Judge Jim Hathaway, who was his nephew.

Carson Morrow often visited the Hathaway Ranch—he and Jim were good friends. Greg Hathaway was an officer and pilot in the Army Air Corp in World War II, and was stationed for a time at Davis Monthan Air Base in Tucson. He was another one of Hathaway's nephews. One story—and Carson Morrow said he had actually seen a place where explosives had blown down some trees—was this: Greg buzzed Jim Hathaway as he rode along a ridge, and Jim shot at Greg's B-25 with a .30-.30 rifle, maybe hitting one of the plane's wings. Greg dropped a bomb near Jim, which blew down some trees, but did not injure horse or rider.

Hathaway carried on a battle of sorts with trespassers coming onto his property. This story needs no verification: Jim fashioned a skeleton out of some cow bones and a bear skull. He dressed his creation in women's apparel, fashioned a hangman's knot, and hanged his skeleton alongside a road. He fastened a sign to the "woman" which declared that his handiwork was a wild woman who had been running amok in the Huachucas until captured and executed. The sign went on to the effect that any trespassers would be dealt with accordingly.

In the 1930s, Carson Morrow brought some Shetland ponies to Whitetail Canyon. For a number of years we cared for and rode them. All but one, which was a stallion named Spotty—obviously a paint—were mares. They were: Chocolate, Fuzzy, and Taffy. Taffy was my favorite. She was a bit large for a Shetland, with good conformation, and a bright sorrel color. She and I got along fine, but she did not extend her good favor to everyone. One morning, Ralph Morrow and an Aunt of mine—Lola Morrow—were in front of my grandparent Morrows' home. Aunt Lola was seated on Taffy. My Dad, Ralph, was an excellent horseman. He said: "Lola, you had better watch out, that little mare is going to pitch with you." Aunt Lola replied: "Why, I've rode lots of horses, and I'd like to see this Shetland throw me off." At that exact moment, Taffy, as bronc riders say, "broke in two," throwing Lola skyward. She hit face down in some sand, with no injury—except to her pride.

When town friends visited my sister Audrey and me in the summers, we all rode the Shetland ponies. One morning we started out, my Dad riding a young horse he was breaking, I was on Taffy, Audrey rode Chocolate, and her friend Ethel Nalley was mounted up on Fuzzy. Stanley Patterson's steed was the stud, Spotty. Stan maybe had not at the time ridden a great deal. Spotty began running down the road, and Stan fell off. Spotty was captured, Stan mounted up, and Spotty again ran, and Stan again fell off. My Dad said: "Stan, sit leaned back with straight back, and

Jim Hathaway (left) with Congressman (unnamed), Nogales, Arizona, circa 1928

Photograph (cropped) courtesy of the National Border Patrol Museum, El Paso, Texas

your stirrups out front. Look right through between Spotty's ears. Don't look right or left at the ground, as that is where you will end up." Stan did as instructed. We came out on the first reasonably flat, open ground at the mouth of Whitetail Canyon, Baseball Flat. There was tall grass and weeds growing high over the ground. Spotty left the road running, straight across Baseball Flat. Stan stayed with him. All we could see was his red hair bouncing above the grass.

It was about 1937 that Carson Morrow brought an appaloosa stallion to Whitetail Canyon. He was around for six months. He was pastured with the Shetland mares, and one of the mares months later produced a colt. The mare was Chocolate. The colt was named Brown Cocoa, which changed to Brown Koko in a year or two. Koko was slightly larger than a good-sized Shetland, and when fully grown could outrun the average cow horse. As he aged, his color changed to resemble an appaloosa. Maybe a decade after Koko's father had come and gone, I asked Carson Morrow what the situation was with the

Michael Morrow on Koko, Ralph Morrow, 1957

appaloosa stallion. He said Jim Hathaway had stolen the horse from a small Mexican circus that had come along near the international boundary, and he needed to "cool him off" for awhile.

The late summer of 1940 Ralph Morrow set out to post a game refuge that took in most of the Chiricahua Mountain high country. I went along, riding the good horse Koko. The first night we camped in South Fork of Cave Creek. Our pack horse was a dun which had the imaginative name of Dunny. After a day of posting refuge signs, we arrived at Monte Vista lookout. The fire season was over, and none of the lookouts and smoke chasers were on the mountain. We corralled our horses, fed them some hay and grain left over from the fire season, and spent the night in the cabin. The next night we camped at the head of Witch Creek, and the following day we rode north along the foothills headed for West Turkey Creek. This was before Rural Addressing days when, during the Clinton administration, some bright people, who no doubt benefited monetarily, renamed roads and trails. Then the road into West Turkey Creek became East Turkey Creek Road; East Turkey Creek was renamed South Turkey Creek, and on and on. The reason given for rural addressing was: Emergency and law enforcement personnel could respond to 911 calls and know the exact location. That was the carrot. The switch was: If you don't have rural addressing, your mail will not be delivered. (Nearly twenty years later, mail is yet delivered to old highway contract mail addresses.)

A resident living on the west side of the Chiricahuas—after rural addressing— saw some vandals setting fires. He called the Cochise County Sheriff's Office in Bisbee, to report the crime. He told the dispatcher about the fire setters, and that the fires were being started in the area of his home which was in West Turkey Creek, but, thanks to rural addressing, the road was called East Turkey Creek Road. The dispatcher then asked: "And where exactly is that?" So much for rural addressing and 911 response.

Back to 1940: Dunny was used to the trip as we headed for West Turkey Creek Ranger Station. In fact, we had quit leading him, and he followed along behind. For some reason, neither my Dad nor I noticed that Dunny was lagging further and further behind. Suddenly, a great commotion brought to our attention that all was not as planned with Dunny. Here he came in an all-out wild run—straight for our horses. Koko ran off into a grove of oak trees before I could get him under control.

On ran Dunny, the pack saddle hanging on his side. My Dad soon roped him. Dunny had decided to lie down and roll, which had twisted the saddle to his side, and sent him on his wild dash. Bedrolls, pots, tin plates and cups, utensils, a small Dutch oven, and our provisions were strung out on the ground for two hundred yards. The pack saddle was straightened, and we spent a half hour gathering up all that had been packed on Dunny. On to the ranger station we rode, and several days later arrived back in East Whitetail Canyon. Dunny was haltered and led the rest of the trip. Incidentally, post rural addressing, the road to East Whitetail was designated: West Whitetail Road.

Koko (@ 11 years old) on 3△ Ranch, Sulphur Canyon, circa 1950

Michael Morrow, Seattle Asian Art Museum, 1990

MICHAEL'S JURY DUTY

After serving as an Air Force officer and F-84 and F-86 fighter pilot for over four years during the Korean War era, I, for some as yet unknown reason, left the Air Force. Several years were spent in a lackluster effort in law enforcement. I returned to the University of Arizona (U of A) for a degree in engineering. One day, the administration said: "If you will just leave, we will give you a diploma." So, I did. Since the degree was a B.S. in Mining Engineering, this was never divulged in the presence of any environmentalists.

Michael Morrow was an exceptional student. He said he was influenced by my hours of study, but as a student he excelled—I did not. Michael graduated from the U of A with "High Distinction," earning a double-major B.A. in Mathematics and Psychology. This was followed by an M.A. in Teaching English as a Second Language. He lectured some at the University, then spent a year abroad, primarily in Spain and Portugal, where he taught English to top IBM executives in Oporto.

Pete Moser had a real-estate firm in Tucson. Pete also had graduated from the U of A with a degree in Mining Engineering. He suggested that I get a real-estate license. For over thirty years I had a real-estate broker's license in Arizona. This was more of an avocation than vocation. Throughout the years properties were sold for others, and the family dealt some in real estate. Michael obtained a real-estate salesman's license. He and I were in partners for awhile, until one day—even though he had lived most of his life in a desert—he said the summers were too hot and he moved to Seattle, Washington.

Microsoft was still in its formative years in 1984, when he went to work for them as their 700th employee hired, first as a technical writer for the manuals that

Michael's SYSTECH Group, Edgewater Inn, Elliott Bay, Seattle, 1992
(Recreating the famous "Fish from Your Window" photo taken of The Beatles in 1964)

accompanied Microsoft software, then later as the supervisor of a technical-support group ("SYSTECH"), responsible for all aspects of the production and publication of those same manuals. Being in the right place at the right time is often very benefi-cial, and Michael quit working for others when he was a young man.

For a number of years he had a winter home in Tucson and a summer home in Seattle, until finally becoming a full-time desert dweller once again. In 1997, during his winter-in-Tucson, summer-in-Seattle days, he was called to "Jury Duty" at Seattle Municipal Court. The following is his day-by-day account of that adventure, sent originally as nightly email messages to friends and family.

(According to Michael, "The Martini" is Hollywood slang for the last shot of the day when filming a movie, so he felt a martini recipe was an appropriate way to end his daily jury-duty musings. *Most* of the recipes have been omitted here.)

Michael's Narrative

Today marked Day One (of Five) of Mr. Morrow's Ordeal, aka "I Couldn't Come Up With Any More Good Excuses to Weasel Out of Jury Duty." The alarm rousted your fickle scribe at the ungodly (since Satan is, after all, the Prince of Insufficient Illumination) hour of 6:00 AM today. The first day of the rest of the week, I said cheerily to myself as I vaulted out of bed. Arrived at the Seattle Municipal Court (12th floor of the "Public Safety Building" between 3rd and 4th, James and Cherry—in case any of you are planning a field trip of your own) at the astounding time of 7:50 A.M. Can't for the life of me understand why people do this voluntarily, especially those who aren't involved in the care and feeding of poultry or hoofed mammals. Caramba! Got my official juror number. Number 418. (Overheard as I was sleepily reading the official "Welcome to Jury Duty" pamphlet: "What's my number?" "Four Two Five." "Is that four two five, or four hundred, twenty-five?" Oh God, please don't ever let me fall into the gears of this system.)

Watched a twenty minute pep video, narrated by none other than Raymond Burr. (I couldn't make this stuff up.) Gist seems to be: "This sucks, but you'll feel so much better when it's over." For six hours read everything I could get my hands on: the entire August issue of *Premiere*; the complete Sunday *Seattle Times*; two back issues of the *Seattle Weekly*; a backlog of clippings from the *Wall Street Journal* and *The Economist*, (the gist of which seemed to be how radical French Deconstructivists and misguided feminists are destroying the American educational system).

Along about 3:00, got herded into the elevator and sent down to Courtroom 3. A solicitation-of-prostitution case involving a young Hispanic male (who required a court translator) and a Seattle police person (obviously female, but I was trying to avoid gender-labeling terminology) posing as a sporting gal.

Judge started the "voir dire" (French for "looky here") process by droning through a set of cue cards on his desk. When he got to the "does anyone have any reason why he or she thinks he or she or it can't render an impartial decision in this case," I had to raise my hand and say "harrumph." Judge (and later, prosecuting attorney for the City of Seattle) and I got into a spirited, if attenuated, conversation about why I thought the gummit didn't have any right sticking its nose into financial transactions between consenting adults, and how Prohibition didn't stop people from drinking in the 20s and 30s, just helped create a powerful new criminal class, blah, blah, blah. This seemed to galvanize a couple of other lumps (two myn, one womyn, one of whom was reading the most recent John Grisham novel, I kid you not) into objecting as well. Just call me a rabble rouser.

Attorney for the defendant, attempting to establish that everyone understood the concepts of "presumption of innocence" and " reasonable doubt" elicited a frightening torrent of hogwash from one grizzled old fart, who opined that since we were dealing with misdemeanors, he would be comfortable returning a verdict of "guilty" even if reasonable doubts were still bumping around his noggin. The reason? Well, since this wasn't as serious as those felony things, even an erroneous guilty verdict could be an "educational experience" for the defendant.

Slack jaws of amazement all around. I struggled against, and finally overcame, the temptation to jump up and thank him (à la *Blazing Saddles*) for his authentic "Western gibberish."

Defense attorney embarked on an interesting tack, involving a famous episode of *Seinfeld*: the "puffy-shirt episode." Actually pretty clever, since even for those who don't watch the TV series, it was simple to summarize: Seinfeld meets a woman in a cafe; she talks in such a quiet, mousy little voice that nobody (except her absent boyfriend) can understand what she is saying; to be polite, Seinfeld says "yes" a couple of times when it appears she is asking him a question, even though he has no idea what she is asking. Turns out he has agreed to wear a ridiculous frilly shirt she has designed on a nationally-televised telethon.

Attorney asks "Is Seinfeld legally—or even morally—obligated to wear the frilly shirt?" Very clever cuz his client doesn't speak a word of English. I think you can see where he was going with this: client was just nodding his head "yes" when solicited by Robo Hooker, even though he didn't have a clue what the crazy gringa was talking about.

Cool, I think. Then he turns to me (why were they picking on me?) and works a variation of his theme.

"Mr. Morrow, do you speak any languages?"

"Besides English, you mean?"

"Well, yes . . ."

"Okay: Spanish, French, Portuguese, and a little Arabic."

"Well, is there a language you don't speak?"

"Oh, hundreds. Thousands. Take your pick."

"Hmm. How's your French?"

"Pretty rusty, I'd say."

"All right then! Suppose you were in Paris, and this guy comes up to you on the street, and starts rattling away. You don't comprehend everything he says, but respond 'yes,' or rather 'oui,' a few times. Later on, you realize you've agreed to buy his car for an exorbitant sum. Are you legally obligated to do so?"

"Oh, you know, verbal contracts aren't worth the paper they are written on."

"Heh, heh. But what about your obligation?"

"Hmmm. How big is this French guy?"

Didn't get chosen for that jury. Dang. End of day one.

"Mr. M Performs His Civic Duty": Day Deux

Roused by the plaintive bleating of my alarm clock. Feeling much less springy than Day One. Railed at cruel fate most of morning toilette, and almost missed the bus that gets me to the courthouse on time.

Jury Assembly Room right down the hall from the Tuberculosis Clinic on the 12th floor of Public Safety Building. We share the same restrooms. Mental note: wash hands thoroughly and refrain from biting nails. Look at clock: 9:05. Pull out several newspapers, some mail, a flyer or two. Finish reading them all. Look at clock again: 10:20. Going to be a very long day.

Was hoping for some excitement today, but even less stimulation than Day One. Actually, experience is more Beckett-like, only set in an airport terminal instead of a trashcan. "Paging Mr. Godot. Please report to your party at Gate 9." Only, of course, Mr. Godot is on a commuter flight to Pasco, and won't be meeting you at Gate 9. Ever.

At 1:30, a breakthrough: my number is called for another trial. All a-twitter, fourteen of us cram into the elevator that will take us down to the courtrooms on the fourth floor. Someone had pastrami for lunch. Darn, I think it was me.

We are herded into another holding pen. Countdown commences: 10, 9, 8, . . . at 3, the bailiff (a kindly woman who looks somewhat like Ray Walston on *My Favorite Martian*) informs us that the parties concerned have decided to settle without going to trial. Couldn't they have figured out they didn't want to go to the moon before getting all suited up?

Back upstairs. Contemplate digging out to freedom with one of the plastic spoons by the coffee pot, but realize I'd then be hanging outside, some 150 feet above the Seattle sidewalks (.com). Ever since seeing *Vertigo* as a child, have had A) intense crush on Kim Novak, and B) paralyzing fear of heights. Scrap digging-out idea. Might even land me in the TB Clinic.

2:30: Overhear a woman in bathroom, being violently ill. She emerges, ashen, announcing to all interested bystanders that she thinks the snack foods in the jury room "are making her constipated."

3:30: To my horror, find myself reading *People* magazine article about "Sexy New Hollywood Moms." Jury foreperson mercifully announces that we can all leave for the day.

On way home from downtown Seattle, marveling at how many pretty women are walking around on the sidewalks. Normal Puget climate of darkness and drizzle not conducive to such sightings, as folks are hidden under layers of flannel, khaki, Gore-Tex, and lumpy leggings. Besides, living on Capitol Hill, home to some of the northwest's most attractive transvestites, has made your scribe hesitant to jump to conclusions (and let's face it, none of 'em look as good as Jaye Davidson).

I'm starting to think I should get out of my car more often, take advantage of this wonderful public transport and the opportunities it provides for enjoying our lovely city. Across the aisle, a woman starts barking at passersby, then leans over and in a commanding voice informs me "Marination. Preparation. Melrose Place. They're all the same: 'MP'."

I manage a wan smile, and get off the bus several stops before my actual destination.

End of Day Two.

"Mr. M Performs His Civic Duty" Day the Third

This is conjuring up some eerie memories from grade-school days, when I would be the last child standing in the group of unpicked players for the softball teams. Oh, I had a wicked swing; unfortunately, the bat never managed to connect with the ball. And the naturally athletic (and much taller) captains of the opposing teams had no interest in bolstering my self esteem, the way they would no doubt be required by law to do these days. (Can you picture Little Leaguers, with mom, dad, and attorneys from the Justice Department cheering them on?)

Three days of warming the bench, and nobody has picked me to play.[1] Today there wasn't even a false start, like yesterday, or the entertainment of a voir dire, like Monday. I would head to the batting cage to see if a little practice helped, but most everyone else in the jury pool is working on a good buttocks crease, too.

Starting to think that the real civic benefit of this jury service thing is to act as a deterrent: "You think you're bored after sitting in this room for three days, think how you would feel if your surroundings shrunk to the size of a jail cell—and your cell mate was large and frisky."

OK, I promise to be a model citizen and obey all laws. Except there are bound to be some I don't know about that I break every day. I'm doomed.

One last chance to help decide the fate of a fellow human tomorrow. Maybe it will be something really interesting, like someone mooning the entire Seattle City Council during one of their televised hearings. And, speaking of mooning just so you will have something entertaining and enlightening to read today:

> **RALEIGH, N.C., Aug 20 (UPI)**—Mooning someone may be tasteless, but a North Carolina Court of Appeals has ruled that it's legal under state law. The decision stems from a case involving a man who dropped his shorts to his ankles as a Charlotte woman walked up a flight of stairs to her condominium.
>
> Mark Edward Fly appealed his misdemeanor conviction for the 1995 incident. The appeals court ruled 2 to 1 that there was no evidence Fly intended to show his private parts. State prosecutors could appeal the decision to the North Carolina Supreme Court. North Carolina's law makes it illegal to "willfully expose the private parts of his or her person in any public place and in the presence of any other person, or persons of the opposite sex."
>
> In a dissenting opinion, Judge Ralph Walker said "the buttocks are a part of the human body which morality and decency require to he covered in the presence of others." Fly's public defender, Karen Eady, says the ruling suggests "we can go around mooning anyone in North Carolina that we want to."

Nice to see that those fundamental liberties are being upheld, so to speak. But which amendment (unreasonable search? freedom of assembly?) does this fall under?

---

[1] Michael excelled in high school track—primarily the 440-yard dash and relay races.

Talked to one of the women who did sit on the jury in the case of the Hispanic dude who was accused of soliciting a prostitute. Said the city did such a miserable job of presenting its case that it took them only 10 minutes to return a verdict of "not guilty."

End of Day Three.

Day Four: "They Like Me, They Really Like Me"

apologies to Sally Field

Was it only yesterday that I was kvetching about not being on a jury? Well, as a good friend reminded me recently, "answered prayers can turn into dangerous realities."

I've evolved legs and dragged myself up out of the primordial ooze of the jury room and onto the craggy beachhead of an actual jury. Yes, they picked little old me, wisecracks and all (more on that with tomorrow's installment).

I absolutely should not, cannot, and *will not* divulge any details of the trial, since it's only in recess now. No way can you get me to tell you anything about it—not even my usual smart-alecky remarks during voir dire, as they would probably reveal too much. Nuh uh. Nosirree. Even if Uma Thurman were to dress up in a skintight black leather outfit and come to my house to interrogate me this very minute … my lips would be sealed. (C'mon, I double dare you! Please.)

I *can* say that the attorneys—both for the defense and the City of Seattle—are putting on quite a display of … incredibly …. slow … cross … examination. The judge man himself nodded off a couple of times.

In honor of the glacial (some might say "tectonic") pace of the proceedings, here is:

Today's Martini Recipe: "The Glacier Blue"
(from the Four Seasons Hotel in Seattle)

1. In cocktail shaker, toss in dash (absolutely no more than 1/4 shot) Blue Curaçao liqueur, 2 shots Bombay Sapphire Gin, and 3 shots Stoli Cristall vodka. Over ice, but doesn't have to be from a glacier.
2. Shake vigorously for approximately 40 seconds.
3. Pour contents of shaker through strainer and over lemon twists in two large martini glasses.
4. Kick back in an easy chair and watch polar bears dance on your ceiling—or see if there's an old episode of *Perry Mason* on the TV.

Day Five: Final Day

Well, in spite of the following exchange during voir dire between yours truly and the attorney for the City, I finally get to sit on a jury:

"Mr. Morrow, do you drink?"

"Yessir."

"About how often do you drink?"

"On a daily basis."

"Can you describe how you get when you have had a lot to drink?"

"I become incredibly witty."

"Um, anything else?"

"Yes, everybody becomes much more attractive."

"Heh, heh. The old 'beer goggles' effect, right?"

"Well, I prefer to think of it as 'wine glasses,' actually."

As you have guessed, this was a DUI (Driving Under the Influence) trial. The judge (a Mr. Holifield, with an "i" not a "y"—as well as two intact lobes), added a couple of chuckles of his own when he asked prospective jurors if any lived in Ballard.

(*Note for non-Seattle readers*: Ballard is an old fishing community consisting mostly of Norwegians and some Swedes, long ago absorbed by the Seattle limits. Ballardites are known for some of the following characteristics: names such as "Thor" and "Ole"; hats with horns on them; "lutefisk," a dreadful paste-like fish dish; and taverns called "The Valhalla." But the real source of their infamy is their reputation as some of the worst drivers in a region not famed for skillful motorists. Ballardites don't think they have done a good job of parking unless at least one wheel is up on the curb; they weave all over the road ["Ya sure, I pay taxes on it, so I'm darned tootin' gonna use it all"]; and they rarely go more than 7 mph ["Where's the fire, sonny?"]. So, in a case that hinged partly on the alleged irregular driving of the defendant, the judge was half facetiously trying to weed out anyone used to that kind of driving as the norm. Whew. Ever notice how long it can take to explain some jokes?)

Some words about the key players.

Counsel for the city: honest to God, if someone in central casting worked with someone else in costuming, they could not come up with a better "lawyer as shark" look. Heavily pomaded hair (slicked straight back); large class ring; brilliantly shined shoes; smart, double-breasted suit.

And the size of the guy: shoulders nearly popping out of his suit, and (well-manicured) hands as big as Virginia hams. Like some NFL linebacker moonlighting as a bouncer in an upscale strip club (not that I would know about these things from direct experience, mind you).

Counsel for the defendant: in contrast to the prosecutor, this guy was folksy understatement personified, from the tips of his sensible shoes to the top of his slightly balding pate. With his owl-like eyes peering out good-humoredly from his glasses, his quiet, soothing voice, and his wry self-deprecating humor, he could have easily been mistaken for a CPA (which in fact his client was). However, if the prosecutor was a shark, this guy was a barracuda. I think I'll give him a call if, heaven forfend, I ever wind up needing a lawyer.

Fellow jurors: belying my snotty observations about some of the people I had been hanging out with in the assembly room earlier in the week, the five other people on the jury were quite impressive in their abilities to grasp the main issues, conduct a logical and friendly analysis, and adhere to the judge's instructions. I was very pleasantly surprised by what an efficient and non-confrontational group this was; no Lee J. Cobb *Twelve Angry Men* scenes, even when it looked like a potential hung jury for awhile. (Well, one woman did have a tendency to break out of the corral and head off for the wild, overgrown chaparral of irrelevant discussion, but we were able to lasso her and drag her back to the holding pen without too much trouble each time that happened.) I conceded foreman duties to one bearded guy when he actually used the phrase "decision fork"—and seemed to make sense. Frankly, I wish most meetings I had to attend when still employed at a Behemoth Software Company That Shall Otherwise Remain Nameless had gone half this well.

One would think that a DUI case would be pretty cut-and-dried, and in the hands of anyone else, that may have been the result. The defense attorney made a good case for disregarding the Field Sobriety Tests (FSTs) conducted at the scene of the arrest: the defendant was tired from working late; he was born with a cleft palate that, in spite of surgery, still caused him to slur his speech when he was nervous; a horrific childhood injury burned his feet and left him with permanent balance problems. So, snick, snick, snick, that part of the case was pretty much cut to ribbons. (In the jury room we all tried the FSTs as described by the arresting officer, and decided we would be toast if called upon to perform the same tests on an uneven patch of pavement, under the glare of a gendarme, while enduring the hoots and jeers of playful passersby.)

Unfortunately, it was not so easy to discount the results of a Blood Alcohol test administered back at the police station. Two successive tests showed BAC readings of 0.127 and 0.128 (grams of alcohol per 210 liters of air, in case you are interested—but there will not be a pop quiz). Legal definition of intoxication in Washington is 0.100, so this put the readings at 27% over that, well above the machine's margin of error. The machine itself appeared to have been carefully calibrated and serviced, with built-in safeguards, and seemed sufficiently easy to use that a trained Chihuahua could probably do it. To foul up the test would have meant that the arresting officer was either A) a vindictive person out to get the defendant; or B) an incredible doofus who shouldn't be allowed near paper clips.

We all liked the defendant, who appeared to believe quite firmly that his driving had not been impaired. He is a nice family man who puts in long hours working on low-income housing projects for the elderly. It was not easy to return a guilty verdict, and we took turns trying to convince ourselves that we had reasonable doubts. But, in the end, the glove did fit, and we could not acquit.

So, what conclusions are we to glean from this rambling account of my time in the halls of justice? Here are a few:

1) Don't always assume that your fellow man and woman is lacking in intelligence just because a majority of them elected [*fill-in-the-blank-with-appropriately-odious-candidate-here*] in the last election (and decided to tear down the King Dome and build a new open-air football stadium for mega-billionaire Paul Allen at taxpayers' expense—but I digress);

2) Bring a cushion if you have to sit in the jury box (those wooden seat backs are killers);

3) Drink at home—the booze is cheaper, the air is cleaner, and you can hear the TV;

4) If you must drink elsewhere, take a cab home—a DUI arrest looks pretty terrifying, even from an outsider's perspective—and imagine how awful you'd feel if you ran over someone's puddy tat.

E. J. HANDS   F. H. HANDS

Hilltop Lead~Silver Mines
HANDS BROTHERS, OWNERS

Dos Cabezos, Arizona, *April 4th*

J. D. Taylor,

Gave Civet Cat away to Calif. party that wanted it from the first but I did not want to let it go if some Ariz. people would take it. I have not heard from Hancock & Welch lately about the resort but the last report the Forest people had not moved altho they promised immediate action and that with them might mean yrs. judging from my experience with them. A little ore is being found in both tunnels so the Supt. told me last eve he appeared to be quite jubilant about it but for my part I could see no reason for being so. There is lots of snow on top of mts. and water everywhere. I am very busy clearing ground for orchard and ought to have had trees planted long ago. Regards to everyone

Yours &c.
E. J. Hands

Letter from John Hands to J. D. Taylor, envelope postmarked 1915

COUNTRY SCHOOLS

The Hilltop Metals Mining Company purchased the Hilltop Mine in 1913 from brothers Frank and John Hands, and later established the West Hilltop townsite in the North Fork of Pinery Canyon. Mine development and mining of lead and silver ore began in earnest in 1924, with an "adit" or tunnel being driven in a northerly direction for 1,800 feet, with drifts running west and northeast, as ore veins were mined. The northeast drift branched, one branch to the east, and another northeast for approximately 1,500 feet from the junction. There the tunnel broke through to the northeast side of the ridge. Those workings were named the Kasper. A mid-level tunnel, called the Gray, was driven approximately 2,000 feet, with a raise developed to intersect the easternmost drift of the Kasper. A third tunnel—the Rehm—was driven at a lower level for approximately 1,800 feet. Ultimately, the underground workings of the Hilltop exceeded 25,000 feet.

From the eastern portal of the Kasper, a trail wound down to the mine road leading to the mouth of the Rehm. A substantial town, also known as Hilltop, was constructed a short distance below and east of the portal of the Rehm Tunnel. The town was situated on several wide benches that had been blasted out of the limestone hillside. A large metal power house and machine shop housed compressors and electrical generators. A number of miners' cabins ranged along the benches. There was a store, bunkhouse, boarding house, a pool hall, and beneath the club house, and below the lower bench level, there was a dance hall. There was a change room and showers for the miners and male employees of the mining company, and separate facilities for the women and girls of Hilltop for bathing.

Hilltop Metals Mining Company Stock Certificate (1,000 shares), 1925

The mine road wound down into Whitetail Canyon. On a leveled area south of Whitetail Creek was the Hilltop School, attended by the miners' children, as well as those from surrounding ranches. All either rode horseback or walked to school. For a time, there were children living at West Hilltop. A steep limestone ridge jutted above the townsite, requiring the children to climb through rough brushy terrain before descending on the Whitetail side of the ridge.

My Grandfather—Jim Kuykendall—was the mine superintendent for the Kasper, and his family lived at West Hilltop for a time. My mother, Juanita Kuykendall, her two brothers, and several other children attended the Hilltop School. Each morning—and returning each evening—the West Hilltop students' path to school was as follows: Accompanied by a miner, sometimes riding a timber car along the mine rails, sometimes walking, they went approximately 3,000 feet through the Kasper tunnel. They then dropped over 1,500 feet down the

West Room, Hilltop School, circa 1923

trail to the road near the mouth of the Rehm Tunnel. Then down the East Hilltop road to a short-cut trail that led to the school house. Afternoons saw them climbing back up the trail and again going through the Kasper tunnel. The total one-way distance was about two miles. Other students rode horseback or walked cross country as far as four miles each way. The dedicated scholars of a bygone era!

Nothing now remains of the Hilltop Schoolhouse but the ruins of a brick foundation. There is a rural electric line that more or less parallels East Whitetail Creek. A branch line runs south to the old Hilltop Townsite. Near the junction of the lines is the place where the schoolhouse stood. It was a large frame-and-clapboard building, with a folding partition that divided the interior into two large classrooms—the East Room and the West Room. At times the enrollment was sufficient to warrant two teachers, assigned to their respective classrooms.

Mining at Hilltop shut down in 1927, except for a brief period in the early 1950s. Classes were no longer held at the Hilltop School when the doors closed for a final time in the spring of 1937. Then the schoolhouse was torn down and salvaged, as was the entire town of Hilltop after it was purchased by Ralph Morrow in

1964. Many of the miner's cabins were moved intact, and the superintendent's house was rebuilt at the Morrow Orchard[1] near Whitetail Creek, where it is today.

My sister Audrey and I were among the last students to attend Hilltop School. The two of us attended Portal School beginning in the autumn of 1937 through the spring of 1941. I returned to the old Portal School house in the fall of 1943 and graduated, along with George ("Pee Wee") Newman, from the eighth grade in 1944.

In the summer of 1937, the Pague family moved to Whitetail Canyon. Beginning that year, Ben Pague drove the school bus. There were school children at intervals all along the roadway down out of Whitetail, up through Paradise, and down Silver Creek to the Portal School. The Pagues—Robert (Sonny Boy) and Barbara—were on the bus when Audrey and I were picked up school mornings.

We four Whitetail Canyon bus riders were sometimes joined by others when the Hilltop Mine was in sporadic operation. Our conveyance was a reasonable facsimile of a bus, but more closely resembled the Toonerville Trolley in the comics. Up along East Turkey Creek, Barbara McGinty and maybe one or two others came on board. In Paradise, Earnest (Sonny) and Gail Lee and a few other students got on the bus. A short distance east of Paradise a small lad was usually waiting alongside the roadway. Then it was down through Silver Creek, with Mr. Pague exercising due diligence to the curving mountain road and ignoring the crowd, which resembled a trainload of East Indian peasants arriving in Bombay. To maintain some semblance of sanity and preserve his hearing, Mr. Pague attempted to shut out his charges as we sped along the road going and coming from school. In the evenings when we approached Paradise, the boy living east of the town would attempt to convey to Mr. Pague where he wished to disembark from the Toonerville Trolley. He spoke very slowly and a typical exchange would be thus: "Mr. Pague I . . . want to . . . get off . . . at my house." By the time he had repeated this several times we would have arrived in downtown Paradise.

In the earlier days both schoolhouses at Portal were used. The smaller frame house—now used as a Post Office—was designated the "Little Room." It therefore followed that the building now housing the library was dubbed the "Big Room." When students advanced to the Big Room, they had achieved a higher station in life. The Little Roomers were from grade one through probably five, with the Big Roomers grades six, seven and eight.

---

[1] As of this writing, now the Colibri Vineyard, managed by Page Spring Cellars.

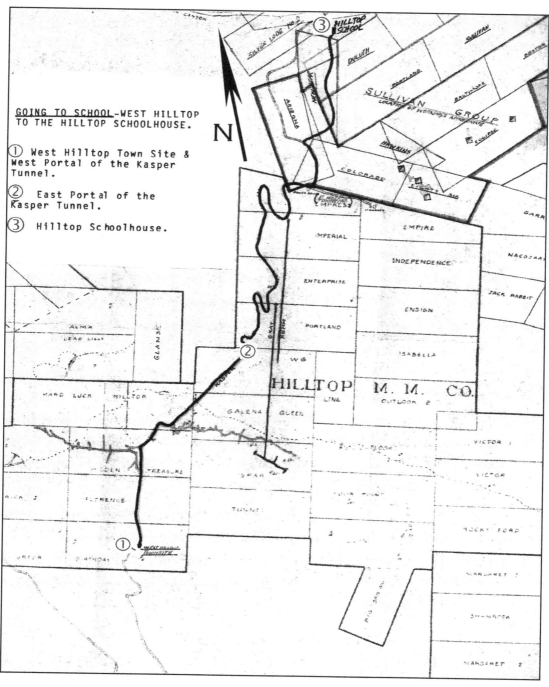

The Route through the Kasper Tunnel from West Hilltop to the Hilltop School

Portal School "Little Room" (now the Portal Post Office), Grades 1 through 5, 1938 or 1939
Teacher Lucille Corbett, back; the author, front row, left; "Pee Wee" Newman, front row, center

Having reached the fourth-grade level of education, I and other never-to-be-identified confederates decided the time had come to try cigarettes: The problem being where and how to obtain them. I shall confess to being the criminal mastermind in this diabolical undertaking. I suggested that one of the AVA Ranch lads go to the Cave Creek Grocery during lunch hour. (There were two stores then: the Cave Creek Grocery and Newman's.) There he was to tell the clerk that Mr. Foster, who was the brother of Doctor Adamson's wife and ran the AVA Ranch for them, had requested the pick up and delivery of two packs of Old Gold cigarettes, which were to be charged to Mr. Foster's grocery bill.

With a supply of cigarettes at least temporarily achieved, we set about organizing the Portal School Smoking and Discussion Society.

The Society was to be short-lived, however: somehow, someone spilled the beans. From the Big Room came Audrey Morrow with a summons to appear.

All Big-Roomers held the Little-Roomers in some degree of contempt. It was a recognized fact that even the Big Room teacher outranked the Little Room teacher. The Big Room teacher was absolute legal authority, disciplinarian, judge, jury, and prosecutor. The omnipotent Big Room teacher required that I be questioned extensively about these irregular goings-on. Since Audrey was an older sister and, more importantly, a member of the higher echelon of Big Roomers, her face was lit up with the pleasure ever derived from seeing a Little Roomer in difficulties—especially when he was her little brother. The other Big Roomers, who were as severe on detected crime as they were wont to "look the other way" when one is merely wanted, engaged in varying degrees of smirking and uttering snide remarks. I denied any knowledge of cigarettes, and when grilled as to the identity of my fellow partners in crime, stated I had no knowledge of any alleged confederates—or words to that effect.

Unfortunately, loyalty and the code of silence, the practice of sub-rosa, are unknown to some when it comes to turning school's evidence. I was tried, convicted, and sentenced for not only taking part in a heinous crime, but also for gross perjury.

§ § §

There was a girl named Willoughby James who lived with her widowed mother, Rose. To Willoughby, we students of the Portal School owed our immunities to several common diseases. Each Christmas vacation, Willoughby and her mother traveled about visiting other places—and no doubt many relatives. Each return from Christmas vacation brought Willoughby once again to Portal School, and with her came: one year measles, another whooping cough, and the list went on. Thus, we were all in the debt of Willoughby for providing us with our lifelong immunities.

Speaking of slight and serious health considerations, there came a time when the Little Room gained stature over the Big Room, and that happened when most all of the Big Roomers were infested with head lice. We in the Little Room escaped that problem.

§ § §

Academics and sports: There is no education quite like that garnered in the halls of rural learning. When Audrey enrolled in Douglas High School, I attended A Avenue School in Douglas for the sixth grade and was at the top of the honor-roll list throughout the year, not through study or inherent wit and intelligence, but for the reason that Portal School had already covered the material presented by the backward urban Douglas school.

As for sports: There were various pieces of equipment on the Portal School grounds, equipment of a kind used by gymnasts, and these were in continuous use. It was mandatory that all students played baseball, and good players could look forward to a career playing for Bob Gresham's team or the CCC team when they oft engaged in baseball games, usually at Sunny Flats. Uncle Bob (he was married to Mary Morrow) was an accomplished athlete and pitcher. Miles Graves, who owned the Apache Store, was his catcher—decked out in full chest protector and catcher's mask. We definitely had something to shoot for in that direction. Of course there was volleyball, and other sports such as dodge ball, which was played for the sole purpose of inflicting as much pain and injury as possible to those in the ring.

One game we played often resulted in something similar to English rugby. Groups of players took up positions on the north and south side of the Little Room. One team then threw a volleyball over the roof to the opposing team, who ran the ball around to the other side of the building. If they guessed correctly, and the throwing team had run the wrong way, they kept control of the ball for another throw. If their judgment was wrong, the teams met head on, and each team tried to gain or keep possession of the ball. My first exposure to this sport was rather peculiar. Uncertain of the exact rules of engagement, I took up a position on the edge of my group. Over came the ball, and—what are the chances of this?—it came down squarely on the top of my head. Maybe I should have considered a career in soccer. I was instructed by my team mates that the object of the game was to at first *catch* the ball.

Baseball at Portal School was initially played with regulation hard balls, but fielding grounders over the uneven schoolyard and the resulting occasional injury led to a change to softball. Some local ladies challenged us to a game. We thought it would be an easy win as most of the ladies were sturdy, and some a bit more than that. Running would not be their game. What we failed to reckon was their hitting strength: after a few hits well over into Cave Creek, the game was lost. We always weaseled out of a rematch.

School at Portal is gone now, and it won't be coming back. It was a different world here in the Chiricahua Mountains of southeastern Arizona, and that world has faded away also.

Portal, Arizona Post Office, 2008
Former "Little Room" of Portal School

Ralph Morrow, Jhus Canyon, 1940s: A juniper tree Nacho left behind

THE SILVER CREEK WRECK

Ignacio Flores—Nacho—was approaching one hundred years of age when the twentieth century passed its mid-mark. He had been in the United States for over sixty years, and was uncertain how many years he had lived. He crossed the line from Mexico perhaps in the year of 1900—of that he was also uncertain. His first job was a contract cutting wood in Tex Canyon and packing it to Chiricahua Station on the railroad approximately 30 miles north of Douglas, Arizona. When the contract was finished, Nacho packed up his axes, saws, wedges, and camp equipment, loaded everything on his string of six burros, and headed east toward Hachita, New Mexico.

Along the way, he cut wood and posts for anyone needing such, and there was always work at hand. Nacho's wanderings took him from Hachita to as far west as Ruby—west of Nogales. He heard that the Yaqui Indians had destroyed his home village and killed all of the people. Nacho and his people were Opata Indians. Some of Pancho Villa's men came to Apache, Arizona, where Nacho was working, and offered him a Captaincy in the rebel army. He told them he did not wish to be one of Villa's crossed-bandolier soldiers, that he was doing good working for his frijoles. Nacho would never return to Mexico.

It was said that Nacho went to an army recruiting station to enlist when the United States entered World War I. He was deemed to be too old for service. The recruiting officer told him to go home to his mountains, that his hair was too white. Dejected, Nacho returned to work and live as before.

In Jhus Canyon there was a group of patented mining claims which encompassed around six hundred acres. The claims were owned by Ralph Morrow.

Though separate from other holdings, a small herd of cattle were grazed there. The claims were surrounded by National Forest, and were not fenced. All of the surface water in Jhus Canyon was on the claims. In the 1940s Morrow contacted Nacho, who was cutting wood in the Peloncillo Mountains of southwestern New Mexico. Would Nacho be interested in cutting posts in Jhus Canyon on contract? He would. Nacho packed his burros, moved to the Chiricahua Mountains and set up camp near an orchard where some people were living and growing apples in Jhus Canyon.

Morrow gave Nacho a new waterproofed tent and some supplies—Nacho's burros were turned out to graze. Large junipers—some nearly five feet in diameter—grew along the creek near the water. Cutting with axe and cross cut saw, Nacho felled the junipers, and with axe, wedges, and sledge hammer, split the logs into fence posts. Nacho's posts were sold and delivered to ranches in a wide area. The work went on for several years. At the time, Nacho thought he was about eighty in those days. He may have been older.

The Chiricahuas were to Nacho's liking, and he stayed on cutting wood and helping out on some of the ranches. At last he set up camp in Whitetail Canyon a hundred yards east of the Z–T Ranch Headquarters—owned at the time by Herman Kollmar. Herman and his wife arranged for Nacho to receive a social security pension. The Kollmars purchased and delivered food and supplies that Nacho requested. Often they brought along a few cans of beer and sat around his camp fire in the evenings while Nacho relived the old days. That was the life he was living when A.R. (Alden Ray) Mooney (brother of Patricia M. Morrow) once again returned to the Chiricahuas and began running the Z–T Ranch for Kollmar.

A.R. began "punching cows" when he was fifteen, working on the Mud Springs Ranch north of Douglas. From there he went a few miles east to the Cull Ranch, picking up more cowboying skills from the old hands, and some of their philosophy and sayings. On any cold, raw day, one of his favorites was: "How would you like to be up on (whatever high point was at hand) with nothing but a wet sheet to wrap up in?" This gem is guaranteed to totally irritate—for some unknown reason—any female to whom it is directed. Use with caution.

From the Cull outfit, A.R. gravitated farther east to the Stevens spread, being at the time run by Melvin McClintock. After a time, Melvin left and Alvin Taylor was the foreman. Alvin said that Alden Ray was one of the best all-around hands he ever had work for him. It was the last days of World War II and A.R. joined the army, serving in the Special Forces in the European Theatre.

When he mustered out, he went to work for the Diamond As, where Buster Samuels was the Wagon Boss. Cowboy life suited A.R. to a "T"—working and riding the range and rodeoing some.

A.R. Mooney and Driscol Martin
Grey Ranch, south of Animas, New Mexico, 1950

It was exactly two weeks from the time that Uncle Sam decided he could not do without A.R.'s services until he was on the front lines in Korea, joining his brother William P. Mooney, who also served a full year in the Army up and down the Korean peninsula. Winter swept across the land in 1950, and the yellow horde came to the aid of their North Korean neighbors. A.R. said it was so cold that machine guns froze and they used any warm fluids available to thaw them. One day he was gunner on a .50-caliber machine gun mounted on a jeep. "I was really on that day," A.R. said. "We were going along at a good clip when I saw a bunker with just a gun slit facing the road. I swung the fifty around and fired a burst.

When we went up to the bunker there were three gooks in it. All of them were stitched right through the head."

Before judging A.R.'s words with "politically correct" hindsight, remember this: There were over 34,000 killed in Korea on the side of the good guys; 157,000 were wounded and maimed; 8,100 fighting men were never accounted for at all. The premise for the war was to halt the spread of socialism/communism. Korea was relegated to never-never land, which stirred no feelings of pride in the American people, unless they or their families were involved. Few now under the age of 65 years of age little know nor care about this so-called "police action."

A.R. and seven others were the only survivors of his company. He said the allied forces were retreating so fast that he did not have time to set up a machine gun. He fashioned a sling from a blanket that he may fire while standing and retreating. He was wounded by shrapnel and rifle fire, but crawled and limped onto a road where a tank fleeing southward picked him up. Thus ended A.R.'s combat in Korea, but he carried the physical reminders with him for the rest of his life.

Prior to leaving the Army for a final time, A.R. was stationed in 1955 at Fort Bliss near El Paso, Texas. At that time your scribe, R.W. Morrow, was in the Air Force flying F-86D jet fighters in the 54th Fighter Interceptor Squadron, Ellsworth Air Force Base, South Dakota. The 54th had two T-33 jet trainers used for instrument flight checks and cross-country flights. These were the standard tandem-seated trainers of that era. They were rigged for installation of two .50-caliber machine guns in the nose section. These had been removed and the section was used for cargo—such as hauling booze for squadron parties.

On a cross-country training and beverage flight to El Paso, I suggested to A.R. that perhaps he would like a ride in the T-33. He enthusiastically accepted. A.R. was in the back seat, chute and helmet in place. Clearance and take-off instructions received from the tower, we took the runway. The intercom is on at all times so all that is transpiring is available to A.R., as well as comments from his brother-in-law. A.R, who was probably a bit tense, does not reply. Down the runway, airborne, wheels and flaps up, and A.R. realizes his pilot—me—is not going to after all kill him. At least not on takeoff. At altitude, A.R. gets to fly the aircraft for a while, and did reasonably well, for an inexperienced flier. We had filed a Round Robin flight to Tucson—one in which the aircraft is not landed. Over Willcox, we turned back, and began buzzing everyone we could think of in the northeast section of the Chiricahuas and southwest New Mexico.

We flew down East Whitetail Canyon, buzzed the Noland Ranch, up East Turkey Creek to Paradise, circled down through Cave Creek at tree top level, buzzed Rodeo, and P.E. Mooney's crew working on the railroad. On to Hachita, where we buzzed the school house, and made a second pass for the benefit of the school kids who came out on the play ground. Back on the ground, A.R. said he wished he had known about the Air Force. He would have made that his career. In later years he qualified for a private pilot license. On final approach, one flight, his old war wounds caught up with him. Caught by some jet wash, his aircraft flipped upside down. He laughed when he told about the tower's transmission telling him he was clear for landing as soon as his plane was right side up.

A.R. was back at the cowboy life, working for Herman Kollmar, running the Z–T Ranch. That was 1960, and Nacho was in semi-retirement and living near ranch headquarters. A.R. often visited with Nacho, and took him along when he was going to Rodeo, New Mexico, for supplies. Usually, they stopped off at the Rodeo Tavern for a few drinks, and one late afternoon, a few became more than a few. The afternoon became nightfall, and at last the two revelers decided perhaps they should return to the ranch. They boarded their pickup truck, and departed Rodeo. Without any problems, they negotiated the highway, and took the Portal Road. And, again, there was no erratic driving. On past Newman's Store in Portal they motored, and came to the Silver Creek Road leading to the town of Paradise.

The old road went along the creek banks, and at times was the bed of the creek. In the 1930s, the CCCs constructed a new road, which skirted the side of what was designated—in surveys of the 1880s—the "Grand Royal Ridge." Three wooden bridges were constructed on the road. The bridges were replaced by concrete bridges and metal guard rails in the 1950s.[1]

The ranch hands approached the first bridge on the eastern end of Silver Creek Road, rounding a slight curve to line up with the bridge. Their pickup was traveling at a reasonable rate of speed, and A.R. seemed to be in complete control of the machine. As they neared the bridge, Nacho declared in a loud voice that he was in dire need of answering a call of nature. Before the pickup slowed, much less came to a halt, he clawed at the door handle and began attempting to exit the fast-moving truck. A.R. saw that immediate and definitive action was called for, and grabbed Nacho's left arm. As A.R. grappled with Nacho, while attempting to slow

---

[1] For more about the construction of the old Silver Creek Road, see "A Road to Paradise" in the chapter "Digging Up Skeletons: Carson Morrow's Chiricahua Bull Sheet."

Old Silver Creek Road between Paradise and Portal, 1931
Before CCCs constructed new road. (Note Model T car approaching at top.)

and control the truck, he lost control. The heavy truck bumper hit the north guard rail, and the truck plunged off the bridge into Silver Creek—a dry wash, except when flooding, which it was not.

The drop was about fifteen feet to the creek bottom, where the truck now rested, with both revelers yet inside. They climbed out, checked themselves for injuries, and found none. They walked back to Newman's Store, and placed a call on the public telephone outside. Kollmar was pulled from a sound sleep, and the story of the Silver Creek Wreck told. Perhaps Nacho's call of nature had been satisfactorily answered.[2]

---

[2] For more about Ignacio "Nacho" Flores, see "La Leyenda de Ignacio Flores" in the chapter "Digging Up Skeletons: Carson Morrow's Chiricahua Bull Sheet."

UNCOOPERATIVE COOPERATIVE

In the year of 1998 a member of our telephone cooperative, for some reason or another, got a burr under his saddle and began stirring up all sorts of irregularities about the cooperative. Your scribe sent a "Letter to the Editor" of a local newspaper. A bright newspaper gal thought it was humorous, added "A satirical account of phone co-op conflict," and put the harangue in the paper as a "Guest Column," as follows:

To the Editor:

Somewhere in the Southwest (Willcox), there is a telephone cooperative (Valley Telephone), where in the year of 1998, there occurred a rebellion. What happened is as follows, and any resemblance to actual events is totally accidental, because most, if not all, of the information was supplied by one devious and dastardly group known as the directors of the board of Valley Telephone Cooperative, whom henceforth shall be known as "The Directors."

Many years ago there were many areas of the county of Cochise that had no telephone service, so, they formed a cooperative and pretty soon they had private touchtone telephone service, and they communicated with each other, and hooked up their computers to the NET, and everyone was happy. Well, not quite.

The Directors began paying themselves a fee for every day or part of the day that they spent on cooperative business. This fee was $150. Take heed all you young people, don't overlook the possibility of a career in directorship. This fee paying was more or less in accord with the cooperative by-laws. (Let us henceforth call the cooperative, for the sake of brevity, VTC, okay?) The Directors were also paid expenses incurred while on VTC business, and this was only fair.

One fine day, one of the Directors, thinking about how expensive medical insurance was, said something like, "Look, fellow Directors, why don't we let VTC pay for a complete medical and dental insurance plan for ourselves and our dependents while we are Directors and when we are no longer on the board, let VTC pay for the rest of our lives and for the lives of our dependents." So they did, and this was a violation of VTC by-laws, and cost, according to the Directors, in 1997 alone, $55,000 plus.

"When you are on a roll, why stop?" asked the Directors and they had good old members of VTC buy each a $100,000 paid up life insurance policy, with all sorts of cash benefits. In accord with VTC by-laws? Not on your life. When asked the magical question, "How much, Your Majesties, did this cost all us lowly peasants?" the Directors laughed and said, "Substantial monies." And, here the "facts" once again become somewhat unclear. The amount paid for the life insurance policies varied with the day of the week, and ranged from near $200,000 to approximately $300,000. In a rare flash of intelligence, the Directors decided to cash in the life insurance policies. Who got the money? All of the Directors raced out and bought new pickups. Well, maybe not all of them.

Along the way, the Directors borrowed a large amount of money from another agency. Then, they bought some "extremely profitable" companies. Since VTC is a non-profit cooperative, some audacious person inquired "Where are the profits going, and are you Directors receiving any funds from these companies?" No answer. Numerous other questions unanswered. "How much do you Directors cost each year?" Answer: $11,000 then $16,000 then $22,000 then as much as approximately $30,000, and the figure begins to, as you mathematicians often say, "increase exponentially." Where will it end?

A band of revolutionaries began to notice all these directorial goings on; these alleged irregularities and possible purloining of funds. These revolutionaries were led by a bandit by the name of El Blanco. The revolutionaries decided that enough was enough and they made certain negative declarations to the Directors, and said the revolutionaries were going to sue the Directors. The Directors upon hearing this went to lunch, and after a large meal and some libation, all at VTC expense naturally, went back to their office. "This could be serious," some of the Directors said. One director said, "Del dicho al hecho hay gran trecho." (Rough translation: "From saying to doing is a long distance.") The Directors became carried away by their somewhat intoxicated brains and began to say all sorts of things. One jumped up and cried: "Chile Relleno!" Another, remembering the one bit of Spanish he had learned in fifth grade said: "Donde está la biblioteca?"

Anyway, when El Blanco and the revolutionaries heard of this buffoonery, they were greatly angered. Some of the revolutionaries wanted to challenge the Directors to a duel, but they decided that wouldn't accomplish much, and they proceeded to sue the Directors in civil court for "failing to fulfill their fiduciary responsibilities to the members of VTC." Or, something such as that. The revolutionaries also decided to impeach all of the Directors, which they could legally do according to the by-laws that the Directors had apparently been violating. The revolutionaries circulated petitions and secured sufficient signatures from the membership of VTC to hold a "Special Election" to kick all the Directors out in the gutter. Only, when the Directors received the petitions, they called various members of VTC and threatened—cajoled—pleaded with them to remove their names from the petitions. Some did, but not enough, so, the Directors ruled that some of the other signatures affixed to the petitions were "not valid."

Now the revolutionaries really were angry. They made some more petitions and had them all signed up and sent in, and the Directors said, "looks good, but you are one signature short." The revolutionaries took care of that, and the Directors said, "well, they did not think they would hold any 'Special Meeting' for the purpose of impeaching said Directors, but they would hold a meeting to tell all of the peasantry how great their majesties were, and if they had been doing things not in accord with VTC by-laws, why they would just change the laws to legalize the alleged crimes."

Okay, El Blanco and the revolutionaries said, two can play that game. We will have a meeting, our lawyers say it is plumb legal like, right after the Directors and impeach these rogues, each and every one of them. Now, it happened that the Directors had contracted to hold a "Special-we-really-are-great-people-and-haven't-done-anything-wrong-at-all" meeting in a particular unnamed spot (the Elk's Club in Willcox), and made arrangements to secure the premises for said purpose until 4 PM on the designated day. The revolutionaries contracted for those environs beginning at 4 PM.

The Directors hearing this, said, quite appropriately, "Hold the phone. We have made a mistake. We need the Elk's Club building until midnight." Man, did this ever make the revolutionaries mad. They made arrangements to hold their impeachment meeting elsewhere. All looked good for the revolutionaries. Enter the lawyers, stage right. Stage wrong? A hurried telephone, now, follow this closely, a telephone conference call involving attorneys for the Directors, the attorneys for the revolutionaries, and a superior court judge. The judge—and this is, as the lawyers say, "hearsay"—says he doesn't want to get involved in a discussion of the petitions, but since the Directors have stated that they will not leave even if the members impeach them; they are not accountable to or representative of the membership and don't have to do what the large common majority want; and the revolutionaries are going to impeach the Directors and put in their own Directors; all of this is going to be very confusing to the members. Thus, supposedly, the judge says that the revolutionaries cannot even hold a meeting as it is illegal for them to do so.

The revolutionaries are really up in arms at this point, and they vow the Directors have not heard the last of them. Some of the revolutionaries suggest storming VTC headquarters and dragging the Directors shrieking, praying, protesting from the building.

(Annual elections were held, and many of the Directors were defeated, and all seemed to be on a steadier course. However, before radical changes are made, one had better first make certain that there is something of value to replace them.)

THE SHOOTING OF WILBUR WARD

Most of the old ranch houses and other homes are gone now, with hardly a trace of their existence remaining. As the mail system modernized, many of the post offices also disappeared from the northeastern Chiricahua Mountain/southwestern New Mexico area. Contract mail carriers have routes of nearly one hundred miles in the modern day, and few post offices to serve. In the old days, that was not the case.

There was a post office at Hilltop—at times in the store run by W.K. and Eva Rosetta Morrow, which was a few hundred yards east of the Morrow Orchard in East Whitetail Canyon. In a grove of sycamores just north of the public road, there is a rock and concrete foundation marking the spot. At Paradise there was another post office, and one at Portal in the Cave Creek Grocery building. A post office at Rodeo, New Mexico, received mail from the Southern Pacific trains, and sent it on to its destination. A mail carrier lived in Whitetail Canyon/Hilltop.

Bob Gresham and Mary Morrow Gresham—my uncle and aunt—had a home on a few acres of level ground next to Whitetail Creek. Now there is nothing to indicate that anyone ever lived there. The Greshams carried the mail for a few years—to Hilltop, Paradise, Portal, and Rodeo. Down along the route mornings, picking up outgoing mail and parcels; back up in the afternoons, delivering letters and packages.

If groceries or supplies were needed by anyone along the mail route, a list was left in a mail box, along with some cash. The mail carrier purchased the requested goods either in Portal or Rodeo, and in the afternoon left the items and any change in or by the mail box. If a lift to any place along the route, or to possibly catch a train in Rodeo, was required, free transportation was provided by the mail carrier.

After a few years in the 1930s, the Greshams left the mountains for a career as Border Patrol. Then Bill Stevens—Sugar Bill—started delivering mail and groceries, and providing transport for passengers. Bill was an expert rifle shot. His services were soon needed by the army in World War II. He was in the invasion forces in Italy, and his skills put to good use. But, before he left for the army, he and his wife lived in the house where Greshams had resided, and he drove the mail.

From time to time the Hilltop Mine property would open, and mining would go on for awhile, until the property once again closed down. There was always a watchman living at Hilltop East when the property was operated. One of the watchmen was named Ward, and he had a son that lived with him for a year or two. The son was seventeen or eighteen years of age, and was named Wilbur Ward. Wilbur had never finished school through the eighth grade, and one of the Portal school teachers encouraged him to attend school at Portal through the grade eight—the highest grade offered at the school.

Wilbur did complete his grade school education, and after a time was seen no more in those parts. One afternoon Wilbur rode in with Sugar Bill as he completed the mail run. Just to the east of the Gresham-Stevens house, well, and outhouse, was the boundary fence enclosing a few acres of the property. Sugar Bill stopped to open the gate, and Wilbur thanked him for the ride and got out of Bill's vehicle.

There are things in everyone's life, maybe changes that would have, should have, been different. Unfortunately, the shooting of Wilbur Ward does not stand out as one of those things. It happened that Robert (Sonny Boy) Pague and your scribe were standing around, presumably awaiting the arrival of the mail car. I had been given a brand-new Daisy air rifle, or, as we referred to them in those days, a "BB Gun." Whether the crime was premeditated and with willful intent, none could ever say.

Without so much as a "Good afternoon, Lads, fine weather we are having," from Wilbur, he said, "Don't you dare shoot me with that BB Gun." And, then added: "You little S.O.B." Downright rude.

The Hilltop Mine Road was across the creek from Sugar Bill's domain, and Wilbur had to climb the grade for a mile or more to the townsite. Wilbur sauntered along, walking along the fence line toward Whitetail Creek. Considering distance and trajectory, it was a long shot for the Daisy.

A deep breath in, exhaled about one-half, sights aligned exactly between Wilbur's shoulder blades, squeeze the trigger and ... the pellet hit Wilbur in the seat of his pants. The rides along country roads are dusty, and a small puff of dust flew out of his pants' seat. He shouted, threw his arms up, and pivoted. Your scribe was already vacating those environs. Whether Sonny Boy, accomplice by association, was captured, was never known. Wilbur never sought revenge, and went on with his life of ignoring us lesser beings.

Perhaps Wilbur learned a valuable lesson that day, and never again made insulting reference to the alleged background of any other person the rest of his life.

SILVERBELL

In the desert northwest of Tucson, Arizona, there is a mine, and in bygone days there were two towns each with the name of Silverbell. The first, and older town had its beginnings as early as the 1860s, when high-grade copper was found in the desert hills. Originally, the copper mining was underground until the 1940s. The mine operated and shut down—dependent on copper prices—from 1860 to 1883; then began to boom again in the early 1900s. The Arizona Southern Railroad from Redrock to Silverbell was completed in 1904. Silverbell soon boasted a population of three thousand, and had achieved the somewhat dubious distinction of being described as the "hell-hole of Arizona."

A smelter at Sasco—ten miles northeast of Silverbell—was erected to process the Silverbell ore. But a shaft fire in 1911, and problems at their Tombstone properties, forced the owners, the Development Company of America, into bankruptcy—thus ending, for a time, all activity at Silverbell. The property was taken over by the American Smelting and Refining Company, or "ASARCO." The property continued to be operated as an underground mining venture by ASARCO until 1921, when lower copper prices halted production.

ASARCO acquired properties in the Avra Valley, where wells were drilled and pipelines installed for the operations they had planned. In 1934, the railroad tracks of the Arizona Southern Railroad to Redrock were torn up and the Sasco smelter was dismantled. It seemed Silverbell had at last faded away and died. The town was torn down until only one large frame building yet stood. It may have been a boarding house, perhaps a saloon—a building of varied uses.

In 1948 a new town came to life approximately four miles east and a small bit south of the old Silverbell. The new town was also named Silverbell. There were homes for married miners, bunkhouses for singles, a boarding house, store, filling station, a complex housing engineering and administration, a large crushing and milling facility, and a mile to the west, a copper-leaching plant. Two open-pit mines were developed: Oxide, near the mill and town, and the El Tiro pit four miles away, where the original underground mine and old Silverbell once boomed. Large pumps on the valley wells forced water through pipelines to the town and mill.

Some of the townspeople tore down the last building of old Silverbell, and used the lumber to build corrals for their horses. Old Silverbell was almost gone. Large electric shovels, bulldozers, and trucks hauling tons of waste rock or ore, changed the desert landscape almost over night, it seemed.

New Silverbell and the two open-pit mines had been in operation nearly two decades when your scribe appeared on the scene. After acquiring a B.S. degree in Mining Engineering, I worked as a field engineer for Pacific Gas and Electric Company, based in San Francisco, but mostly in the field as an engineer on extra-high-voltage electrical-transmission lines. City life, and a different existence had disagreed with a family of desert rats, and we moved back to Tucson. I began working for ASARCO at Silverbell in the engineering department. After four months, the Mine Superintendent said he needed another pit supervisor—or shift boss—and said the job was mine if I wanted it. A step up the ladder and considerable more money overrode any hesitancy in accepting.

Two, and sometimes three, large electric shovels operated in El Tiro Pit. One shovel was placed in Oxide Pit. On day shift and swing shift, one shovel loaded ore in trucks which transported eighty tons per load to the crusher, as the other two shovels loaded haul trucks with waste or low-grade copper ore, which was sent to dumps to be leached. Usually five trucks were assigned to the four-mile ore haul to the crusher. All trucks arrived at the shovel shortly after the shift boss had delivered the shovel crew. By the time the last truck was loaded and underway, the first truck loaded would have made the eight-mile round trip, and be in place for loading. One shift boss took care of the ore haul, while a second was in charge of stripping waste and low grade material. Two rotary drills were in operation every shift in El Tiro Pit, and one drill worked Oxide. These drilled 9-inch holes to a depth of fifty feet—the benches in each pit were forty feet in height. There was considerable organizing, and details of operation, and unless you are planning on being a pit supervisor, probably would not be all that interesting. Graveyard shift ore was hauled from Oxide Pit—a short haul requiring only three trucks. One shift boss stayed with the Oxide operation, while a second ran El Tiro, where waste and low-grade ore were being mined. There existed a somewhat democratic situation with pit supervisors and engineering doing most of the planning. Most of the time the Mine Superintendent sat around in his air-conditioned car up on the rim of the pit. He was a pretty heavy drinker off the job, and needed sleep and rest while on duty—which suited everyone.

The shovel operator on one of my crews seemed to always have a bit of a glow on when he came on shift. One night on swing shift he was running one of the shovels in the El Tiro Pit. Basically, there are few things involved in operating a mine shovel, but they do require some skill, and good coordination: crowd (takes the bucket toward or away), hoist (elevates or lowers the bucket), and swing (pivoting the bucket left or right). There were two heavy sleds upon which there was a tower at each shovel. A heavy cable carrying electricity to the shovel was looped over the towers, that trucks could back into position for loading. Truck drivers usually left their trucks while loading took place.

As a driver climbed down the ladder from the cab of his truck, the shovel operator swung the bucket loaded with tons of rock. The bucket had not been hoisted high enough to clear the side of the truck, as the operator crowded to position the bucket over the truck, it hit the side of the truck, which knocked the driver off the ladder. He fell some distance and hit on his back. Fortunately, he did recover from his injuries, and came back to work. I sent the shovel operator in for a conference with the Mine Superintendent. The conference was probably about which brand of bourbon they preferred. That was the most serious accident I ever had on any of my shifts. One night, though, I sent a dozer and operator to a high point above the pit to shape up a diamond drill site for the geologists. Panic set in when I looked up and saw the lights on the dozer and considerable amount of track hanging over the edge of the pit. Back went the dozer as I raced up pit benches some eight hundred or more feet in my pickup. The drill site would have to wait until daylight. Unfortunately, there were fatal accidents from time to time.

There was always some jockeying for position by the truck drivers as shut down time neared. If at all possible, particularly on the long ore haul to the crusher, most drivers tried to avoid the last load—they referred to as the "S*** Load." The primary crusher was a huge gyratory crusher. It was a cone-shaped structure with a large pestle of sorts that crushed rock against the sides of the cone. At times, not all of the rock generated from a blast was of a size that the crusher could accommodate. One shovel operator would purposely load a large boulder which would plug the crusher. The crew on that shovel would then sit around until the crusher was back in operation.

A large rubber-tired tractor was assigned to each shovel. It cleaned up around the shovel area, and pushed material that had trailed out onto the bench floor when a blast was set off. If material needed to be moved on a waste or low grade dump, it was used for that. When a shovel was moved—either on a particular bench, or to another level in the pit—the sleds and cable towers were pulled by the tractor.

Even moving to a different location on a bench required some work, and truck drivers assigned to the shovel assisted the shovel oiler, coiling the heavy electrical cable on one of the sleds as they followed along behind the shovel. Truck drivers did not like the job, particularly on a hot summer day. The shovel operator, who had deliberately sent material that plugged the primary crusher, was soon broken of his ploy: the shovel was ordered moved to some waste area, and the ore trucks began hauling to a waste dump. As soon as the crusher was operational again, the process of moving back to the ore area was undertaken.

None of the pit-supervisor pickup trucks or the haul trucks were air conditioned. Everyone became conditioned to the heat, which was at times intense down on a pit floor in mid-summer. Temperatures in haul trucks—on the long haul—neared 140 degrees Fahrenheit. But the job disliked most by all crews was moving a shovel up or down one or more benches. This led to a great amount of grumbling as the giant shovel rumbled along—followed by its clean-up rig towing the two sleds and cable towers, with truck drivers and shovel oiler coiling the heavy cable on one sled. Gloves, of course, were supplied to all, but the job was tiring and disagreeable.

There are two men who always come to mind when thinking of the mining days. Louis Richardson—Louie—was hands down the most skilled dozer and motor-grader operator I have ever seen. He was closely followed by Ed Young, who may have been on an equal basis as a motor-grader operator. Ed would open a fresh tin of Copenhagen Snuff, put it in the sun until totally dry, and then saturate the snuff with Jack Daniels Bourbon. This concoction was always in his mouth when he was on the job. Ed was operating at a high level at all times.

Louie was a good artist of western paintings, and penned several books. Louie and Ed were not prima donnas, but they were not given orders. If something needed to be done, they were told what the job was, no more. Most of the time

Louie was operating a D9 Caterpillar crawler tractor. Among a multitude of jobs, Louie would prepare diamond-drill sites wherever the company geologists indicated. The sites were surveyed in by the engineering department, with great care and accuracy. Louie would sight from several different angles, and remove the pin and stakes set by engineering. After smoothing the site he would replace the pin and stakes. This caused some anxiety on the part of the geologists, but the location would be within inches of the surveyed spot. Louie was an observer of human behavior, and with his talent for writing would produce some rhymes of some of the people working in the mine. One truck driver that Louie set into verse was named Alejo, and was called Alley Joe—naturally. Whenever a gripe was heard by Alley Joe, his response was always the same: "It all pays the same." On a hot summer day a shovel was being moved far up on the rim of El Tiro Pit to begin stripping waste material that the pit could expand northward and some copper ore mined. It was a long move, and as Alley Joe became tired, and perhaps bored with the task of coiling heavy electrical cable, he began cursing and grumbling and complaining. Those subjected to Alley Joe's incessant, "It all pays the same," were quick to remind him, "It all pays the same." This verse went on for several pages—as set down by Louie.

Another lengthy verse by Louie was about the Pit Man or Dump Man. Sometimes at night or stormy weather, a man was stationed on the edge of a dump wherever material was being hauled. He had a small open door house of sorts which was on skids that it may be moved about. A bank of lights were set up in the area where waste or low grade was being dumped. Between trucks, the dump man could shelter in his house. When a truck arrived, and began to back toward the edge of the dump, the dump man guided the truck with hand signals and indicated where to stop, set brakes, and dump. Louie's verse described this poor soul, battered by the elements, chapped, red-rimmed eyed, freezing of winter and sweltering and eaten up by gnats in the summer.

Louie's poem of several pages then described how on one night a fierce wind was whipping up and over the edge of the dump. Shot rock was wet down to suppress dust before loading, but old dump material and fine particles were pelting the dump man with great force. At last he reached his limit, sought out the union steward, and filed a grievance against the wind—or as Louie described: the Dump Man, Guardian of the Rim, filed a grievance against the blow. This case was reviewed and discussed and kicked up the ladder until it came to rest on the United States President's desk, LBJ. President Johnson considered the case and responded that he and his aides had determined that the wind had seniority, further, the dump man would have to appeal to the one who governed the elements, and outranked even LBJ.

As time went by, a large dump of waste rock marched relentlessly toward the site of old Silverbell, and buried the town beneath hundreds of feet of rock and dirt. Old Silverbell—the "hell-hole of Arizona"—was gone forever.

Years went by—five—and a small company made plans to operate a copper mining and leaching operation. It was the San Juan Mine located in the Peloncillo Mountains north of the town of Safford, Arizona. The chief metallurgist at Silverbell had gone over to the San Juan and asked your scribe to head up mining, which happened.

THE PIRTLEVILLE ALLEY SPRINT

My first job with the Sheriff's department of Cochise County was a combination affair as a deputy sheriff and cattle inspector. This went on for about eight months and I was transferred to Douglas to work as a deputy. That job also ended when we moved to Tucson, and I returned to the University of Arizona.

Some good things happen in law enforcement, but, unfortunately, not all is in that category. Domestic violence usually was rather sad. Generally the husband was the culprit, although it did occasionally happen that some Amazon was doing some serious kicking of the husband's backside—and maybe in some instances, deservedly so.

When Ralph Morrow was a Cochise County deputy sheriff in the early 1930s, there was a case that he told of and his solution to the problem. Seems there was a certain man about town that would become inebriated. He would return home and proceed to beat up his wife and daughters. They made a complaint to Deputy Morrow. He considered the matter and told the wife and daughters to do this: They were to arm themselves with broom handles or light-weight clubs. When the borracho [*drunkard*] returned home, and before he had time to prepare for his entertainment of beating the household females, they were to station themselves by the door. As soon as the borracho stepped inside they were to club him as hard as they could. This they did. One episode of "running the gauntlet" was all that was required. No further beatings took place in that household.

One afternoon a call came in from a woman who said her husband had abused her, and she wanted him arrested. I took the call and proceeded to the address given. We carried blank complaint forms, which we filled out and had the person filing the complaint sign. Probably not proper procedure as determined by lawyers and judges. Since we had not witnessed the crime, as in most cases, a complaint was needed. The husband was at home, and all seemed to be relatively peaceful when I arrived on the scene. The wife signed the complaint form. The husband was handcuffed and we had reached my vehicle when the wife burst from the house, screaming and crying. She was blubbering and saying: "Don't leave me, please don't leave me."

To this the husband replied: "Are you totally out of your mind? I'm hand-cuffed and on my way to jail because of the complaint you made, and you are saying, 'Don't leave me'?!"

At that point, a conference seemed to be in order. After asking the woman if she wished to drop the complaint—she did—the matter was discussed, and both wife and husband agreed they would get along. No further complaints were made by the wife, so perhaps they did.

One night another domestic-disturbance call came in to the police station. The husband had been beating his wife. The husband was a very large person, and I figured I was going to possibly need some assistance if he gave me any trouble. The three of us sat down at their kitchen table for a talk.

Neighbors had called in the matter of a domestic altercation. The couple started off with all the things they did not like about one another. After steering them away from the dislike segment, they detailed what they liked about one another. They agreed there would be no more disturbances in the house or in the neighborhood. When asked if they thought they wanted to continue on without separating, they thought they would. After pointing out that the husband's conduct was unacceptable, not only to their home, but was also disrupting the peace of the neighborhood, he agreed to change his ways. The next morning both came to the police station and conferred with the judge—Justice of the Peace—and told him they appreciated all the deputy had done for them. Maybe they had not been communicating. Who knows? There were no more complaints from them or their neighbors.

After a routine cruise around town one night, I came back to the police station. Harry Selchow was the highway Patrolman stationed in Douglas then. He had come in to the police station, when a call came in from Pirtleville—just northwest of Douglas. A man was arguing with two women on a street corner beneath a street light, and worse, hitting one of them. Selchow took the wheel, and I the passenger seat in his patrol car, and we sped to the scene.

Two women and one man were indeed on the corner as described by the caller, and as we zoomed in to the spot, the man hit one of the women. Just then he noticed Selchow's patrol car bearing down on him, and he ran, going across about a quarter block of vacant land. Selchow was in hot pursuit. The culprit was inches in front of the car, and I was urging Selchow to run into him, but Selchow wouldn't do it. Just as we were coming to a street, the runner doubled back and began running toward an alley. Selchow was slow on braking and the car was still moving when I bailed out, carrying a five-cell flashlight in my left hand. Half falling, half running, I got a good start off the blocks—so to speak. I took off after the runner, who turned down the alley, with your scribe now in hot pursuit. We had run maybe half a block when I ran up alongside of the culprit. For awhile he just kept running. There we went, side by side, down the alley. I grabbed him by the arm, and after a brief struggle, got him under control

About then the absurdity of the entire situation caught up with me, and I began laughing. The culprit probably thought a maniac had him by the arm and was soon going to bean him with the flashlight. About then Selchow arrived, and he was laughing. "Man," he said, "I could see that flashlight beam just flying. I doubt Jessie Owens could have outrun you down that alley." For awhile after that, whenever I saw Selchow he would refer to me as "old Jessie Owens."

THE VISITOR

In the Chiricahua Mountains of southeastern Arizona, near and along a stream called East Turkey Creek, a town came to life. It was 1901, and the town was named Paradise. There are two differing stories of how and why the town was named. The realistic version was as follows: George Walker and other prospectors located some mining claims in the basin west of what would become Paradise. They named the group of claims "The Leadville." Old-timers said that Walker and his partners began mining some high-grade lead/silver ore. They had shipped three railroad carloads—apparently from San Simon—when Walker declared: "Boys, this is Paradise." Another version, the romantic one, had George and his young bride—one of the Reed girls from Cave Creek above Portal—strolling beneath the towering sycamores that grew along East Turkey Creek, when she murmured "George, this is Paradise."

Paradise began to boom with the formation of the Chiricahua Development Company, and by 1904 there were thirteen saloons, three general stores, a meat market (W.K. Morrow's), a hotel, a barbershop, and a jail. Across the creek there were seven houses where cowboys and miners might while away an evening. A "money panic" in 1907 spelled the doom of the Chiricahua Development Company, and the huge boilers that were in place west of Paradise were never fired.[1]

---

[1] The Panic of 1907—the fourth such panic in 34 years—was triggered by a failed attempt in October of that year to corner all the stock of the United Copper Company. Banks that had leant money to the scheme began to fall, leading to a credit crunch that spread across the nation—and more closings of banks and businesses. The severity of the downturn was such that it prompted the United States Congress to form the Federal Reserve System.

Paradise: Morrow Butcher Shop at right, early 1900s

There followed a frenzy of activity. The big companies were just playing a trick on everyone. When the dust settled, they would sneak back in and locate mining claims all over the California Mining District—in which area Paradise was located. Prospectors rushed to locate and patent claims, and small mining ventures sprung up everywhere. After a time most ceased operations.

The mineral in greatest abundance was, as an uncle, Marshall Kuykendall said: "Leverrite. Leave 'er right there." He became quite well off from mining ventures, and if you don't think money matters consider this: Both he and my aunt, as of this writing, will soon celebrate their eighty-first wedding anniversary. Both are active—physically and mentally—and will also be celebrating their one-hundred-two-year birthdays.

So, Paradise rocked along and reached a low point about 1960, when there were only two full-time households, and each had but one and sometimes two people living there. Some Hippies, as they were then called, bought some property and took up residence in and around old Paradise. They hung around, some in a seemingly dazed condition, for several years, and then it snowed. The Chiricahuas are unpredictable. One year it may freeze ice a few nights. The next it may see

Paradise: Boozers Place Saloon and Hooligans Tonsorial Parlor, 1904

four feet of snow, or, as happened in the winter of 1978–79, the temperatures for two weeks did not pass the freezing mark. Most nights the temperatures dropped to as much as 18 degrees below zero F. It was not short-sleeve weather.

The Hippy Snow came in the 1960s and it was deep. Nothing moved, days went by, and the Hippies ran out of food. One of them struggled through the drifts and reported the situation. Food was air-lifted to the camp, and the Hippies saved. When the roads thawed, most left and were never seen in those parts again.

A cowboy and dude wrangler acquired some property in and around Paradise, and set up a facility for horseback riding and entertaining guests. One summer he decided to stage a trail ride into the Chiricahua Mountains, going along forest trails to the high country, where there would be a genuine old west cookout. He hired a good Dutch oven cowboy cook out of Tucson, and he set up in Barfoot Park, high in the Chiricahuas. Now, the organizer, dude wrangler, did not know much about the Chiricahuas so he asked my dad, Ralph Morrow, and a cowboy named Claude Fortenberry if they would go along on the trail ride. A pretty large bunch of trail riders trailered their horses to Paradise, and the ride began.

Paradise: Stage office (low building behind riders) and stage-line hotel, Market Street, circa 1904
Passengers waiting in front of the hotel for the stage to arrive

Claude Fortenberry was a good cowboy; had been a deputy sheriff for a number of years; managed cow ranches, and hunted lion with Dale and Clell, the last of the Lee Boys, legendary lion and jaguar hunters. One day I met up with him.

"Sit down here," Claude said, "I want to tell you about that trail ride of Scotty's that your Dad and I went on back a few years. Most all of the guests rode good horses, and since we were going along forest trails, none were going to have any trouble getting around the mountains. Your Dad was a hard man to follow horseback in those mountains.

"From Paradise and up to Soldier's Flat and then through the pass in to North Fork of Cave Creek. Then we took the trail going by Boogerman Springs.[2]

"The trail was not too good, and at one place a log had fallen across the trail. One girl was riding a good-looking palomino horse, and he wouldn't cross the log. Your Dad said he would get her horse over the log. He got on the palomino and the horse fell over backwards and down the hillside. We were sure enough lucky. Neither the horse or your Dad had a scratch on them. He got the horse over the log, and the ride went on across to the trail at Herb Martyr [*Dam*].

"Climbed out on the Snowshed Trail past Deer Spring and headed north going past Chiricahua Peak; past Cima Ranger Station, Round Park, Fly Peak, took a short jog to Tub Spring to water our horses, and near sundown made it to Barfoot Park. It was a long ride, but everyone came through in good shape. Along the high country trails, the palomino girl—probably about twenty—asked me about all the Forest Service signs that had pieces ripped out of them. You know how those bear will take a bite out of one, or give it a swipe with a claw. I told her the bear were doing it, and it was a contest with them to see which one could reach up the highest. Darn near every one of those signs have been bit or swiped. Forest Service is right proud of them, always putting redwood stain on them. We were mighty lucky that girl's horse didn't get hurt." And then Claude added: "Or your Dad for all that."

Typical cowboy: first the horse, then the rider.

Some years later I would remember Claude remarking about the Forest Service redwood-staining their signs.

Patricia and I, after years of town living, moved back to the Chiricahua Mountains and settled on part of the Morrow ranch holdings—the Coryell Place. We had forgotten country living and did all the things city folks usually do when they become country folk. We planted fruit trees and gardens and raised horses and cattle, and one day asked: Why are we doing these things? Sunset magazine had an issue mostly dedicated to deck building. Why don't we build a deck? A redwood deck. So we did. No use being sensible about it. The deck was planned and constructed—all 16 feet by 60 feet. It was oiled and coated and it looked like some of the *Sunset Magazine* decks—at first. (An aside: Advice to those who would build decks—don't.) A surround and foundation went around the deck to keep out any rattlers thinking of taking up residence, and time went by.

---

[2] In old Paradise days, a whiskered wild-looking character had camped and lived there for awhile. He had no known name, but was called the "Boogerman" or "Bogeyman."

Deck repairs became an annual event, with boards replaced and the entire affair coated with various highly-recommended substances. This was all accomplished in a carefree and nonchalant manner with a total absence of profanity involved. One year a redwood oil and stain was decided upon—the kind used by the Forest Service on their signs. The product was slathered onto the deck. Empty gallon cans were placed outside the yard beneath a tree.

"What are you going to do with those cans?" I was asked by the "consejera" [*adviser*].

"Why, you never know when you may need a good metal can."

Work finished, and perhaps a celebratory after-dinner sip of bourbon finished off the day. Patricia's mother was staying with us at the time, and retired to sleep soundly throughout the night. Around midnight Patricia said, "Wake up! There is something out on the deck!" Out of bed and into the living room and a quick peek out by the drapes. There was an exceptionally large black bear wandering around sniffing the deck. "That's about the biggest black bear I have ever seen," I said. "What are we going to do?" Patricia asked. The scene was lighted by a bright full moon, with no lights required.

"Well, I don't think we had better do anything. The breeze is blowing from the dog houses toward the bear, and they obviously don't know about our visitor." At the time we had three dogs. Two were Lab-Ridgebacks and real hunters, the other a Lab-Cattle dog. "If we stir up the dogs, they will jump that bear, and they might get hurt. Let's just sit tight."

About then the bear wandered over and took a bite out of the deck railing. A few more exploratory nibbles, and our guest wandered off the deck—fortunately, not in the direction of the dog houses, where all were sleeping as soundly as Patricia's Mom. I went into our office and looked out.

There was the bear, looking up at me.

In a loud voice, I said: "What do you think you are doing?!"

At that, the bear ran off into the night.

The next morning Patricia told her Mother that a bear had been on the deck. Her Mom said we were teasing her. Outside, we showed her the bear tracks running away from the house, and a large pile of bear scat. We pointed out the porch rail, where it had been sampled. The empty cans were torn apart and scattered. The mystery of the bear-damaged Forest Service signs, so carefully coated with redwood stain, seemed to be solved. Apparently the smell attracts the bruins. Redwood stain was never used again. Our visitor has never returned.

HARD SCRABBLE AT THE SAN JUAN

January 1970 I left Silverbell and ASARCO and began working for a small company north of Safford, Arizona at the San Juan Mine. It was an old property that had originally been an underground operation. A company out of El Paso was in the business of selling sulphuric acid to petroleum refineries. In some process or another, the acid removed large amounts of hydrocarbons that resembled tar. The company had to take back the spent acid with all this goo in it. Disposing of the acid and tar-like substance now became a substantial problem. It cannot be dumped on the ground, not prudent from an environmental standpoint.

The San Juan Mine offered a solution. The ore found there—for the most part—could be dissolved by acid and the copper recovered by a process collectively referred to as leaching. Basically, what transpires is this: Water and acid are put onto the copper ore, which goes into solution. This is then run through a series of rectangular tanks in which metal cans or other small metal items are placed. There is an ionic exchange with the copper dropping out of solution, and the iron traveling on with the now "barren" solution. Thus a useless product, such as the spent acid, could be converted to something profitable. In the case of the San Juan, metal was loaded and removed from the tanks, referred to as launders, by a crane with a large electric magnet. At intervals, tanks were drained and washed as the crane stirred, then transferred washed iron to another cell. The water and copper mud ended up in a settling tank—from which wash water was pumped during that operation. The copper settled over a few days time; the water was pumped out and the copper spread on a drying pad where it dried and was then shipped. The result of this was a copper powder that assayed 80% to 90% copper.

The El Paso company, with headquarters back east—naturally—leased the San Juan from the then owners. The lease was for ninety-nine years, and had some conditions written in that caused lawyers to salivate. Example: Words to the effect that the owners could cancel the lease if the El Paso gang did not operate the property in a "miner-like manner."

The mine manager, when I arrived, had been the chief metallurgist at Silverbell (get the connection?) and he was assisted by another metallurgist that had worked for him at Silverbell. Perhaps a "Chinese Fire Drill" or the Keystone Cops in one of the old silent films in hot pursuit of some gangster aptly described the situation. There were crushers; there were conveyor belts (this is always a requirement for the benefit of investors inspecting the operation); all, a frenzy of activity. A contractor using an air-track drill was in charge of drilling and blasting. A mid-sized Caterpillar front-end loader was being used to haul shot rock to the crusher, and away from the crusher to form dumps on which the acid-water solution was being placed.

Soon we acquired a large air-track drill, some haul trucks, and two more loaders. The metallurgists had a D8 crawler on hand before my arrival. The manager and his assistant had installed a large-diameter concrete pipe to return copper solution—this was termed "pregnant solution" as opposed to "barren solution" after it left the launders. Your scribe suggested that perhaps a ditch would suffice to carry the pregnant solution to the launders. After all, you metallurgists must know what happens when lime and acid get together. No problem, said the two.

Except for the acid eating the pipe up post haste.

There were large centrifugal pumps powered by diesel engines that forced barren solution to which acid had been added back to the leach dumps. Periodically the impeller shaft on a pump would break and send the impeller into a large plate, with the result that the impeller would be destroyed. There is a design flaw here in that the stainless steel (pumps all stainless because of acid) shaft is nearly three inches diameter, and this is necked down to a threaded end of about three-quarters of an inch. It needs to be redesigned. No action. Junior mine manager goes to town to buy some tools. Reports back to mine manager that hardware store owner is thinking of selling. Let's buy the store, says the mine manager. Material is being hauled from pit to crusher and stockpiled. Material is picked up and fed to crusher. Medium crushed material is being hauled to dump. My and my associates' job was to take care of mining and to build the leach dumps. The metallurgist-manager was directing operations. Look, we in the mining and hauling business said, you have us loading, hauling, dumping, and repeating the process for the same material four and five times, do you realize how much this is costing? No reply. What are these four men doing that you have hanging around the office? Answer: They are writing a history of the San Juan. We don't need any history writing going on, we are out here to run this operation as efficiently as possible, and to make a profit.

Conference called: Listen, Manager C.C., this is a lesson in economics that needs to be passed along. Do you remember the TV series *Maverick* that starred James Garner? He was always quoting something or other his Old Pappy said. Well, my Old Pappy's Economics Lesson was as follows:

Chapter 1: Spend less money than you make.
Chapter 2: Before you buy something, be sure you need it and can pay for it.
Chapter 3: Don't borrow money unless it's for a sound business venture.
Chapter 4: If money is owed, it is much better to have it owed to you.

I think we can apply those principles to our little operation here, don't you?

Apparently not. Time marches on, and the manager and his associate are no longer in evidence. It seems the old saw, "Don't let the gate hit you in the butt on the way out of here," has been applied. The promoter/CEO of the acid plant and the San Juan, which he has renamed the "Peacock Mine," sends out a mechanical engineer who has been designing and overseeing the construction of desalinization plants in Saudi Arabia. He ought to be able to cope with the Arizona desert. Time drags on for the mechanical engineer, now Peacock Mine Manager. One day the chief geologist and I wish to discuss something or other with this new manager. He is sitting behind his desk, we sit down opposite, and say whatever it is that we came to say. There is no reply, and the mine manager seems to have fallen into a state of catatonia. Suddenly he grabs his desk telephone and frantically dials a long-distance number. He then exclaims in a loud voice: "Fred, get me out of here!" He pauses a second, then adds a frantic "*NOW!*"

Soon a replacement is found and a new mine manager arrives. He has an airplane. When anything that the airplane is capable of hauling is needed, he transports the item and charges the company. A civil engineer shows up one day. He says that he has been partying with the CEO back in New York and has been hired. What am I supposed to do? He asks. No one knows the answer.

As is sometimes the case, things got bad, and then things got worse.

Seems all of our suppliers were not being paid. We needed some parts from the Caterpillar company in Phoenix. They said we had to pay them some money before they would ship us any more parts. The CEO is visiting—he often did with various investors—he directed the chief accountant to cut a check for a substantial amount, which he would take to Phoenix and deliver to the Caterpillar dealer. Days passed, and no parts arrived. The Caterpillar dealer was called. Have you shipped the parts that we need? His reply was just as soon as he received the promised money. Where did the money go?

Fewer and fewer workers remained and it seemed the Peacock had molted. A message was stirring across the high desert, and it said it was time to depart.

Sparks Faucett lived in the Chiricahua Mountains around Portal at the time. He had been a contractor, building highways, and also had a stable of race horses at one time. When I was about thirteen years of age, I was a jockey, riding race horses for Sparks around southern Arizona. I often prayed I would not grow larger, but alas, one day I was six feet tall and weighed in around 175 pounds. That was long after the jockey days.

When I left the San Juan (Peacock) Mine, I said thanks for the job, and, as Sparks used to say: "Here is wishing you all the luck in the world, because God knows you are going to need it." I did not intend to return, but fate moves in some mighty strange ways. I picked up a real-estate license and went to work for Pete Moser and Jody Zeller in a real-estate firm they owned in Tucson.

Jody had a Master's degree in English Literature, and used to grade our contracts and put "Failed" or a gold star on them. She was a wise woman, and taught us beginners some useful real-estate things.

A RETURN TO THE SAN JUAN

Real estate was going along with some fairly good transactions from time to time. When anyone in the office closed a lucrative deal, everyone, as per Jody's directive, retired to a nearby pub for a round of drinks at the successful person's expense. If no deals had been made for awhile, sometimes the drinks were on Pete or Jody. Things rocked along for close to two years, and the telephone call came. It was the chief accountant for the El Paso acid—and other—companies calling. After the usual bits about health, how are things going?, etc., etc., the accountant said they needed some help. They had been hanging on to the San Juan Mine, and were being sued. "Let me guess," I said. "The owners are suing you for not operating the property in a 'miner-like manner.' Correct?"

"You have it," said the accountant. "The old CEO was trammed, as you mining people like to say.[1] The new CEO, put in by the banks and investors, is a chemical engineer and retired vice-president of Exxon. He is coming out to Tucson, and wants to meet with you. Wants you to do some work for him in preparation for the lawsuit against us."

"Okay, I will meet with him and see what exactly he has in mind. When is he going to be here? And, where does he wish to meet?" The response: "Tomorrow night at the Marriot downtown." No use stringing this out, it seems.

The meeting: New CEO wants to know any and everything that your scribe can tell him about the San Juan. Where is the manager that was on site when I

---

[1] The term actually dates back to old-time English coal mines, and refers to iron cars running on tracks.

left? CEO says he fired him, and has a crew of a few people running a leaching operation. The chemist is yet there and running assays and some tests in the lab. CEO wants some exhibits made up for the trial, and requests that I visit the property for a look around.

Who exactly is suing you? CEO says that a large manufacturing company that makes various products for the automobile industry has decided they will open up some small copper properties and not have to buy copper from other companies. They have approached the owners of the San Juan and told them if they could break the ninety-nine-year lease they will buy the property. Further, the would-be buyers have engaged the services of some geologists and some diamond drill holes have been drilled near the San Juan property boundaries.

Property visited and situation assessed. Old chemist says that there is only one man who can straighten out the situation and that man is the one who has recently been fired. Diamond-drill holes investigated: turns out they have been drilled not *near* but *on* the San Juan property itself.

Findings are reported. Displays for the trial or made up, and another meeting is scheduled—this with one of the CEO's lawyers and the CEO's wife. It is a pleasant day in the Old Pueblo, we are having lunch alfresco. Your writer suggested this, as northeasterners may have you eating hotdogs on the street—as happens in *The Producers* when Max Bialystock (played by Zero Mostel) suggests to his accountant, Leo Bloom (Gene Wilder) that they "dine alfresco." (Max also tells the hotdog vendor, "Please tender my compliments to the chef.")

The CEO pretends he is conferring with the lawyer, but he is actually listening to his spouse grilling your scribe. How many tons of iron and acid are required per ton of copper produced? What information, and how was it obtained, was used in mine planning? What is the stripping ratio waste to leach ore? And, the questions went on and on. Is she coming up with this on her own, or is she following a script? Lunch finished and meeting is over.

CEO telephones. I would like for you to manage the San Juan during this trial period, and afterward. I think we can get this property on a paying basis. Okay, but you have to furnish me with a trailer to live in at the mine, and I will order what that will be. And other matters are agreed upon. It is also decided that not only will we defend against the lawsuit, but will sue the large company for trespassing on the property, and various other charges.

The owners lost their case against us, and the manufacturing company paid all costs and handed over a half million dollars to the San Juan crowd, which gave us a bit of cash to begin with, plus certain other considerations. Backing up a bit, the lawsuits were not—surprise—resolved overnight, but dragged on for about two years. During that time the San Juan equipment consisted of a D8 tractor, a front-end loader, and the crane at the launders. The entire work force consisted of no more than a dozen men, and everyone worked—including the chief wetback, yours truly. The problem with the pump impellers was resolved by a local machinist's work. A large tank was set up to store diesel and gasoline (President Jimmy Carter's regime said there was a fuel shortage). Stainless and plastic rainbird type sprinklers began to be used to sprinkle acid solution on dumps and the open-pit walls. There was no blasting of new ore as there were no drills on the property. Some of the people who made everything work were Larry Johnson (cowboy and heavy equipment operator); A.R. Mooney (cowboy, ranch manager, Army NCO, etc.); Wooster Whitmire (expert mechanic and inventor); Herman Garcia (exceptional worker who was illiterate but would follow to the letter work outlined for a week). Those were but a few.

The old chemist, who opposed anything we proposed to do: "You can't leach the pit. You can't pump the pregnant solution out of the pit. You can't glue PVC pipe together and hold under that much pressure. You can't run this outfit as it should be run, and only the man the CEO fired can do that." Was more or less urged to quit, and he did, much to the relief of everyone.

Shipping cement copper by truck was expensive. Johnson and A.R. suggest, since a train ran from the main line near Bowie to Globe a couple of times a week, that we pour a slab by the railroad tracks and ship on the railroad. This was done and substantial savings resulted.

The western-most end of the open pit narrowed down. Using the front-end loader, we closed it off with a dam about four feet in height. Solution sprayed on the pit walls and along the rim flowed down into the pit and became a lake of copper water. At first we used a gasoline engine to pump the solution out of the pit and to the launders. The lake had to be crossed to go to the small island where the engine and pump were nestled against the pit wall. Johnson and A.R. used a small metal row boat to cross the lake. A.R., on one trip was standing in the front of the boat as Johnson rowed. The boat struck a rock and A.R. plunged into the pit lake. A hasty shower and no damage done.

One night the fog had filled the pit, and A.R., wearing waterproof gear, was crossing the pit. As he neared the pump, the gasoline engine blew up in a terrific explosion. "Pard," A.R. said, "I thought I was back on the front lines in Korea. I had to stand right there and smoke a cigarette." We replaced the pump and powered it with a diesel engine.

We were making a modest profit rawhiding the operation, so we began a scaled-down mining effort. With a drill and some equipment, we made an average profit of about fifty thousand per month, and this would be our downfall.

A.R. studied up on running assays, and in addition to other jobs, did that work. The old chemist was not missed. Word came down from the higher echelons to the effect that if you can make that much money with so few employees and little equipment, think what you can do with more equipment and many more employees.[2]

"CEO, we are working for you, and will do what you order. This is a small operation, and historically speaking, leaching as the central business is not successful."

The CEO says: "Full speed ahead, and damn the tortillas." He doesn't know that some of us are part Mexican, or more.

A.R., cowboy philosopher ("How would you like to be up on Chiricahua Peak in a snow storm with nothing but a wet sheet to wrap up in?") says a difference of opinion makes horse races and missionaries. You would expect none less from A.R., whose favorite saying as he pulls in a poker jackpot is: "When you come right down to it, life is just simple arithmetic. A hard working man adds, a rascal subtracts, a wise man multiplies, but only a fool divides."

"Maybe," I reply, "We are kicking up before we are spurred."

We were not. A.R. bailed, as did Johnson—but I stuck around as mine manager a shade too long.

This is what happened, and it ended my mining days, and I began living full time in the Chiricahuas with Patricia M. While I was off for a week, the CEO had hired a new chemist—and this chemist was a strange character, to say the least.

One morning I hauled a new drill helper to the pit. Returning to the office area I drove past the launders. There was an elongated pit west of the crane level where iron was dumped, to be fed into the cells as needed. The crane sat on a strip of

---

[2] This still-common management error is described in the 1970s classic, *The Mythical Man Month*. It later became known as "Brooks's Law," after the book's author. In simplified form, Brooks's Law maintains that adding more people to a project will, after a certain point, make the project-completion time *longer:* not only does a larger workforce result in a more cumbersome chain of command, but it also takes time as new workers come up to speed. As Brooks put it, the fallacy is analogous to assuming that since it takes one woman nine months to produce a baby, it therefore follows that hiring eight more women will reduce the baby-production time to just one month.

level ground between the pit and the launders. The new chemist was out of his parked pickup and was looking at the launders. I drove on by and stopped at the foot of one of the ramps leading up to the crane level. The sump pump engine was running as the settling tank was being drained prior to laying out copper on the drying pad. I opened the pickup door and got out, remembered I had several things I wished to discuss with the chemist, and turned back for a note pad. I had taken a step or two when the back of a pickup came into view beneath the bill of my hard hat. The pickup hit me in the chest, arm and leg, and crumpled my pickup's opened door. As I fought to recover such basic functions as breathing, the chemist trotted down the ramp, saying he did not know he had left the emergency brake off on his pickup. The truck had been parked on perfectly level ground; at the moment that was not uppermost in my mind.

I was rushed the 90 miles or so to Tucson Medical Center. At the time, the wife of one of my cousins was the Chief Emergency-Room Nurse there, so I perhaps received more attention than most do upon arrival at such facilities. She informed me that it looked as though I had a compound fracture of my right arm and would soon see some bones piercing the skin. That was good news. She hustled off and brought an orthopedic surgeon back. He said X-rays were in order (turned out the arm was badly bruised and gashed a bit, but not broken).

"Any other complaints?" asked the doctor. "Only my leg," was the reply.

Surgeon checked the leg in question and asks: "You didn't walk in here did you?" The answer was I had. "If you let me, I could bend your leg out at a ninety degree angle. We must operate. I can do it first thing in the morning." After many weeks in a full-length leg cast—summer, of course—I turned in my resignation to the CEO who was urging me to reconsider. Nearly eight years of the desert hills of the Peloncillos and the San Juan were enough.

The chemist had taken the hint and left before my last visit to the property.

Months later I received a telephone call from a man in Salt Lake City. He began asking me about the chemist. The chemist had been working for the lab this man in Utah owned. "What do you want to know about your man?" I asked. And told him about my little accident and that I suspected the chemist had actually pushed the pickup to start it rolling. "This is what happened here in my lab in Salt Lake: This So-and-So got into an argument with one of the women working in the lab and beat her up pretty badly. He has assault charges against him, but the nut case is threatening to sue *me*."

Suspicions confirmed.

A METEOROLOGICAL FORECAST

Grant Godfrey, prospector and successful finder of ore deposits, worked for the chief geologist at the San Juan when the property first began operations in 1970. And he stayed on during the lean lawsuit years, and was on hand when your scribe arrived back on the property in 1974. Grant and his partner had discovered a substantial ore deposit and sold their claims to Phelps Dodge for a sizeable amount of money.

Grant bought an airplane—which crashed in a grove of pine trees, shearing off the wings. The instrument panel scarred Grant's face up enough that, when he looked in the mirror, it reminded him that perhaps he should not take up flying again. He tried the trucking business, but that did not work out, so, he set about partying and gambling a bit, until one day he was out of money. Occasionally someone remarked about how Grant, in their opinion, had squandered so much money. His reply was always: "At least I had the money to spend." One morning he seemed to be somewhat dejected; when asked what was the matter, he replied: "Old So-and-So is mad at me, and I cannot figure out why. I have never done anything *for* him."

Desert dwellers are quite zeroed in on the weather and what has happened and is going to take place. Most conversations are started with an inquiry as to amounts, if any, of precipitation and future prospects of more.

Weather forecasts via satellite were not available at the time, and the San Juan was far from Tucson and the weather people there. We did not even have a wise old Indian like the one who was asked each morning about a weather forecast. He would deliver an opinion, and nine times out of ten he was correct. One morning he was asked what was in store and he replied: "No forecast today. Don't have any idea what is going to happen." When asked why he had no weather information he said: "Radio broke."

Speaking of Indians: I hired some Apaches who lived on the San Carlos Reservation, and they were hard workers. One who comes to mind is Tex Robertson, who was a darned good hand. Tex was not fat, but he was big—about six foot four and maybe 230 pounds. His face was scarred from fights he had been in—some apparently involving knives. Tex liked to drink. After one such bender, he did not show up for work, so I fired him. A couple of days went by and here was Tex, accompanied by his wife. She was a good-looking woman, and like Tex, she wasn't fat, but was around six feet tall, and pretty fit. She said if I would give Tex another chance, he would be at work and on time. I gave Tex a job, and he was very reliable after that.

It was a bright September morning without a hint of the winter to come. We did not look forward to that time. Freezing winds that whipped across the slopes of the Peloncillos were harsh working conditions. But, that day was clear—no clouds, not even a thin streak of one. Grant and I were standing on the uppermost rim of the pit. "What do you think, Grant, will we be getting anymore rain before the winter?" Grant looked around full circle, thought a minute, and said: "No, no chance of rain now. The rainy season is definitely over, and you can take that to the bank."

Noon came, and it appeared as though the old prospector was on target. There would be no more rainfall until the winter storms came. An hour passed, and suddenly, massive black clouds rolled over the high ridges of the Peloncillos north of the San Juan. It rained—over four inches in less than an hour. Desert washes and arroyos were not only running bank to bank, they were overflowing. Sheets of water covered the desert hills several inches in depth. It took several days to repair the flood damage.

Grant was never again heard to deliver a meteorological forecast.

A MECHANICAL GENIUS

If one man could be singled out of greatest importance in getting the San Juan up and running during the rawhide mining and lawsuit days, it was Wooster Whitmire. He redesigned the impeller and pump shaft and the problem of breakdowns ended. A large tank that had been used for water storage by the manager/metallurgist-run operation was cleaned and placed into service for storage of fuel—a Wooster project. He overhauled the crane and magnet used at the launder. If a part was not available, he drew up the specifications and had a machinist manufacture it. When a new pipeline was required for acid, he said the metallurgists were wrong in that only stainless steel would hold up. Black iron pipe was cheaper and would probably last out the contract.

Most of the time, Wooster worked alone, unless some muscle was required for a project. In retrospect, the list of his accomplishments was extensive.

A.R. Mooney, though not alone, bore the brunt of many of Wooster's pranks. A.R. acted as our supply runner, in addition to other duties. Each Friday at midday he was given a list of supplies for pick up in Tucson. Before he left Tucson for the San Juan the following Monday, he called for any additions to his list.

A.R. got up early one Friday morning. Before preparing to leave for Tucson, he checked the large engines and pumps that forced barren solution and acid to the pit or leach dumps. He then got into his pickup for a nap before he left.

Wooster saw A.R. in his truck sleeping. He gathered some short lengths of 4-by-4-inch boards and arranged them front and back of A.R.'s truck tires. Wooster was careful that none of the boards could be seen with a cursory examination. Wooster went to the engineering office where he could observe. After a time, A.R.

finished his nap, started his truck engine and attempted to drive away. The vehicle would not move. He tried again, and again the truck failed to move. A.R. got out, inspected the vehicle, and tried once more with the same result. Next he opened the hood, and then looked beneath the vehicle. There he saw the problem. His voice could be heard as he drove away—curse words punctuated by Wooster's name. Wooster then made a point to call A.R. "Old Lumber Yard" every time he saw him.

Many when a job is finished satisfactorily take a moment to reflect upon their good work. Inevitably Wooster would make certain vulgar gestures—the kind you may get if you happen to inadvertently cut off someone in city traffic—directed at the recently completed work. His vocabulary was at least thirty percent curse words of varying degrees of vulgarity. One morning I asked Patricia if she would like to ride up to the pit with me. Wooster was seated with his back to the road next to something he had been repairing. Another man had been helping him and he faced the road. I stopped, rolled down a window and said something to the two men. Wooster did not look around, but immediately began his usual tirade. His partner was trying to shut Wooster up as he had seen Patricia in the truck with me. Finally I drove off, Wooster none the wiser, Patricia red-faced, but laughing.

Every few days Wooster would tell of some adventure he had experienced. We could never determine whether he did this for our presumed entertainment, or actually believed his stories were true. It did allegedly tempt some of the men to go along with Wooster shopping.

The anecdotes went something like this: Wooster would have stopped off at the Safeway to pick up some supplies. As he walked down an aisle—and this was always the case—an exceptionally beautiful woman flashed her well proportioned bosom at Wooster. Once this also happened as Wooster was walking up the steps to the post office in broad daylight.

The most outrageous yarn he came up with was this: I was up at the pit, when Wooster came along. It was a cold, raw day, a brisk wind blowing across the slope. "About half hour ago I saw something that is hard to believe." No telling what was coming, Wooster kept you guessing. "What was that, Wooster?"

"Well, to the west of the pit on the road [*this would have been over a quarter mile away—and remember, it was really cold*] there was a car stopped. There were two of the best looking-women ever, and they were out on the hood of the vehicle sun-bathing, without a single stitch of clothes on. They saw me admiring them, sat up, smiled, and waved to me. Isn't that the blank, blank, thing you ever heard?"

Mighty darn close, Whit, that's for sure.

JUNIOR BIRDMEN

In the 1950s, there were contract primary flight schools scattered across the country. One of them was Malden Air Base, near Malden, Missouri, which is down in the southeastern part of the state—the "Boot Heel." The Government furnished airplanes—T-6 Gs, the advanced trainer in WWII—military check pilots, and various other personnel. Flight instructors were civilians, as were food-service personnel, etc. Contract Primary flight schools were where many fledgling cadets and student officers were introduced to the strange and wonderful mysteries of flight.

Malden was a cold, wet place when your humble scribe reported to "Malden Air Base, United States Air Force Primary Flying Training School, Headquarters 3305th Pilot Training Squadron (Contract Primary), Anderson Air Activities Contractor To U.S. Air Force." With a title like that, how could you go wrong?

My class was 53-B, which indicated about when we would graduate from basic and receive our wings and be commissioned as second lieutenants. We began reporting to the flight line when preflight was finished. About forty percent would not make it through primary—"washed out"—and a few more left when we went on to basic to fly the T-28 and then our first jet, the T-33 trainer.

There followed six weeks of Pre-Flight academics, P.T. (physical training), and no doubt some other things. All of this was done under the constant supervision and harassment of some of the cadet corp. It was not until later that we realized these malcontents were cadets who had washed out of the program and were awaiting orders to somewhere else. Throughout primary, any infraction of the rules resulted in demerits, which had to be walked off on Saturday afternoon.

Flights of cadets marched in formation to and from the flight line, to academics, and physical training. Usually there was a great deal of singing as everyone marched along. This was done for entertainment purposes and to show the military officers that they were not going to succeed in breaking our spirit. Also, and this was if we did not particularly like the brown-noser cadet lieutenant, rather ribald songs were sung when we were in the vicinity of any officers. The cadet lieutenant was usually chewed out for our conduct. After all, we were studying to be officers and gentlemen.

One song, of many, even some taught to us by the French Cadets, went like this: "Up in the air Junior Birdmen; up in the air upside down. Up in the air Junior Birdmen, get your feet up off the ground. And when you hear the big announcement, that your wings are made of tin, then you'll know, Junior Birdmen, that you have all been taken in."

I had the misfortune to catch a bad cold—desert rats are not used to places where it rains. The cold became a sinus infection, and I was grounded while my fellow cadets began to fly. I reported to sick call; something had to be done. The base medical facility was a bare-bones operation, and ultimately I was sent to specialists at Scott Field near Saint Louis.

Travel to Scott Field was via a C-45 that was one of the aircraft assigned to Malden Air Base. The nose doctors did various things, decided they could clear up the sinus situation by various and sundry procedures, and after about ten days they had succeeded. A call was placed to Malden requesting some transportation. There is a fuel shortage at the moment and we cannot send an airplane for you. Meanwhile I left the hospital and resided in a barracks. Trips were made to baseball games when the Cardinals were playing. Food was quite acceptable. Things were agreeable. Time went by. Another call was placed, and the story was the same: fuel shortage. The Kingston Trio song about the man who boarded some public transportation system in Boston and due to not having enough money to pay, never returned. It was looking more and more as though that would be the case. A desperation call: I don't have any money, have not been paid for some time. Can you arrange for finance here at Scott to let me have some money, and I will take a Greyhound Bus back. Okay, will do.

Finally—got back to Malden. "Morrow," the section commander on the flight line said, "we are going to have to wash you back to Class 53-C as you have too much catching up to do." Reported to new section with the 53-C cadets and student officers.

Primary, Malden Air Base, September, 1952
Left to right: Griffiths, Morrow, Gardner (instructor), Polimas, Golonka.

The civilian instructors would brief their charges before departing for the flight line, sometimes using airplane models to demonstrate various maneuvers. Four of us were assigned to Gene Sackey.

Sackey had been a P-38 fighter pilot in WWII, and in addition to his flying instructor job, had a crop-dusting business. He was a color-coordinated dresser. One day he might wear a green cap, green shirt, green pants, or another day all blue or some other color. He did not hold briefings prior to departure for the flight line. He would come out of the instructor's room, chute over a shoulder, and announce whichever one of us he was flying with first. On the way to the aircraft you were told what the day's lessons may be. Once in the aircraft, you were instructed, and you remembered.

Occasionally, the instructor would pull the power back on the T-6's 550 horse-power engine, and announce: "Forced Landing!"

There was then a checklist to go through that included having the gear up. At the time, being a beginner, I did not have that much feel for the aircraft, and I had lined up on a farm field—there were many to choose from in Missouri—and completed the checklist. Sackey applied power and almost immediately called for another forced landing.

I rattled off the checklist—not realizing he had put the gear down, which I declared to be wheels up. The "instruction" that came from the back seat is with me yet.

A/C R.W. Morrow, Malden Air Base, 1952

My first solo flight in the T-6 was 30 July 1952. Sackey took a vacation and I completed primary with a P-40 pilot named Fred Gardner. After 260 hours of academics and 130 hours in the T-6, we were deemed ready to advance to Basic. That was to be at Webb Air Force Base, Big Springs, Texas.

FASTER FLY THE JUNIOR BIRDMEN

West Texas in winter, and the winds sure can blow out there.

Webb Air Force Base had two parallel runways—one for T-28s and the other for the jet trainers, T-33s. Webb AFB also served as a civilian airport. One day, a twin-engine private plane went missing. The search went on for several days—but when the dust clouds finally settled, the plane was found between the runways.

The T-28 was a tricycle-gear aircraft with a 750-horsepower engine. It was designated a transition aircraft between prop and jet aircraft. We flew them some 60 hours. My T-28 instructor was the bottom of the barrel in that department. He was not, when I looked back after a few years, even a very good pilot. You can't win them all. Two cadets were lost in a mid-air collision while flying T-28s.

In spite of our rather inept instructor, I and the four other cadets assigned to him managed to begin learning instrument flying and formation flying. None of us were sad to be leaving the T-28 phase of the program. Now, we began to fly the T-33 jet trainer. It was a fine aircraft built by Lockheed. Seating was one behind the other, with the instructor sitting in back, unless we were practicing instrument flying beneath a canvas hood simulating weather conditions that required instrument flying. Four of us were cadets and one student officer assigned to Foch J. Benevent—instructor, T-33s. Foch was a dapper fellow, always wearing aviator glasses, a bright scarf, and his cap tilted at a jaunty angle. He had flown P-38s in combat during WWII, and he announced—quite honestly—that he would much prefer to be back flying combat missions than flying with the five of us. But, he was an exceptional instructor, and even though at that late date some students were washing out, he put us all through the program.

Perhaps prejudiced, but I always thought we were a bit ahead of the other junior birdmen because of Foch's instruction.

He cautioned us not to think we knew it all when we received our wings. He said he had thought he was pretty hot—until he got into his first dogfight with some Japanese Zeros, and then he had a sudden change of mind.

A fly-over was made for some ceremony at San Angelo, Texas, and a number of T-33s with students and instructors were involved. Foch let me do the flying, even though it called for some close formation. Any of his students could have done as well, but when we were back on the ground, one of the other instructors said he saw Foch tucking in pretty close and followed suit. Foch said he wasn't flying the aircraft, that Morrow was flying.

Before we graduated, Foch broke out a "little black book." It was filled with the names of ladies scattered across the United States, along with their telephone numbers. He insisted that we copy down all of the names and numbers.

Somewhere along the way, after Patricia and I were married, Foch's list disappeared. I wonder if any of his students called on Foch's girlfriends.

There were no fatal accidents when we were at Malden. Unfortunately, that changed at Webb.

In addition to wing tanks and an aft fuselage tank, the T-33 had a large tip tank on each wing tip. I can vouch through personal experience that, by landing smoothly and hot, with some aileron added for lift on the heavy side, the T-33 could be landed safely with one full tip tank.

One of the fatalities at Webb was because someone—who did not know what he was talking about—came up with this procedure in case one of the tip tanks on the T-33 did not feed: 1) fly between the two runways at five hundred feet and three hundred knots (345 MPH), then 2) release the tip tanks. An instructor and his student followed the designated procedure. Once released, the full tank rolled up the wing, hit the canopy, and the aircraft flipped over and crashed.

Another, and this dated back to primary at Malden, and instructor Sackey. Sackey had put one of the cadets for elimination from the program. Somehow, Sackey was bothered by doing this, and on the way to our aircraft told me that he was sorry to have to put So-and-So up for elimination, that there was no specific reason he did so, but something told him to do it. The cadet passed his check ride and was assigned to another instructor. He then made it through T-28s and T-33s, with two hours of night flight left before graduation.

His aircraft crashed straight in on a clear Texas night.

Webb AFB, 1953: two weeks before being commissioned USAF officer and receiving wings

In May of 1953, class 53-C graduated, received our wings and commissions, and went off to various assignments. I and some of my compatriots went first to Laughlin Air Force Base at Del Rio, Texas, for air-to-ground gunnery. It was there that a pilot named Weisberger tore off a few feet of his plane's wing tip, when he hubbed a mesquite while shooting up some old cars on the tactical range. He managed to land the craft back at base. Air-to-air gunnery, Luke Field near Phoenix, he hit another F-84 while rat racing (an all-out zooming around the sky, trying to stay on first then another aircraft's tail). Weisberger drove a tip tank into the fuselage of another aircraft, just back of the canopy. Both planes made it back and landed safely. The other pilot had to be restrained, until he calmed down a bit.

There was an incident happened one day that was rather humorous—in that no one was injured. Two pilots in training lined up on the runway for takeoff. We usually took off with one airplane flying formation on the wing of the other. The lead aircraft had a malfunction of the ventilation system and carbon monoxide impaired the pilot's judgment. Down the runway the F-84s raced. Mid-point of the ten-thousand-foot runway was reached, and on they went, faster and faster. Take-off speed was reached and passed, and on they went. The end of the runway loomed, and the two still did not become airborne. Off the end of the runway, with the wing man in tight formation as they raced across farms and ended up in an irrigation canal. The wing man said that he had been told to always be in formation—supposedly he said.

SMOKE CHASERS

In the high country of the Chiricahua Mountains there is a place called the Cima Ranger Station. Perhaps some of the log buildings remain and have not completely rotted and fallen down. The main cabin was a large structure, with two bedrooms, two fireplaces, a long room with a kitchen area at one end, and a shower room. Water was heated as it circulated through coils in the firebox of a large wood burner cook stove, and was stored in a forty gallon tank. A smaller log structure housed firewood, tools, and fuel for lanterns. A barn and corrals completed the compound. Fresh water flowed through pipes from a spring above Cima.

"Cima" in Spanish means a summit, peak, or top—and Cima Ranger Station is near the summit of the Chiricahuas. In winter months, as was the case with lookouts and the ranger station at Rustlers Park, no humans were in residence. In early spring that changed. Soon the fire season—before the summer rains—would begin, and the Forest Service Administrative Guard, the packer and his string of mules, and perhaps two or three others arrived at Rustlers Park. Supplies arrived and were stored in a metal-lined building. The barn was filled with hay and grain, and the packer took food and hay and grain—where needed—to the soon-to-be-occupied lookouts and Cima.

Your scribe was on the mountain and at Cima for awhile in 1949, before going on to Fort Huachuca and the buffalo. When I left Fort Huachuca in 1951, Ralph and Juanita Morrow were back living at Hilltop in East Whitetail Canyon. The district forest ranger needed some people for lookouts and smoke chasers, and gave me a job. At first, there were three of us smoke chasers at Cima. One man went to

Fly Peak as a lookout, the other to Sentinel Peak Lookout. Sentinel was a small house and tower about fifteen feet above ground level. The lookout and smoke chaser lived in the probably 14-by-14-foot lookout.

John, the smoke chaser recently assigned to Cima, told the Administrative Guard, Nig Moore (seems anyone in those days had the nickname and was called by such if they were dusky complected), that he sure would like to get another assignment.

The lookout slept on a cot, and John rolled out a sleeping bag on the floor. The quarters were cramped. Nig wanted to know what the problem was. John said old Whit, the lookout, took a big dose of Black Draught laxative every night and was up stumbling around at three every morning headed for the out house. Nig said he would see what he could do.

Fly Peak Lookout, Chiricahuas, circa 1937
Cabin later rebuilt by Civilian Conservation Corps

For a week or so I held down the plush environs solo. Then two more men arrived, and one of them left to be smoke chaser at Monte Vista Lookout. The other hand had a history as a malcontent, and after a few weeks he came up with a reason to quit his job. Once again I held down the fort alone, and it was right peaceful.

I found two strange things at Cima Ranger Station: first, even though Cima was miles from any road, someone had packed in around fifty or sixty "pulp" books, mostly westerns; second—and more puzzling—in one of the bedroom closets, hanging from several rods, were probably a hundred neckties.

Who packed all those neckties over to Cima, and why, I never knew. They were there when I left at the end of the fire season.

There were at that time lookouts that were manned day and night during fire season: Sentinel Peak, Silver Peak, Monte Vista, Fly Peak, Barfoot, and Sugar Loaf, which was in the National Monument. Smoke chasers were at Sentinel and Monte Vista, and at Cima and Rustlers Park. In each lookout tower there was a compass rose with a sighting device. All stations had a large map with a compass rose centered representing all of the lookouts and other locations. A string was fastened in the center of each rose. When a fire was seen by a lookout, a sighting was made and the bearings from their position to the fire reported. When two lookouts had reported a fire and the bearings from their location, it was a simple matter to use strings crossing the bearings reported, and where they crossed was the fire. A simple but effective system.

Once the location was determined, the smoke chasers saddled their horses and rode to the fire—usually, with early reporting, a tree or dead snag that had been struck by lightning. The ride, at the time, was made even at night, with lightning shaking and thundering across the mountains. Sometimes a mist of rain would be falling, but not enough to put out the reported blaze or blazes.

On an exceptionally dark night, I was going back to Cima, and crossed Round Park below Fly Peak. On the south boundary of the park, the trail went into an area of dense forest. Even with night vision established, I could not see anything. The good horse I was riding pulled on the reins, putting his nose down smelling horse and mules tracks on the trail. In about a half mile, we broke out into enough light to hurry along back to Cima.

One afternoon a thunderstorm began and lookouts were reporting fires in a number of locations. All smoke chasers and the packer were out hurrying to first one fire and then another. In late afternoon, I was headed toward Rustlers Park and met Nig Moore, Admin Guard, and Melvin McClintock, who was the packer. Nig said they were headed for Sentinel Peak, but first there was a fire burning east of Fly Peak. It was almost dark when the three of us had finished with that blaze. We hastened on to Sentinel Peak and joined the smoke chaser from there on a fire of several acres. Late that night we had dealt with that, and no other lightning strikes had been reported.

Back at the Sentinel Peak Lookout, Whit wanted to know if anyone would like a shot of Peppermint Schnapps, and was taken up on the offer. His idea of a shot was more like a water glass, and the ride back to Cima was with no pain. Nig and Melvin had a ways to go to Rustlers, but I was back home. In twenty-four hours I had been to several fires and rode over forty miles along forest trails.

§   §   §

Early suppression of forest fires coupled with prescribed burns has always seemed a reasonable approach to preserving the national forests. There are few if any lookouts left in the Chiricahua Mountains. The district forest station is in the desert at Douglas, miles from any forest land. Perhaps the omnipotent Department of Agriculture and the Forest Service attitude as guardians of the forests for the good of the people is best summed up by a statement made by the District Ranger several decades back: "We don't have to work the roads. We don't have to maintain the trails. We don't have to keep up and maintain the public camp grounds."

THE MOUNT GRAHAM FIRE

This was to be the last forest fire for many who were of another era. It was the summer of 1956, and Patricia and I had left the Air Force and were back in the Chiricahuas. A large fire was burning in the mountains southwest of Safford, and the call went out for some crew leaders. My Dad, Ralph Morrow, and I drove over and up to the high country where a large fire camp had been established. Efforts to stop the blaze had been unsuccessful, with high winds driving it over fire lines. As it turned out, there were crew chiefs enough. We were joined by Frank Price and another man at some corralled horses that had been rented out to the Forest Service. We each picked out a mount. There was a big blue roan horse that a local lion hunter had rented out, and I picked him. He turned out to be a good mountain and saddle horse.

A local was at the corral with his horse, and when we all mounted up, he led us off to the west fire line. We apparently had no particular mission, as we just rode along on forest trails that dropped to lower elevations and then climbed to the mountain tops. This took the entire day, and chowing down that evening, and signing out with the time keeper, we turned in for the night. The next day was a repeat of the last, but on the third day, our guide was no longer in evidence.

On the far north area of the fire there were no crews at work along the forest trail. The fire had not quite reached the trail. A good breeze was blowing from the trail toward the fire, and we decided to back fire. We set fires all along the trail, and began patrolling the trail. My Dad and Frank were off a distance, and we other two "fire fighters" were watching to see that nothing rolled across the trail.

Suddenly we saw a flare up back toward Frank and my Dad. In a few minutes here they came on horseback.

After getting their section of the back fire going, they had lain down to take a nap. As Frank said: "That fire sure enough got to roaring. We woke up and jumped on our horses, and got out of there."

That night we stayed at a camp that had been established in the foothills.

We had unsaddled, fed and watered our horses, signed in with the time keeper. After supper we were sitting around a camp fire, and noticed a Forest Service man leading a couple of mules off toward an enclosure that had been thrown up as a corral. He had a mule on each side and had their lead ropes up short. About that time a helicopter came in to land, and scared the mules. They stampeded with this fellow hanging onto them, and his feet were hitting the ground every twenty to thirty feet. "Man," someone said, "That reminds me of a story I was reading my little daughter about some cat wearing twenty-league boots."

A couple of days later we left and went back to the Chiricahuas. Our fire line was the only one that held until it rained and put the fire out.

R.W. Morrow and 1st Lt. (later Col.) Bill Newell on alert, Ellsworth Air Force Base, 1955

WAR STORIES

The Korean War was winding down that summer of 1953. We were not scheduled to go there, and those fighter pilots in classes ahead of us were disappointed when they arrived in Korea. The Wheels, pilots with combat experience, wanted to fly as many missions as possible, and set down some Catch-22 rules for new arrivals, who left Korea with fewer hours than those of us who stayed behind.

We reported to the ready room before dawn, and were in the air over the range firing before sunup. Flights of four set up a race-track pattern, firing on a 9-foot-by-30-foot target towed behind a B-26. Two fifty-caliber machine guns were all that were used for practice. Each plane's guns were loaded with different colored bullets so that hits could be determined for each pilot's score. Different colored "rags" were in use making a study of how readily various colors could be picked up in the early morning light.

The pattern was as follows: A flight of four would be in echelon, the leader rolling in on the first turn of an "S" pattern. As he rolled into the second turn of the "S," his wingman began his pass. The leader would be in firing position—down and over 15 degrees angle off the tow plane's flight path. The leader fired, crossed over the target, paralleled the tow plane, and began climbing back to the perch. Meanwhile, his wingman was firing, and the element leader had rolled in. Leader's wingman off the target, element leader firing, and his wingman rolling in. This went on until ammunition was gone. Formation flying, instrument training, and rat racing completed most of flying. The tow plane dropped the rag back at Luke Field and we counted up our hits. A minimum score of fifteen percent hits

F-86Ds of the 54th Fighter Interceptor Squadron, Ellsworth AFB, South Dakota, 1954

was required to qualify. All the shooting of shotgun and rifle I had done from childhood paid off for me, and I more than qualified on the first sortie I flew.

By afternoon, there in the Arizona desert, one tended to be ready for a siesta. Academics were scheduled for each afternoon. There was a bird colonel—US Army—that taught one class. He had an Ml rifle—fortunately loaded with blanks—stashed behind his desk. When several of his pupils had given up trying to stay awake and had dozed off, he would point the Ml up and out over the class room, and fire off a round. This made a deafening sound in close quarters, and brought everyone to full alert.

In September, Patricia and I were assigned to the 54th Fighter Interceptor Squadron of the Air Defense Command at Ellsworth AFB, near Rapid City, South

Dakota. That is to say, I was assigned, and Patricia was support personnel. The 54th were at the time flying the F-84G jet fighter, which was actually designed to be a fighter-bomber. It was a good, dependable aircraft, and I flew it for several hundred hours before the squadron started flying F-86D all-weather interceptors. That aircraft was armed with 24 rockets that were carried in the belly in a retractable pod.[1]

Colonel Benedict, the commanding officer of the 54th, had arrived two weeks prior to several of the Luke graduates. Colonel Benedict was originally a Royal Canadian Air Force pilot before the United States entered WWII. He was a spit-and-polish commander. The flight line was swept clean. Operations building was freshly painted, and the atmosphere summed up by a conversation overheard. The First Sergeant was talking to a Tech Sergeant in a hallway. The Tech leaned and put a hand on the wall. "Sergeant," said the First Sergeant, "Get your hand off that wall or you will find yourself painting the entire hall."

A lesson in conduct: Prior to Colonel Benedict commanding the 54th, a T-33 from his then squadron had some mechanical problems and was left with the 54th for repairs until it was repaired. Time went by, and the aircraft had not been repaired. Colonel Benedict flew in and demanded to know why his aircraft had not been repaired after so much time had passed. The Captain in charge of engineering, which performed such duties, got rather snotty with the Colonel, and said

---

[1] The 54th FIS began life in 1941 as the 54th Pursuit Squadron, based at Hamilton Field, California. They were then equipped with a variety of pursuit aircraft, including the P-36, P-40, and P-43. When World War II broke out, the 54th moved to Paine Field, Washington, then north to Alaska, where they were assigned to the 343rd Fighter Group. Flying Lockheed P-38s, they remained part of the guardians of the north until they were inactivated in 1946.

In December 1952, now known as the 54th Fighter Intercept Squadron, they were reactivated at Rapid City AFB, South Dakota. There they were initially equipped with F-51D Mustangs, before converting to the jet era in F-84G Thunderjets, as part of the 29th Air Division. In 1954, they finally got a "first-rate" jet, the F-86D Sabre Jet.

In the fall of 1957, the 54th traded in the almost-supersonic swept-wing F-86D for the older and slower straight-wing F-89J Northrop Scorpion. The squadron flew the Scorpions until Christmas Day, 1960, when the Air Force once again inactivated the 54th. The squadron was reactivated for the final time in 1987, flying F-15 Eagles out of Elmendorf AFB in Alaska. The unit was inactivated again in 2000.

From "The 54th FIS," Ralph Morrow & Larry Davis,
Sabre Jet Classics, Volume 22, Number 1, Spring 2014

certain things he should not have said. Surprise! Guess who a few weeks later was the Captain's commanding officer. Soon there was a new officer in charge of engineering, and the Captain was no longer in evidence in those parts.

One flight of F-84s flew north each morning toward the Canadian border, and then along the border to Great Falls. On my first flight along the "High Line," I was number four man in the flight of F-84s. The weather closed down to zero after we landed for refueling at Great Falls, and we spent the night. The next morning the weather had lifted, but the direct flight back to Ellsworth was in the weather. The flight leader and his wing man took off, with the leader flying instruments and his wing man in formation. I took off on the wing of the element leader who flew instruments in the weather for the time it took to return to our home base. The element leader and another F-84 had been in the weather at night and the wing man made a separate instrument let down. A critical point in an instrument let down and landing is the transitional time from Instrument Flight Rules (IFR) to Visual Flight Rules (VFR). As VFR began to develop, IFR continued, as primarily instruments continued to be flown; VFR conditions began to be included in each cross check, until full VFR could be flown. Something happened, and the wing man crashed off the end of the active runway. There was a tremendous explosion that flashed up through the night clouds.

The leader, now my element leader back to Ellsworth, required another aircraft to be scrambled, and he then flew in formation down through the weather. Having heard of this, I was somewhat nervous about my leader. We were in solid clouds for over an hour, and I began to experience vertigo. It felt as though we were gradually banking to port. A quick look at the instrument panel indicated that we were straight and level. This went on until we let down out of the clouds at Ellsworth.

In October of 1954, a month before Michael Morrow arrived at the Ellsworth hospital, I was promoted in rank, and became a flight leader and alert team captain. Also, was designated an instructor pilot in T-33s. The squadron was still flying F-84s.

The alert hangars were located near the end of the runway at Ellsworth, which was three hundred feet in width and two miles in length. Four bays housed the aircraft on alert. Overhead doors could be closed if the weather dictated. When a team of four pilots reported to the alert hangar, the aircraft were given a preflight inspection. Parachutes were placed in the cockpits, and all readied for scrambling the aircraft. Two-story living quarters were centered between the aircraft bays. Crew chiefs and pilots were usually downstairs. Weather reports were updated, and all made ready for scrambling, and code sheets for that day given to the pilots. In the afternoon, or evening, usually a card game of one sort or another started—sometimes penny ante poker. When operations rang the alert bell indicating aircraft were to be scrambled, and the number of aircraft to go, the action began. We stood five-minute alert—meaning from the time the bell rang we had five minutes to get in our aircraft, start up, take the runway, make our take-off run and have the gear up.

One of the pilots on alert remarked that five minutes cut it close to scramble the F-84G. I already knew how quickly the F-84 could scramble, so it was a sucker bet. I will bet you a bottle of Jack Daniels that I can scramble in less than three minutes. This brought hoots of derision, and the bet was called.

We are sitting around a card game when the signal came to scramble two aircraft. Out through the door into the hangar; crew chief already has the auxiliary power unit running as the ladder to the cockpit is climbed; hit the start engine as the side of the cockpit is cleared, and the engine begins to wind up; by the time chute is fastened and shoulder and lap straps fastened, the engine is nearing 20%; quick check to see that pins are removed on ejection system; at 20% throttle around the horn, and signal for APU unit disconnected, chocks removed, and ladder removed; power increased to start aircraft rolling; canopy closed; engine instruments cross checked as power increased; tower called notifying two aircraft scrambling; power pushed to 100% as the aircraft takes the runway; several checks of engine instruments on takeoff roll; flight occurs; wheels and flaps up.

Time: 2 minutes, 45 seconds—and guess who is drinking free bourbon.

The squadron was receiving F-86Ds, and some of the pilots were checking out in that aircraft, but we were also flying the F-84s. On initial approach for landing, I had one wing man on the right wing—traffic pattern was left hand. An F-86 was high and to our right and was figuring to bounce us in the traffic pattern. I told the wing man to loosen up a bit, and we broke into our attacker. A low-level dogfight then occurred off the end of the runway, with the tower in a full-swivel panic.

One night, and the squadron was complete F-86s, a war game exercise was on, and this could go on for several days. Aircraft were continuously being scrambled to intercept Strategic Air Command bombers flying in from the north—presumably the route the Ruskies would take. There was no wind, and aircraft were taking off and landing in opposite directions. An F-86 landed and was rolling down the southern most side of the runway. I took the runway for a takeoff in the opposite direction of the landed aircraft. My plane was nearly airborne as we passed, and in a moment of silence from the distressed tower, the other pilot—Captain Ulfers—said: "I knew you were going to do that."

It seemed your turn to scramble had barely gone past when you were up again. Everyone tried to grab a short nap when they could. A pilot had fallen asleep on one of the cots in the alert hangar, and it was near to his turn to fly again. Someone had some firecrackers—a couple of cherry bombs. Several of us gathered around, lit the fuse on a cherry bomb and threw it beneath the sleeper's cot. He opened his eyes, wondering what was so interesting. The explosion was loud, and a few choice words were heard.

A favorite trick of some pilots was to lurk around at altitude, and bounce aircraft shortly after they had taken off, and were not up to speed. This would happen if aircraft were taking off to the northwest where there were no buildings. Southeast takeoffs went over the base entrance and some of the housing area. The terrain dropped down off the runway at Ellsworth. While rolling, a quick check of the operational channel may reveal some anticipated attack. I would keep the F-86 in afterburner, and drop down low off the end of the runway. When sufficient speed was reached an Immelmann was executed[2]. The attackers were usually met head on.

There is a large repair and tire business in the small town of Animas, New Mexico. People come to this facility from a radius of sixty miles. The operation is owned and operated by Ronnie Ward—business man and professional rodeo hand, team roper. I arrived early for an appointment for vehicle repairs. Ronnie's helper had gone to lunch, and Ronnie was eating. We were entertaining each other with various yarns, and some about Air Force days. He asked if I had ever considered going on in the Air Force as a career, and why did I not do so.

"Ronnie," I replied, "After fifty years, I still have not figured that one out."

---

[2] A maneuver involving a half loop and a half roll at the top, putting the aircraft in the opposite direction; named after German aviator Max Immelmann (1890-1916).

THE INEFFABLE PLEASURE OF DINING AND DRINKING AT SOMEONE ELSE'S EXPENSE

One night, when my flight was on alert, the weather was socked in with a light snow falling. I put my name up—as flight leader and alert team captain I scheduled the order of pilots scrambling—first in line. It seemed less stressful than being concerned about other pilots in the flight going up with conditions so unfavorable. We had already lost one member of our flight while standing alert with another team. A new pilot was then assigned to the flight.

A scramble of one aircraft was received, and soon after takeoff, IFR was necessary. Leaving the tower channel, I contacted the area GCI radar site for directions. The F-86D was equipped with radar, and rockets were fired at the appropriate time and range by the aircraft's electronics. Nothing to compare with the aircraft and weaponry of the present. But the GCI directed aircraft to the target transmitting headings, altitude, and speed of the craft to be intercepted.

Two events direct thoughts back to that night: As the F86 climbed through the night storm, the plane's surfaces and the atmospheric conditions created an electrical charge. Thin blue streaks of miniature lightning flashed across the canopy and wings. Quite spectacular. This went on for probably a quarter hour, and at that time the target began to paint on the aircraft's radar. The clouds at altitude thinned, but conditions were still IFR. The boogie was visible about three hundred feet ahead. Coming in closer and alongside, revealed a commercial airliner. The aircraft type was radioed to the GCI site, who then said they had finally received notification of the aircraft's clearance. The second occurrence of the night came a few days later when the pilot of the airliner filed a complaint that his craft had been endangered. The matter was reviewed, and ruled in favor of the Air Force pilot.

The 54th Squadron flew to Yuma Air Base, Arizona, for training exercises. A B-45 towed a reflective target, flying over the gunnery range. Flights of two F-86Ds were directed to the target abeam—at 90 degrees—to the target heading. Shortly after takeoff, the lead plane's pilot fastened down a canvas hood and began flying instruments to simulate actual IFR conditions. The chase plane checked for aircraft that may be in the area, and to monitor conditions prior to and at the time rockets were fired.

The airplane radar began to paint the target and tow plane. The target was locked onto, and a display appeared in the airplane's radar scope. The aircraft was then guided by the pilot using the radar scope. Firing in twenty seconds was indicated, and when cleared by the tow plane—making certain that they had not been locked onto as target—the trigger was held down until firing occurred, with the pod dropping and six of the twenty four rockets fired. The pod then retracted. The scope presentation was continuously filmed; a camera mounted under each wing began filming when the trigger was depressed. The flight of the rockets was recorded, and hits on the target—if any—could be readily seen.

The squadron stayed at Yuma for a month, before returning to Ellsworth. A wager was placed with flight leader Captain William Norris. Norris had been a combat pilot in Korea, and later served in Vietnam, retiring as a two-star Major General. The bet was that the flight I led would score more hits than his flight. The losers would have to pay for dinner and drinks back at Rapid City, and this would include spouses, or girlfriends, as in the case of an unmarried member of my flight.

Norris did score the most hits in the squadron with fifteen, and was followed by the squadron commander, Major Fairbrother, who retired as a Brigadier General. I was third in hits with eleven, but the rest of my flight brought our flight total ahead of the Norris flight. The losers paid the wager, and, since my gang chose the place and dinner, it was not inexpensive. We would have expected none less from the Norris flight.

A fine evening was spent, and even the losers were somewhat happy by evening's end. Ah, the ineffable pleasure of dining and drinking at someone else's expense.

CATFISH, BULLFROGS, AND CHRISTMAS TREES

By the late 1970s, the John Slaughter Ranch in southeastern Arizona had been held and operated by various owners. A family that had been in the grocery business in Tucson had purchased the property and set about restoring the ranch house and property. Along the way, they decided to leave and began efforts to market the ranch. Efforts were directed toward possibly selling the ranch to the Nature Conservancy. Some in various walks of life believe that entity is a noble cause. Others, on close inspection of their "non-profit" real-estate transactions, find it to be a well crafted real-estate scam of world wide proportions.

Beneath towering cottonwood trees there was on the ranch a small pool of water. The pool was fed by a flow of artesian water, and in the pool there were several small fish—Yaqui Chubs. These were deemed to be nearing extinction by the Conservancy and must be preserved at all cost. It is said that the subject fish inhabits the streams of Old Mexico by the thousands.

As the conservers of all things great and small—particularly their lucrative non-tax paying, non-profit business—ruminated and considered, other potential buyers of the Slaughter Ranch appeared on the horizon. One real-estate broker headquartered around Santa Fe, New Mexico, often visited the ranch, and thought of perhaps buying the ranch, lock, stock, and barrel. My client flew in to Tucson from his headquarters in the eastern United States. We met in Douglas and drove out to the Slaughter Ranch, where we met Ed Williams, erstwhile college professor, now a real-estate broker.

John Slaughter Ranch Headquarters (restored)

Along the road from college professor to real-estate broker dealing primarily in ranch properties, Ed had taken on the garb, demeanor, and lingo of a genuine cowboy. His new bright red Lincoln Town Car was somewhat at odds with his western persona.

We toured the property; saw the old shallow concrete storage tanks; the reservoir, Yaqui Chub pool; the fields, and agricultural remains of bygone days—some probably dating back to John Slaughter's time. The remodeled ranch house was inspected, attention being called to the bathtub installed in Slaughter's days in a corner of the kitchen. The table where John played poker, with his large-gauge shotgun loaded with buckshot resting on the table. The spot where Slaughter's foreman had been killed just in back of the main house was pointed out. The story of the Indian baby girl that Slaughter had rescued and brought back to the ranch to be raised as his daughter, and her tragic death—all were told.

Again we toured the range and stopped once more at the Chub pool. This was real-estate broker Ed's favorite place on the entire ranch. He said he had hoped to put together sufficient capital to purchase the ranch, but had been unsuccessful in his efforts.

My client said he had read some about John Slaughter, and this brought on some comments by your scribe and Ed. It was told that when Slaughter set out on the trail of some outlaw or outlaws, he was always accompanied by a large, formidable black man, African-American, Afro-American, man of color, whatever. He apparently was completely devoted to Slaughter, and was referred to as "Slaughter's Nigger." Totally unacceptable in modern times. Slaughter and his companion would often return with the outlaw horses, firearms, and gear, but the outlaws were never seen or heard of again. Slaughter did not believe in the inconvenience of bringing them back alive.

John Lawrence Sullivan (John L. Sullivan) was born in 1858, and ruled as the heavyweight champion from 1882 to 1892. On tour in the west, he stopped in Tombstone and fought a few exhibition matches. He was challenged by Slaughter's Nigger. John L. said Slaughter's man gave him "a few bad moments," and he decided he had better "put him away as quickly as possible."

My client thought some and said he was not in the land-speculation business, and did not see how the Slaughter property could be financially viable. Why, said Ed, that should not be a problem at all, and my client asked what Ed had in mind. With this artesian water, the topography, the fallow fields there was a commercial undertaking that is sure fire, says Ed. It is this, he continued: Catfish, Bullfrogs, and Christmas Trees. My client looks around a bit, and back at Ed. Catfish, bullfrogs, and Christmas trees, he says, in a somewhat puzzled voice.

This is the way it works, Ed says: With this artesian water it is a simple business to put in ponds in which the catfish will be farm raised. When the catfish are harvested, the offal from them is fed to the bullfrogs, which are, of course, in ponds entirely separated from the catfish. The bullfrogs are harvested, frog legs processed—maybe frozen—and the remainder of the frogs ground up for fertilizer which is spread around the Christmas trees planted on the once fallow fields.

The client appears interested, and repeats "catfish, bullfrogs and Christmas trees" a few times, as though getting used to the idea. He did not make an offer on the Slaughter Ranch, and it was ultimately sold and preserved for the general public to visit.

Know all Men by these Presents:

THAT *J. H. Slaughter of Tombstone Arizona Territory* is

held and firmly bound unto *Fred Beebee of Tombstone Arizona Territory*

in the sum of *Forty thousand ($40,000.00)* Dollars, *lawful* of the United States of America, to be paid to the said *Fred Beebee* *his* executors, administrators or assigns; for which payment well and truly to be made *we* bind *ourselves Our* heirs, executors and administrators, firmly by these presents. Sealed with *our* seal and dated the *22d* day of *April* A. D. one thousand eight hundred and ~~seventy~~ *eighty One.*

The Condition of the above obligation is such, that if the above bounden obligor shall on the *22d* day of *May* A. D. one thousand eight hundred and ~~seventy~~ *eighty one* make, execute, and deliver unto the said *Fred Beebee* or to *his* assigns (provided that the said *Fred Beebee* shall on or before that day have paid to the said obligor the sum of *Forty thousand five ($45,000.00)* Dollars, *in lawful Money* of the United States of America, the price by said *Beebee agrees* agreed to be paid therefor), a good and sufficient deed for conveying and assuring to the said *Fred Beebee*

free from all incumbrances, all *their* right, title and interest, estate, claim and demand, both in law and equity, as well in possession as in expectancy, of, in or ~~to that certain portion, claim and mining right, title or property on~~ *in* certain vein or lode of rock containing precious metals of gold, silver and other minerals, and situated in the Mining District, County of and ~~and described as follows, to wit:~~ *to the following described mining Claims, and Mining Rights to-Wit; the "Cow Boy" Lode or Vein, being a Silver bearing Vein also the "Square and Compass," and the "Victoria" Each being Gold bearing lodes or veins, of quartz rock All of said lodes or veins, & Mining rights are Situate, lying and being in the San Jose Mountains in the State of Sonora.*

Then this obligation to be void, otherwise to remain in full force and virtue.

Signed, Sealed and Delivered in the Presence of *William Wilkerson* *J. H. Slaughter* [SEAL.]

San Jose Mountains (Sonora, Mex.) mining-claims sale to John Slaughter, 1881

Territory of Arizona, ss.
County of Yavapai.

On this *twenty second* day of *April* A. D. One Thousand Eight Hundred and *eighty one* before me, WILLIAM WILKERSON, Clerk of the District Court, Third Judicial District, in and for said County and Territory, duly commissioned and sworn, personally appeared

J. H. Slaughter

personally known to me to be the individual described in and who executed the foregoing instrument; who acknowledged to me that *he* executed the same freely and voluntarily, and for the uses and purposes therein mentioned.

IN WITNESS WHEREOF, I have hereunto set my hand and affixed my official seal the day and year in this certificate above written.

William Wilkerson

Clerk.

San Jose Mountains (Sonora, Mex.) mining-claims sale to John Slaughter, 1881 (page 2)

The Chiricahua Journals

136   ARIZONA.

Fort Whipple,

Yavapai Co, (see Whipple Barracks)

Galeyville P O,

Cachise Co, 60 miles n e of Tombstone, is a thriving mining town in the California district. It occupies a picturesque site in the midst of shady oaks, on a green sward mesa-land, in a cool corner of the Chiricahua Mountains, with the cold and clear waters of Turkey Creek coursing through its streets. In the vicinity are numerous mines, which are being energetically developed, and yielding high-grade ore. Among the number is the Texas, the owners of which have recently put up a smelter, and are now shipping bullion. The mountains on which the town is situated are noted for the grandeur of their scenery, and will no doubt soon become a favorite resort for tourists. A daily line of stages maintains communication with San Simon, a station on the S. P. R. R. 25 miles distant.

Avery Frank & Co, lumber, doors, windows and blinds
Babcock N J, liquor saloon
Barnhart & Reeves, liq'r saloon
Broughton W W, attorney-at-law and notary public
Burdick J F, boot and shoemaker
Carr David P, attorney-at-law
Cummings D W, livery and feed stable
Davidson D E, watchmaker and jeweler

Ellingwood George, justice of the peace
Galey John H, president Galeyville Town-site Co.
Galeyville Hotel, S M Wessels proprietor
Galeyville Townsite Co, John H Galey, president; H B Maxson, secretary
Garcia H A, butcher
Greenwood A P, milk dairy
Harrington W C, blacksmith and wagonmaker
Herring & Spencer, house and sign painters
Higbee A C & Co, general merchandise
Holterman & Hollings, liquor saloon
Johnson Rosa Mrs, restaurant
Kattenhorn George, liq'r saloon
Kelly Thomas, blacksmith and wagonmaker
Kennett P, restaurant and liq'r saloon
Kimbell Charles J, assayer
Lewis J H, physician
Maxson H B, secretary Galeyville Town-site Co, and U S deputy mineral surveyor
McAllister M & Co, butchers
McCandless F & Co, general merchandise
McCandless Frank, notary public
McCarthy —, liquor saloon
McClelland & Pearson, liquor saloon
McConnachie J, liquor saloon
New Mexico and Arizona Stage Co, A C Rynerson & Co, agents
Pascholy & Ray, lumber, doors, windows and blinds
Rynerson A C & Co, general merchandise
Sessions C D, attorney-at-law and notary public

Galeyville, 1881: *The Arizona Business Directory and Gazetteer of Manufacturers & Professional Men in the Territory of Arizona*

GALEYVILLE

On the eastern side of the Chiricahua Mountains, in the late 1870s, a mining rush began that would continue into the twentieth century. The California Mining District was organized, encompassing the mines and prospects. A boom town rose up in a flurry of activity. The town was named Chiricahua City and was located a mile north of the spot where Galeyville would be established a year after Chiricahua City came to life. Tucson's *Daily Arizona Citizen* newspaper reported the boom as follows in its November 24th, 1880 edition:

"I will say that a new camp with a boom is springing up here and a town is being laid off. The people in camp commenced to take and improve the lots as fast as marked off. It is located on a beautiful mesa or plateau of land, with at least 200 acres without a break, and slightly undulating toward San Simon Valley. The rush for lots became a stampede. Tents went up every fifteen minutes; fence poles, wickyups, hockells and all kinds of cheap improvements were in order . . . . The new town of Chiricahua City looks more and more like New York City every day; and then it looks some like Rio Janeiro [*sic*], having a large plaza 300 feet square in the center of town, with an avenue eighty feet wide on each side. And around this plaza the racket commences. A.C. Rynerson Co. are going to move their store on to the northeast corner; the Dickson House will adorn the southeast corner, as Mrs. E.A. Dickson is now putting up temporary houses so as to be ready to accommodate with restaurant and lodging house in a few days; Douglas Gray will have his assay office at the southwest corner, and other business houses will soon fill up the rest of the space. There are from 30 to 40 people coming into the camp every day, most of them from the eastward. . ."

BUSINESS DIRECTORY AND GAZETTEER. 137

Shotwell C S & Co, groceries, liquors, mining supplies, etc

Small B, proprietor Small's Hotel

Smith A E, groceries and provisions

Smith Seward, justice of the peace

Thomas Martha Miss, laundry

Tomlinson J H, liquor saloon

Vaughn Thomas, bakery

Waring & Co, baths

Waring S W & Co, liq'r saloon

Weidenhofer F, fruits and tobacco

Wessels S M, proprietor Galeyville Hotel

Gila Bend P O,

Maricopa Co, 60 miles s w of Phœnix, is a station on the line of the Southern Pacific R. R.

Carscadin Frederick, groceries

Noonan Daniel, general merchandise and postmaster

Gillette P O,

Yavapai Co, 60 miles s e of Prescott, on the Agua Fria Creek. Here is located the mill of the Tip Top Silver Mining Co, which is constantly in operation, crushing the rich ore brought from the mine, nine miles distant. Stages from Phœnix and Prescott pass daily, and a branch line runs to Tip Top.

Anderson John, general merchandise and postmaster

Burfeind Martin, boardinghouse and saloon

Curtis G W, boarding-house and saloon

Larsen James, blacksmith and wagon-maker

Trotter J, justice of the peace

Globe P O,

The county seat of Gila County, situated on the banks of Pinal Creek, near the eastern base of the Pinal Mountains, 60 miles, as the road goes, or 45 miles in an air-line, northeast of Florence, is an incorporated village, well built with numerous stone and brick buildings, and possessing a population of about 1,400. Settlers and prospectors closely followed the expulsion or pacification of the Indians, and in their mountain fastnesses, by their "tanks" and watering-places, and in their pleasant valleys they have discovered the vast deposits of ore or the fertile intervale, and there have made their homes and proceeded to develop the wealth so long concealed from the industries of the world. Thus were the rugged regions of Gila penetrated, the mines of Globe discovered, a district organized, and a village built. The first discoveries were made in 1875; the building of a town commenced shortly; then came that unvarying evidence of enterprise and enlightenment, the newspaper; and on the 4th of January, 1881, was held an election for mayor and all the officers necessary for the exercise of city government. Such advancement is only witnessed in the rich mining regions of the West. The growth of Globe has been rapid, and its

10

Galeyville, 1881: *The Arizona Business Directory* (page 2)

Chiricahua City was very short lived. The Morrow family has for many years owned the land where it was located; no trace can now be found of this boom town. Less than a year after the *Daily Arizona Citizen*'s exuberant article, *The Arizona Business Directory and Gazetteer of Manufacturers & Professional Men in the Territory of Arizona* (published by W.C. Disturnell, San Francisco, 1881) showed only one lone listing for Chiricahua City, "assayer and engineer" John W. Gray.

In the meantime, John H. Galey—an oil man from Titusville, Pennsylvania—and his partners organized the Texas Consolidated Mining and Smelting Company. Their first ten-day smelter run late in the year of 1881 produced 80,000 pounds of lead—and an undisclosed amount of silver bullion—from ore that assayed 45 percent lead and 60 ounces of silver per ton.[1]

The nearby town of Galeyville—with its mine and smelter—soon absorbed the people and buildings of Chiricahua City. By January 6, 1881, Galeyville had its own post office, with Frank McCandless as both postmaster and notary public. Later that year, *The Arizona Business Directory* listed no fewer than 46 entries for Galeyville—including the A.C. Rynerson store originally planned for Chiricahua City.

An article appearing in the *Galeyville Bulletin* newspaper in 1881 (and quoted in the *Arizona Business Directory*) echoed the effusive tone of the Tucson paper's earlier article about its now-defunct sister city:

> The grandeur of the scenery in many of the mountain ranges of Arizona is unsurpassed. On the occasion of a visit by a party of pleasure seekers, including Congressman Springer, of Illinois, to Cave Creek, a romantic spot in the Chiricahua Mountains, the *Galeyville Bulletin* says:
>
> "In this region is a climate affording a perfect sanitarium of perpetual summer, and a wealth of natural scenery excelling in gorgeous beauty the most attractive resorts in Europe or America.
>
> "To the southeast, south and west, there towers nigh unto the clouds a thousand columns, peaks and domes, interspersed with massive structures resembling castles, from which steep declivities, studded with pine, in terraced sections merge from

---

[1] A little-known fact about ore smelted in Galeyville was that tons of extremely high-grade silver ore were being mined and transported to Galeyville from the Josephine Mine in the northern part of the Chiricahua Mountains. The Josephine was a small surface bonanza that soon played out, and this may have been instrumental in the demise of Galeyville.

For an alternative explanation of the source of John Galey's high-grade silver, see the section entitled "Galeyville Days, 1880 to 1908" in the chapter "Digging Up Skeletons: Carson Morrow's Chiricahua Bull Sheet."

either side into a level valley of irregular width, through which the sparkling waters of Cave Creek flow until lost in the sands of the broad acres of San Simon Valley.

"The valley, on entering the mountain gorge, resembles one vast orchard, with now and then a towering pine to dispel the illusion, while along the base, at convenient intervals on either side, are numerous caves that have evidently, from their smoked condition, been the home of the Indian, and from which it took so many years of tedious warfare to dislodge them.

"The scene, the magnificence of all its surroundings, so charmed Mr. Springer that he concluded to use his influence to have the entire Cave Creek region set apart as a public park, save and except the valley, where he believes, sooner or later, will rise a city of no mean proportions. To use the language of our distinguished visitor, 'I have made the tour of Europe, visited all the enchanting spots of Switzerland, crossed the Alps, and climbed the Pyrenees, that I might view the places so appreciated by man, and returned home to find a spot more lovely, and attractive, and sublime than I had witnessed in all my travels.'"[2]

In 1882, ore shipments were delayed and the Texas Mining and Smelting Company went bankrupt. Galeyville miners attempted to continue operations, but soon suspended mining and smelting efforts.

The post office was discontinued on May 31, 1882.

The town of Galeyville, which had contained a post office, six stores, eleven saloons, two restaurants, two meat markets, two blacksmith shops, two corrals, an assay office, a doctor's office, over forty houses, a number of tents, and various places of residence scattered for miles along East Turkey Creek, soon fell abandoned. By 1911 nothing remained of Galeyville but the smelter slag dump and benched areas where buildings and tents once stood.

---

[2] Congressman Springer's true impressions of the Chiricahuas—or at least, Galeyville—may have been less favorable than those reported in the *Bulletin*. In a letter written September 17th 1881 by Joseph Bowyer, the manager of Galey's Texas Consolidated Mining and Smelting Company, Bowyer laments the behavior of the outlaw "Cow-boy" gangs (whose best-known members were probably the notorious "Curly Bill" Brosius—also sometimes spelled "Brocius" or "Brocious"—and the Clantons of Tombstone's infamous OK Corral):

"The cow-boys frequently visit our town and often salute us with an indiscriminate discharge of fire arms ... sometimes going to the length of shooting the cigar out of one's mouth; this produces a nervous feeling, among visitors especially. ... I would refer you to Hon. Wm. Springer of Illinois ... who probably remembers the situation as it appeared to him at the time of his visit here."

(Quoted from a letter printed in John P. Wilson's *Islands in the Desert: A History of the Uplands of Southeast Arizona*; Las Cruces, N.M., 1987)

In the 1900s a family named McGinty filed a homestead that included the old Galeyville townsite. After they had lived on and used the land for agricultural purposes for the required five years, they obtained title to the land. The property was sold to the then owners of the Z—T Ranch, and at last was owned by Herman Kollmar. His widow, acting upon the advice of Herman's lawyer, was convinced that she could become wealthy by not only selling the ranch, but by creating a subdivision of what had become known once again as Galeyville. In later years when asked how she had become involved with the subject lawyer, Mrs. Kollmar replied because he had been Herman's lawyer. She further stated that she had in the early 1960s paid the lawyer $50,000.00 to "get rid of him."

Galeyville was surveyed and divided into over one hundred lots—most of which were suitable for perhaps nothing more than grazing Alpine goats. A commercial area was set aside where there would be restaurants, hotels, and various stores. A travel trailer was placed near the public road through the property. The year was 1961. Mrs. Kollmar moved to Scottsdale, Arizona, and awaited the flood of anticipated wealth. Several real-estate sales people occupied the travel trailer and lurked like trap-door spiders waiting for moneyed customers. On warm summer afternoons they were oft seen lounging beneath sycamore trees, in varied states of intoxication from the copious bottles of beer they had consumed.

One day one of the would-be sellers of real property said it looked pretty grim. No lots had been sold and it was a long drive over rough roads—at least in part—to reach any town where food and drink could be purchased. Everyone agreed, they hooked up their trailer and left.

The years went slowly past, strangers came, but none wanted to call Galeyville home. I had taken a couple of weeks away from the San Juan Mine, taking a crash course in 1976 for required hours, took the state exam and was issued a real-estate broker's license. On a part of the Morrow ranch holdings, Patricia and I had taken up residence, and one of our borders was shared by Galeyville. After leaving the San Juan, I was now a full-time resident. My sales experience—for the family as well as clients—was over a broad range which included Santa Cruz, Pima, and Cochise Counties, and many different types of properties. When someone wanted to sell a property, and they contacted me, and I preferred to sell their property, I would list it.

Mrs. Kollmar solicited my services as a real-estate broker, and in 1981 the Galeyville property was listed for sale. Some cattle ranches had been divided into forty acre parcels and were being sold. Audrey Morrow Miller was involved in selling the parcels. A telephone call came, and I was informed that some lookers had come by, did not like the forties, and she had mentioned that I had listed Galeyville. The presumed customer said he could not handle such a property, but his neighbor in Tucson probably would be interested. Audrey said I should expect a telephone call, and she deemed this to be a referral (that would be twenty percent of the commission I would be paid). I replied that was fine, remembering the client her firm was showing a property. The client said he was not interested in their listing. He had seen a sign advertising a property with R.W. Morrow the agent. That, in the estimation of Audrey's firm, constituted another "referral." On the flip side, she threw some lucrative deals my way from time to time.

The telephone call came, a meeting place was arranged—actually on the site of old Chiricahua City. The customer and spouse arrived. He looked around and declared that this area did not look at all like the pictures his neighbor had given him. It was explained that those pictures—in the brochure of the firm his neighbor had talked to—were of Cave Creek Canyon which was six miles away. The presumed buyer then said Turkey Creek looked like any one of many ravines running out in to Death Valley. He was already beginning to be an irritation, and I said that perhaps he should go and look at property in Death Valley.

He and his wife did buy the property—Galeyville—for an all-cash price, which suited the elderly Mrs. Kollmar.

The buyer was not a bad neighbor, as he was always on a mission to correct first the school system, then the Telephone Co-op … and the list went on, as he continued—as he oft stated—"To fight the good fight."

THE MYSTERIES OF ADVERTISING

Louise's physician husband had died, and she stayed on for a few years living in their country home. It consisted of 45 acres of land, a custom-built manufactured home, well, garden plot, and an older house. Louise decided to sell and move away. She called and wanted to know if I would be interested in acting as her agent. A trip was made to the property, information collected, and the property listed for sale. It was located on the Arizona/New Mexico state-line road approximately 50 miles from the town of Douglas, Arizona. A well done-up property with great sweeping views of the valley and the Chiricahua Mountains.

Seeking a buyer close to home, an advertisement of the property was typed and delivered, along with proper payment, to the *Douglas Dispatch*. The first run of the ad would be for four days. The *Dispatch* at the time was printed and circulated six days a week.

The Ad (as delivered):

IN THE SHADOWS OF THE CHIRICAHUA MOUNTAINS CUSTOM BUILT MANUFACTURED HOME AND TWO BEDROOM OLDER HOME ON 45 ACRES. WELL, SEPTIC SYSTEM, GARDEN PLOT, LANDSCAPED, 50 MILES FROM DOUGLAS, BORDERS A PUBLIC ROAD. FOR FURTHER INFORMATION PLEASE CALL R.W. MORROW, BROKER. [*telephone number stated*].

Rural mail delivery is at times sporadic, and the receipt of the *Douglas Dispatch* even more so. A few days went by and the much-anticipated advertisement of Louise's property checked.

The Ad (according to the *Dispatch*):

IN THE SHADOWS OF THE CHIRICAHUA MOUNTAINS

This was followed by a blank space, of size to accommodate the remainder of the advertisement, of which there was not a single word. A call to the advertising department of the *Dispatch*: "The advertisement of a property I have for sale that begins, 'IN THE SHADOWS OF THE CHIRICAHUA MOUNTAINS'." A moment of silence, then: "Okay, I have it. What's wrong with it?" Stunned silence for a moment as this is digested. "Several things are wrong. It is not complete. There is nothing about *what* is 'IN THE SHADOWS OF THE CHIRICAHUA MOUNTAINS,' *where* it is located, and *whom* to call for further information." Nothing from the *Dispatch* people for a moment: "Okay, we will correct the ad and run it for the allotted time—no further charge." We would hope not.

Time goes by and the *Dispatch* arrives once again. The Ad is again checked. It now sets forth some of the information, but not all. Another call is made and the *Dispatch* people give their solemn pledge that all will be "taken care of."

"Listen you Dispatchers, and set down something that we may challenge the words of Omar Khayyam, 'The Moving Finger writes; and, having writ, Moves on: nor all thy Piety nor Wit Shall lure it back to cancel half a Line, Nor all thy Tears wash out a Word of it'."

"I don't know no Omar, but the ad will be in the paper beginning tomorrow." The paper arrives via rural delivery. Unbelievably, everything is correct—except the name and number to be called are not listed. Yet again another call to the *Dispatch*. All is reviewed, and when the advertising people say all is okay, they are asked to please read the advertisement. They are then asked to read The Ad once again. The *Dispatch* arrives and at long last—two weeks—all is set forth in print, and correctly. Day one and no calls; day two and still nothing; day three, nothing, maybe the wrangling with the *Dispatch* is after all for nothing.

Day four—the last—and a call comes from Douglas. "We have been away on vacation, just returned yesterday, and saw your Ad this morning. We are interested in looking at the property."

We met at Louise's property. They looked. They considered. They offered. Louise accepted. The property sold. Verily, the world of advertising moves in strange and wonderful ways.

WHITE MARBLE

In the northern end of the Chiricahua Mountains, a few miles south and east of Fort Bowie and Apache Pass, there is a marble quarry. Along Highway I-10 between Bowie and San Simon, on the south side of the highway in a field, there were, and perhaps are still, two large white blocks of rock. They are marble that was hauled on wagons pulled by metal-tired, steam tractors, to that place from the quarry.

In 1909, Denver investors formed the Arizona Marble Company, with initial capital reported to be $250,000.00. Mining claims were located—usually placer claims[1]—in several locations, but the principal production came from the claims near Fort Bowie. Active work, with John G. Kerr as manager, began in the summer of 1910. The marble quarried and processed was described as white, with dark veinings, and a flesh tint. Construction of bank buildings in Denver, Colorado, Missoula, Montana, and Champaign, Illinois, used marble from the quarry.

Total production figures for the Arizona Marble Company were reported to be 5,043 cubic feet, valued at $10,086. The Santa Rita Granite, Marble and Mining Company's successor company was the sole firm quarrying marble in southern Arizona in 1966.

In the Chiricahua Mountains, in East Whitetail Canyon, the Arizona Marble Company located and patented a placer claim of 143 acres, which is approxi-

---

[1] In the United States, a placer claim grants the right to mine on public land to a discoverer of valuable minerals (usually gold) contained in loose material such as sand or gravel.

mately a mile and half east of the Chiricahua National Monument. The placer claim was named the White Marble.

The H Y L Ranch acquired the Chiricahua Mountain claims from the Marble Company. The claims were of little use to the owners of the ranch—Sam and Josie Lawhon Moseley—and they sold them. Ralph Morrow hoped to trade land in Whitetail Canyon for Forest land in Cave Creek, and he bought the White Marble with that in mind. It seemed a logical trade for the Forest Service as the White Marble is surrounded by National Forest land, and Morrow would trade the 143 acres for substantially less Forest land which was adjoining deeded land he owned in Cave Creek. In the bureaucratic intelligence ever evident in things government, they refused to trade. The White Marble was sold at a giveaway price to one of Morrow's friends.

The friend visited the property often, dreamed of various things to do with the property, drew up a will, and one day died. After a few years, the heirs of Morrow's friend decided they would sell the White Marble Placer Claim, and I became their agent. The price they asked was a substantial amount for the time. Probably no buyers would be found nearby. An advertisement was placed in the Los Angeles newspapers. A college professor and his wife, who was a speech therapist, lived in Pennsylvania. They saw the advertisement, and called. The professor flew west, we met on the property, and he inspected the claim.

This is the property we have been looking for, the professor declared. Isolation, surrounded by National Forest. The professor's field was anthropology. His spouse was working on a PhD. They had sold a farm, and wished to move west. Enjoy a somewhat Robinson Crusoe existence. They bought the property.

The White Marble has a picturesque setting, not readily accessible. The purchasers built a house, drilled a well, installed solar panels. There are times when an imagined life becomes reality, and reality is not exactly what was imagined. Sometimes something is heard about the professor. The property has been on the market for several years. Dreams dreamed, and dreams lost.

A FEW RULES OF THUMB

Rules of thumb, red flags, whatever the designation, this perhaps should head the list as "Rule Number One": If a seller, if a buyer, do not proceed in good faith, then contracts and agreements as thick and as detailed as the United States Tax Code are of little value. So many years past, when I was introduced to the world of real estate, we used a one-page, legal-sized, small-print document that met almost every need. The years went by, and the contracts were expanded. Each two years brokers and sales people were required to attend real-estate classes on various subjects before a license could be renewed.

A new residential sales contract had surfaced in Tucson. The instructor, explaining in detail the merits of the new contract caused a broker and member of the Tucson Board of Realtors to voice his disapproval. He had opposed the new contract, and went on to name a particular broker who had championed the new contract. The named broker, the fellow classmate said, was trying to cover all possibilities as he was the most-sued real-estate dealer in Tucson. True or not, whether the convoluted contracts now in use protect both buyer and seller and real-estate agents, may or may not be true.

Rule Number Two: Avoid at all costs the "I don't know exactly what I am looking for, but I will know it when I see it" buyer. This is a tough one, as this usually does not surface until numerous properties have been presented to the alleged buyer. Determine what the buyer is looking for when first you meet him-her-it. If the "I don't know what I am looking for, but I will know it when I see it" surfaces, suggest that when he-she-it have figured that one out, you may have a property to show them. That will probably put the subject in the "Be Back," category, and they will never be heard from or seen again.

Rule Number Three: Beware the "Money is no object" situation. Some examples: Mary, saleswoman, says she has a customer who is looking for a large farm, ranch, or combination of both. "Will you go along and help me out here?" she asks. The customer volunteers that "Money is no object." Farms and ranches are inspected. Mary's customer asks reasonable questions about many things pertaining to each property. Evening nears and it is decided, before driving the distance back to Tucson, that some nourishment is required. The customer also, since we agents are paying, partakes of several alcoholic beverages. Mr. Customer, you mentioned that "money is no object," exactly how much money do you have to invest? Why, says Mr. Customer, I have $3,500.

There was a seller of real estate whom I had represented for several years. She had split off and sold several parcels of a choice mountain property that she owned. Approximately 26 acres with all the improvements—house, shop, well, etc.—remained. With regard to legal divisions of property, it was either–or time: either all was sold or all was kept by my client.

Would-be "buyers" come to look at the 26 acres: We are looking for a property on which we will live, perhaps have a bed-and-breakfast business, conduct bird-watching tours, that sort of thing.

What sort of money are you thinking of investing? My client—I represent the seller, however, everyone involved in any transaction will be dealt with fairly—is not interested in carrying back a note secured by a Deed of Trust on the subject property. You will have to come up with the cash, or arrange financing. Lending institutions are generally reluctant to finance remote properties.

"Money is no object," say the potential "buyers." As Mr. Toad in the *Wind In The Willows* classic said: "I've heard that song before."

Here, say the prospective "buyers" on their second visit to the property, is what we have in mind: First, we suggest that the seller pay all closing costs. We will enter into an agreement to purchase the property, with the condition that we live in the home. We will make no down payment. The purchase will be so structured that we can split off four-acre parcels, which we will sell, and the funds will be paid directly to the seller, who will release the parcel to be sold. We will price the four-acre parcels such that the seller will realize her full purchase price, while we retain ten acres with all of the improvements. This seems most satisfactory, the alleged purchasers say.

The "buyers" are asked to repeat their proposal. Your scribe then says: "I do not wish to be excessively rude, but your proposal has just won a place in my top ten most ridiculous real-estate schemes and scams list." The "buyers" leave and were never seen again.

Incidentally, the property was eventually purchased, improvements made, and the land preserved.

Rule Number Four: Watch out for perennially bickering "couples."

Sometimes a couple, a man and woman who have been married a number of years, detest one another, but for some unknown reason—perhaps trying to live longer than their partner—stay together. They will never buy a property. What one likes, the other objects to—they play "good buyer-bad buyer." An offer had been made contingent upon a survey. The agent is advised to be on hand when this is done. The "buyers" arrive to inspect the survey of the mountain property. They are given copies of the surveyor's plat. Here, says the agent, is the surv cap for this point, with the proper notations inscribed. "How do you know that is the point?" The answer is that I witnessed the survey and setting of corners. "That doesn't make any difference. The point could have been moved." And this banter goes back and forth, with first one defending and the other opposing absolutely everything. They did not approve of the survey. There are stepping stones crossing a shallow creek. As the female, Wicked Witch of the West, crosses, she slips and steps both feet in the running water, filling her shoes. This sends her warlock husband into gales of laughter. Another day in the peculiar land of real estate.

Rule Number Five: In commercial and business properties, there are often several buyers or sellers involved. Land transactions in the hinterlands rarely succeed under those conditions.

This is a fill-in-the-blank situation: My brother-sister-girlfriend-boyfriend-shoe-shine-boy is going to come in on the property, and (usually) put up the down payment. Sometimes this does happen.

I have dealt with and been acquainted with a fellow for a number of years. He arrives with his latest going-to-last-forever "female of interest." The mountain parcel does not interest them, but another of twenty acres does. We will buy it in partners. They do. Another adjoining parcel of twenty acres is for sale. We will buy that, also in partners.

My friend, acquaintance, client and customer—in some instances—has a history of a divorce, and each time we meet over twenty years' time, a different girlfriend. I say, listen, this is none of my business, but do you really want to go in partners on these deals? Both parties have considerable money, and they do not finance anything. Certainly, is the reply.

History does sometimes repeat, and the romance ends. How can this mess be cleaned up, I'm asked. There is a lawyer who may be able to help you, give him a call.

Time marches on, and a call comes from the attorney: Mr. So-and-So is my client, and I understand Ms. So-and-So has you as her agent in that she wants to sell her interests in the properties. That is correct, I reply. My client, says the lawyer, is going to sue Ms. So-and-So. Listen, Señor Abogado (Mr. Lawyer), I suggested Mr. So-and-So call you to get this mess straightened out, not to muddy the waters with a bunch of lawsuits. (I am not going to go so far as old Will Shakespeare's character "Dick the Butcher" in *King Henry VI*: "The first thing we do, let's kill all the lawyers.")

A call to Mr. and one to Ms. I am going to send you a Quit Claim Deed clearing the title on the first twenty acres—this to Ms. in favor of Mr. To you, Mr., I am sending a Quit Claim deed in favor of Ms. on the second twenty acres, which Ms. wants to sell. Sign them, have them notarized, and send them back to me. When I receive both Deeds, I will record them, and we can go on about our business.

And everyone lived happily ever after—maybe.

OUR SPECIAL BOYS IN THE MOUNTAINS
WE WILL ALWAYS REMEMBER

In a grove of trees, west of the house, are buried the mortal remains of those fine dogs that have lived and enjoyed life here. Flat creek rocks cover the graves, and there is a marker with each named and the time they were here.

Their spirits live on. These are a few of Patricia's thoughts about, as she says, "Our Special Boys In The Mountains":

ANDY	Pembroke Corgi	1970–1984	Loyal and brave.
HOOT	Lab–Ridgeback	1977–1990	Loved his naps and rabbits.
ROCKY	Lab–Ridgeback	1977–1993	His own man.
CISCO	Lab–Australian Cattle Dog (?)	1984–2000	Loved his family and chasing cows.
PANCHO	Shepherd–Wolf (?)	1984–1990	Loved hunting and running.
NATHAN	Black Lab	1990–2003	Loyal and loving to family.
ALEX	Black Lab	1995–2005	Loved his food and his family. Very sweet.
ELI	Black Lab	2001–2006	Lively and loved running off.
OWEN	Great Pyrenees–Anatolian	2005–	Big dog—*very*. Big heart. Loves family.
TOBE	Black Lab	2007–	Adventurous. Loves running and hunting.

⇑ Cisco, walking along East Turkey Creek, circa 1998

If it had not been for Bonnie and Puff, Andy would have never come to live with us. While we resided at our first Tucson home, one day Patricia brought home a large, red guinea pig, complete with a large cage. She named the new-comer Bonnie. It would be a lonely solitary existence for Bonnie, it seemed. That is until about a week after her arrival, she gave birth to a daughter, which was then named Puff. In contradiction to directions about guinea pigs, they lived in the same cage throughout their lives. Guinea pigs have a life span of about four years, but they lived for over seven, and when Puff died one night, Bonnie lived but two more days. But, that time was seven years in the future.

Bonnie and Puff had supervised outings in the back yard, and in the evenings were often allowed to range about in the living room. There they bucked and ran, jumping over newspapers that were strategically placed. Often Michael or Mollie would be leaned back studying or reading in their rooms, and Bonnie and Puff would be settled on their chests, not moving, sometimes dozing off, or gazing up toward their faces. There was a piece of furniture that was a favorite of Patricia's. It is yet in our household. Several solid walnut rails connect the legs of said furniture. It seemed that Bonnie and Puff sometimes took extra time in their circuit beneath this item, and it was soon discovered the reason. Their teeth were sharpened on the hard wood, and on close inspection, their teeth marks can still be seen.

A new family home was designed and built on the edge of the desert. Bonnie and Puff moved, and their old home was sold. In their new home, they had their own room for them and their cage. When Patricia returned from shopping, her path from vehicle to kitchen was through Bonnie and Puff's room. When they heard her unlocking the outside door, they began to whistle, asking for the grapes or apples or whatever she had brought in addition to their special rations. The new home was constructed on a large lot, which was mostly enclosed by a block wall. A patch of grass was planted for the exclusive use of the guinea pigs.

There was a pet and pet supply store that was owned by two ladies who obviously liked animals. Bonnie and Puff required special rations and special litter, and frequent trips to the store were made. In the pet store there was, among other puppies, a Pembroke Welsh Corgi. The lady pet store owners said they had been able to purchase him from some breeders of Corgis who were in Kansas. His name was "Peats Creek Andrew." For the time, he had a rather high price, and because of this, there were no buyers.

To my associates, the purchase, care, and feeding of dogs and horses, is very important. Where they are concerned, "money is no object." And, with this, I concur. Each trip to the pet store increased their need to purchase the Corgi puppy. One fine day, they could resist no longer, and they returned home with guinea pig supplies and Andy the Pembroke Corgi.

After that, Bonnie and Puff were often exploring their yard and lawn, while being herded around by the hard-working Andy.

§ § §

It was not long after he lost his herd of guinea pigs that Andy left the city, never to return again. It was the mountains and creek where he sometimes joined his Lab companions for a swim and his own herd of cows. They soon learned with whom they were dealing. It had snowed, and Andy was engaged in one of his favorite activities, herding cows. One took exception to such activities, and succeeded in rolling Andy in the snow. She soon was given a proper heel biting by the valiant cowpuncher.

For several years after we settled back in the Chiricahuas, there was extensive fence repair and building to be done. Andy always went along when such recreational activities were taking place. Occasionally, the fence line was on such steep slopes that Andy could not climb them. They were a hard struggle for his fence repair gang. When these places were encountered, Andy waited as he was picked up and set ahead, his person struggling up to repeat the process until the summit was won.

The first years back, we were yet in our "city dude" mode, and had not built a yard fence. We were all free range. One morning I mounted up on a big dun horse, Juan by name, going several miles to another pasture where we had some horses. It was warm, and considering the distance, it seemed advisable to sneak away, leaving Andy at home. His partners at the time, Hoot and Rock, were off hunting rabbits.

Down the road a half mile to the creek, then across another half mile to the first wire gate. Through the gate, fastened again, and Juan and I went onward. Andy had been successfully left behind. Across some more country, and down along Round Valley Wash, and through our second gate. Leading south along a ridge line, there was a trail worn out by animals heading to the spring for water.

Juan was a skittish horse, and scared some riders.

Once in awhile you may get that little shock that usually comes right before a horse is going to buck. He won't pitch, but makes some riders think he will. Juan started acting really nervous like that, looking back as though something was sneaking up behind him. I swiveled around in the saddle, looked all around, and I couldn't see anything. But Juan kept fidgeting and looking back, and I would again check the back trail. Cedars were scattered on the ridge, but not enough for much cover. Finally, on a check behind, I looked *down*, thinking maybe a jumping cactus had somehow caught in Juan's tail.

There was Andy. He had trailed and trotted along to catch up to us. With almost each step Andy's nose bumped one of Juan's rear heels. There was no leaving Andy behind. He may be needed to assist in cow work. Lying in the shade of a big juniper tree was not going to happen, when there was ranch work to be done.

Hoot   Andy   Rocky
Late 1970s

Looking east from the home of Patricia and R. W. Morrow, late 1970s
Corgi Andy deep in tire ruts, with Black Labs Hoot and Rock following

Spirit Dogs racing over the Chiricahua Mountains, 2004

HOOT GIBSON AND ROCKY BALBOA

The Ad, in a Tucson newspaper, stated there were two male puppies, Lab and Ridgeback cross, that needed a good home. The home must be approved by the placers of the Ad, but the puppies would be free. A call confirmed that no one had taken the puppies, and we said we would take one if the owners approved of the home the pups would have. An immediate drive to Tucson was undertaken, and both, not one, of the pups came to live in the mountains. They were named: Hoot and Rocky.

A first memory of the desert dwellers was the evening after they arrived. It rained, and Hoot and Rock, having never experienced rainfall apparently, raced around and around the house as the rain fell. At the time, the dog houses were individual, though with raised wooden floors and carpeting. It was several years past 1977, when Hoot and Rock arrived, that a six-inch-thick concrete slab was poured, to which four-by-four boards were bolted. Wood floors, carpeted of course, completely sealed except for doorways, with roofs with metal roofing, and all painted to match the human home. There were three compartments nearly four feet by four feet in size. That was ample room for cold nights when short-hair dogs may sleep with a hairy companion.

But the new arrivals, in their excited state, did not shelter in one of the individual houses.

Soon Hoot and Rock, with some training from Corgi Andy, settled in to mountain living. Often, when on an outing with the trio, Hoot and Rock displayed their hunting prowess. One may be coursing along a creek or arroyo bank, while the other flushed rabbits out of the bottom land. Working as a team, they caught cottontails and even the fleet-footed jackrabbit. In the springtime, when young rabbits were yet in their nests, Hoot would disappear from his companion hikers. He would arrive home with his sides near bursting, filled with rabbit. Stiff-legged circling and growling by all the dogs would then take place as Rock and Andy accused Hoot of sneaking off without them, and not sharing in his meal of bunnies. Patricia did not like the idea of Hoot murdering young rabbits, but it apparently did not distress Hoot to any degree whatsoever.

Even though Hoot was almost fourteen when he left us, summer heat was not kind to him. Mountain cedar, juniper, oak, and planted pine, spruce, and cypress shaded Hoot on warm afternoons.

It was hot that day, once again at our pastime of fence repairs. Hoot had stayed behind, sleeping beneath a blue spruce. A moment of rest where the fence cornered, and downhill to the creek. A noise beneath a nearby low-growing cedar. There was Hoot and he was in distress, unable to walk. Well, I told my companion fencer, nothing for it, but I will have to carry Hoot to the creek. All on the downward slope. Hoot did not struggle, but his seventy pounds were pressing down for the quarter mile to the creek. Unfortunately, the creek had dried back south toward the high country as it would do in the dry times. As my Dad used to say when riding the mountains, "These horses need to blow a bit." It was time to leave the shade of the sycamores. On up the creek for maybe another four hundred yards, and water. Hoot drank, was sponged, but was unable to travel. More carrying, stopping, sponging, resting, and Hoot began to recover. Now he could travel alone, but the half mile from the creek to the house, with the afternoon sun bearing down, would probably finish him. Those were the days before we had pocket-sized two way radios, and there has never been cell phone service in our area.

Hoot relaxed as he was carried home, perhaps wondering at all the heavy breathing and frequent stops in the shade of any handy tree.

THE CISCO KID AND PANCHO

There is another dog that must be mentioned, though she, as one other, was a tragedy. Her name was Rose, and she was Mollie's Lab. When Mollie's career in the United States Air Force began, she left Rose with us, and we failed her and Rose. Rose was excessively friendly. She liked everyone. One morning she and Hoot and Rock were messing about, and apparently went so far as the road which runs through the property. It is a half mile from the house. Traffic was heavy on the public road. Javelina hunting season was on, and for some reason, an unusual number of hunters were driving about. Someone picked up Rose and drove away. We drove and searched the area, but Rose was either being carefully hidden, or was by then far away.

None were sadder than Andy. Of all the dogs, he was most attached to Rose. When out together, Rose was always near Andy. In one of the pools along the creek, all of the dogs would swim on hot days. When Andy was paddling about, Rose would be in close attendance, ready to lend assistance, if necessary. Within a few days of Rose's dognapping, Andy's health began a downward trend. His appetite was gone. He was interested in nothing, not even in herding cows. He was fading away from a broken heart. One evening he lay down in his house and went to sleep. During the night he died. We dug his grave, wrapped him in a new sleeping bag, and buried him in the grove of trees west of the house. His was the first grave.

Perhaps we should get another puppy, someone said. It was good luck finding Andy in a pet store, maybe we can again be so fortunate. The place was so depressing that we would have taken every dog they had, if possible.

Rather than one puppy, we settled on two. One was supposedly a pure-bred shepherd of some sort, and the other a Labrador Retriever pure bred. Neither were as represented, but that was of no importance. The black Lab was named Cisco, the shepherd Pancho, after the Saturday Matinee adventurers of bygone days.

Pancho, as he matured, we deemed to be part wolf. Cisco was probably Lab and Australian Cattle Dog. It was late the evening we arrived home from

Bath time for Cisco, Pancho looking on, 1984

Tucson, accompanied by the new pups. A flower garden had been fenced in and a dog house, Andy's, placed in the enclosure. The puppies were fed, water set out, and blankets placed over the carpeted floor of the dog house. A light snow began to fall. Welcome to the mountains, Boys.

Morning, noon, and night, Patricia fed, picked up and petted each pup, and cleaned their enclosure. They were taken for several walks each day. The weather was unsettled, and when Cisco and Pancho became tired or uncomfortable, they complained. Each were then picked up and held beneath our raincoats, with their heads peeking out as they enjoyed the outing in solid comfort. Hoot and Rock did not pay much attention to the new Boys. They had other things to do.

On a spring day, Hoot, Rock, Cisco, and Pancho were adventuring afield, followed by your scribe. We had walked down to the creek, cooled feet and parched throats with water brought down from the melting snows. We were skirting around a small point that narrowed down the path homeward. The Boys were all out ahead as I trailed along, carrying a length of sotol [*also known as "Desert Spoon"*] stalk as a walking stick. Suddenly Hoot came around the point, and he was running all out directly toward me. The other dogs were out of sight but in full voice barking. On came Hoot, and just behind him were a half-dozen javelina. Hoot dashed by, and I began poking the javelina with my stick, and they separated, running past me.

Hoot had jumped into a low-growing mesquite bush. His pursuers, bristled and teeth popping, trotted away.

Now Rock, Cisco and Pancho appeared, and a large bunch of javelina was also chasing them. It seemed prudent to move aside and I ran up the hillside. The javelina saw a slower prey and dropped their pursuit of the canines. More stick work was in order as they ran by on each side. The javelina trotted on toward the creek. Every handy mesquite bush had a dog centered in it.

One afternoon at the Morrow home in East Whitetail Canyon, a border collie my parents had at the time saw a couple of javelina and gave chase. Soon the tables were turned and the javelina chased the collie hack toward the house. My Dad was watching this play, and when the javelina were near, he would kick dirt at them and they would again run with the collie in pursuit. And, then all was repeated again.

The Encyclopedia of Dog Breeds lists life spans of many types of dogs, with Labs at 10 to 12 years. Hoot Gibson was almost fourteen when whatever had caused his health problems at an early age caught up to him, and once again we had not heeded Rudyard Kipling's: "There is sorrow enough in the natural way From men and women to fill our day; But when we are certain of sorrow in store, Why do we always arrange for more? Brothers and Sisters, I bid you beware Of giving your heart to a dog to tear." But, then, if you are to dance, you must pay the Piper.

Cisco was a loyal fellow. If other dogs chased after rabbits, he stayed at home. When he and Pancho reached four months of age, and summer was coming on that year of 1984, their walks were a bit longer. Hoot, Rock , Cisco, and Pancho were being accompanied by their manservant. We were going along a wide sand wash where some large oaks offered shade from the warmth of the day. Pancho was a short distance behind. Flood water had carved out a rincón in the sand, with walls about a foot and a half in height. All had skirted the sandy nook, but Pancho came up against the sheer wall of hard sand. He set up a great fuss, ignored by the other dogs, except Cisco, who sped back and dove off the precipice to save his pard.

§   §   §

It was not well thought out the day that we had corralled some cattle and hauled a barrel of water for their overnight stay. Cisco and Pancho rode along in the back of the truck.

The emptied barrel skidded across the truck bed as we rounded a curve. It cut across Cisco's right rear foot, and almost severed the outside toe. A flap of skin held. He was quickly placed in Patricia's lap, and she wrapped the foot in her handkerchief. "If we go ahead and cut that toe off, Cisco will probably limp the rest of his life. There is no dirt on it, let's see if we can do something when we get back to the house." Patricia agreed. We checked to make certain nothing contaminated the wound, applied some antibiotic, set the toe in place and secured it with surgical tape. "I have never seen a dog," Patricia said, "That would leave something like that alone."

The afternoon passed, and Cisco did not so much as lick the bandage. A week passed, and he had not chewed or disturbed the bandaged foot. We waited several more days, and carefully unwrapped the foot. The toe was beginning to heal. It was gently cleaned, a small amount of antiseptic applied, and rebandaged. When the bandage was again removed, the toe was healed, and Cisco seemed none the worse for the injury. A most unusual dog.

Pancho was six years of age. He appeared to be healthy. He was active, ate well, had his required shots, and was wormed when required. One day he was his usual self, but as evening came, he wandered off a short distance from the house. He came back, spent some time in his house, and the evening being warm, lay down in the yard. During the night he died.

Now Rock and Cisco were the last of the four.

THE ARRIVAL OF NATHAN

"Patricia, Rock is going to be fifteen. He can't live forever, and when he goes, Cisco is going to he left alone. We better think about another dog. Why don't you call Custie? She knows everything that is going on around the country, and maybe someone has some pups close to home." Custie (Elizabeth Adell [Miller] Mauzy) and her husband at the time owned the Rodeo Grocery. Custie was our niece, Audrey Morrow Miller's daughter. Everyone liked Custie, and she liked almost everyone. Loyd, her husband, was a both a working cowboy, and a professional rodeo cowboy. Custie was a good horsewoman, and fair roper in her own right.

Custie said she would check around, and in a few days called to say that Dusty Mason had a puppy that needed a home. Dusty was having a house built, but the project was taking longer than anticipated. If we would give the pup, a Lab, a good home, he would give him to us. A trip to Douglas, and to the home of Dusty's parents who were keeping the pup. In from the backyard came the fine black Lab, and took a farewell pee on the carpet, much to the chagrin of Dusty's mother, and the delight of a couple of her granddaughters.

Immediate bonding began as Nathan—Patricia had already named the puppy—rode home in Patricia's lap. A short stop at our creek crossing for Nathan to drink and attend to whatever other business he had. We drove into the yard, which was now an acre fenced around the house. Up ran Cisco in greeting. Patricia's door opened. Cisco saw Nathan and fled around the house.

The nights were growing colder, and Nathan insisted on sleeping on the open back steps. Each evening he would be put to bed in his dog house, and his human would then wait until he was asleep and slip away. Finally, he began sleeping with

Rock. Nathan was loyal and devoted to his family, but suspicious of strangers. As the vet observed when he dropped by to vaccinate the Boys: "That is the first Lab that has ever tried to bite me." Whether horseback or on foot, Nathan and Cisco were always nearby.

Rock was past sixteen years when he gave up on living. He had lived a good, long life. Maybe this applied to him: Once, when I asked my Dad about one of the great hunters and guides, and my Fort Huachuca buffalo punching partner of the summer of 1949, Clell Lee, "How is Clell doing these days, up there on his ranch on the Blue River?" My Dad, Ralph Morrow, thought a moment and said: "Not very good. Too many cold mornings around the camp fire." It seems to happen to man, woman, and beast.

The Boys were leaving and going on to the happy hunting ground. They were all there but Cisco and Nathan, the last of the Mountain Boys. And, then, it looked as though Cisco may be the last. A tick caused an infection in Nathan's ear, and but for the work of the vet as Nathan lay on the kitchen table, he would have died. It was winter, and Nathan and Cisco slept indoors as Nathan recovered. Cisco slept on a bed of blankets Patricia arranged for him. At first, Nathan slept on a couch, until that arrangement was stopped—then he began sleeping in a large easy chair. Patricia gave up. When Nathan needed to go outside, and Michael was visiting at the time, any handy sleeper would be nudged by a cold nose in the ear. When Cisco and Nathan had taken care of outside business, they promptly settled down once more indoors.

Alex was born on Mother's Day in 1995. His owners drove down from Tucson and delivered him to us. They left with tears flowing. Alex was a great dog in heart, temperament, loyalty, and size. He grew into a blocky, strong individual of 110 pounds—mostly muscle. Though all her dogs were held in high esteem, Alex had a special place in Patricia's heart. Though not demonstrative, Alex was affectionate with his family and somewhat reserved with strangers. His only failing was his appetite. He did not tear up shrubs, carpeting, hoses, or any other thing, as some may do; he did like food, and he would eat anything. He did not kill things from mice to larger animals for sport, he wanted to eat them, and he did. If you tried to take away a dead bird, a dove that may have hit a wire, he would swallow down the entire bird, feathers, beak, and all. He could scarf down a squirrel he had killed with about two bites and a huge gulp.

Cisco was within a few months of seventeen years. There was a day bed for the Boys on the porch, beneath the roofed area. It was surrounded by two-inch by six-inch boards and the mandatory carpeted floor. Days, or mild nights, the Boys liked to sleep there. The December nights were cold, and it was difficult for Cisco to go up the sloping yard to the doghouse condominium. Each evening he rested and waited to be carried up to bed.

Cisco had a good appetite. One evening, Patricia diced a large steak, cooked it, and he ate it with his usual enthusiasm. He would rest a bit before being put to bed. Suddenly there was a noise as something bumped against the house. We dashed outside. Within a minute, Cisco had died.

Now there remained Alex and Nathan.

Another black lab arrived, and he was named Eli. Buttercup, his mother, was an outstanding, sweet, yellow Lab. Somehow, as oft happens, his father, Buster, was not in attendance and was elsewhere on the premises. Held in Patricia's lap, Eli complained most of the seventy-mile drive home. He soon was comforted by Nathan, and they became bunk buddies, much to Alex's satisfaction. Alex was a warm sleeper. Nestled down with his head and shoulders in his compartment door, he tried to discourage would-be bunk partners; however, sometimes they would squeeze by him and bed down, until Alex moved to another compartment, and all was repeated. He did not beat up on his fellow canines, but they all had a deep respect for him. If younger dogs were becoming excessively rowdy in Alex's opinion, one low growl and a quick look stopped inappropriate behavior.

And Eli was a rowdy. Very athletic, and fleet of foot, probably faster than any dog before his time. He was also destructive, chewing up carpeting, and taking bites out of any woodwork that was at hand.

Owen "fixing" the hose, 2005

ONE REMAINED

Cancer and age caught up to Nathan, and we lost him when he was thirteen, almost fourteen. Alex and Eli were left to hold down the fort.

Coyotes had been killing and eating some goats, so their owners obtained some Great Pyrenees and Anatolian Shepherds. (The name Shepherd in conjunction with Anatolian is incorrect. They have never been used as herders, but are guardians of both livestock and people, as are the Great Pyrenees.) The goat people began to cross the Pyrenees and Anatolians, and from time to time would sell a few puppies. They were contacted about a puppy, and said they would pick out one for us and deliver him when he was a couple of months of age. Are these exceptionally large dogs, the goat-dog people were asked? Oh, they are not too big, they said. And then added: sometimes one will be a bit under three feet at the shoulders and weigh maybe 170 to 180 pounds. That doesn't make much difference, we said, but we really don't need a dog that large. No problem, they said.

One day Owen[1] arrived. He was small, and probably younger than two months. Much holding, comforting, and careful feedings went on for days, and Owen began to grow. Alex and Eli made certain that Owen was well attended at all times. Eli at last had a companion that was as lively and willing to scuffle as he. He would scissor Owen and throw him down, until one day, the tables were turned. Owen was growing. That did not end their play, except when reprimanded by Alex, and then temporarily.

---

[1] There are several origins given for the name "Owen": "young warrior" (Welsh); "young fighter" (Celtic); "born to nobility; young warrior" (Irish); "well born" (Latin). All are apt descriptions of this fine dog.

The year Owen came to live here in the mountains was the same year that we lost the great dog Alex. His eating habits did not contribute to good health, though he was never a Fat Boy. Perhaps, being a large dog shortened his life span. His favorite summertime tree was a blue spruce. When we returned home on a warm day, he would be sleeping and resting beneath his tree, though he had over thirty to choose from in the yard. His greeting was a few thumps

Owen, a very young warrior, 2005

of his tail. Later, when all was settled, he would present himself for petting, conversation, and some massaging.

Eli by then was mature, and Owen grew. How he grew! Ultimately, contrary to the goat people, he was large. Unless you consider an animal with almost no fat weighing 170 pounds, and standing 34 inches at the shoulder, and a length from head to root of tail of 48 inches, *not* large. His protective instincts also developed. If something had raised his suspicions, and you went to investigate, he always put himself between you and the boogie, and leaned into you making sure you did not move. He also believed in an ordered world. Owen was never excessively destructive. However, if a padded bed was placed over the carpet in the dog house, he removed it and ripped it apart. Hoses had been left strung out to water trees. One evening they were coiled, but left near the faucets. The following morning they were stretched out, and three feet of one hose had been bitten off. They were either coiled and stored, or left strung out, and there was no further damage done.

§ § §

Our nearest neighbor was a mile and one half away, living near the public road. He is gone now, but unfortunately not soon enough.

Michael Morrow and Owen, 2008

The telephone cooperative has an annual membership meeting, and in bygone days, that is when a new director from each of the three districts was elected. There are a total of nine directors who serve three-year terms before standing for re-election. A friend who had attended a meeting some years back was asked about the neighbor. It was understood that he had attempted to be elected—but failed in his attempt—to the board of directors.

"That's true," said the friend. "Your neighbor [*if 1½ miles away constitutes being a neighbor*] gave his campaign speech. He said he was new to the area, and wanted to be a director because he wanted to meet people. Land sakes, what a Dumb Old F***." Forever after, until the failed candidate moved away, he was referred to as "DOFF."

This poor excuse for a human had a reputation of shooting other people's dogs. They did not have to be on his property, or involved in any mischief.

One evening Eli and Owen wandered off, and did not come home that evening. Though it was never proven, this is what happened: As the two came along the road, homeward bound, DOFF shot at them. Owen escaped without a scratch. Eli was not so lucky. It must have been torture for him, but Eli made it home. He had been shot across his back near his hind quarters, and his left shoulder was shattered.

Bleeding was stopped, and a sleeping bag spread in the living room. Eli lay down, closed his eyes, and made not a whimper. The vet was called, and he drove the seventy miles from the city as quickly as possible. Eli lay still and did not complain as he examined him. His shoulder is shattered, and he will probably lose his leg. Tucson is the nearest that such can be done. He has obviously lost a great deal of blood, and the gunshot across his back is worrisome as it probably damaged his kidneys. It would have been too much for Eli, and without Eli's stirring or opening an eye, the vet ended his suffering.

Now there was Owen. We had come full circle from the loyal and brave Andy to but one dog, Owen—big dog, big heart, loves family.

Tobe swimming in Turkey Creek, 2008

Owen faced a lonely life, but for his family, until Tobe arrived.

An advertisement in the Tucson paper stated that among many dogs for sale, there were some Labs. A call went out to several, but none would agree to holding a puppy until it was four months of age and could be vaccinated for rabies, as well as other shots. One said he would probably do as we requested, when told where the pup would live. We met, on delivery day, at Willcox, and another sad owner parted with a puppy. Tobe, now nearing three years, is a great companion to Owen. Though Owen yelps occasionally when Tobe bites too deeply as they wrestle, he never hurts his young charge. It is frightening to see Tobe's head in Owen's mouth. They sleep together, and Tobe uses Owen as blanket and pillow when napping.

We hope to have them both for a long while.

Owen and Tobe napping, 2008

Ralph and Juanita Morrow, 50th Wedding Anniversary, 1975
With The Family

A LAST FAMILY GATHERING

Audrey Morrow Miller and Guy Miller, through hard work, good business, years in the saddle, and the wheel of fortune spinning in their favor, finally owned most of the ranches on which they had worked and punched cows. Now Guy could buy as many saddles as he wanted. As he said: "I don't want to sit down for a bowl of chili, and wonder if I have enough money in my pocket to pay for it." He bought twenty head of roping steers each year. He and his compadres practiced team roping on the critters, and Guy became a recognized team roper. Their living quarters evolved from the primitive home they first lived in to a complex of home, guest home, and other refinements.

To celebrate Ralph and Juanita Morrow's fifty-year wedding anniversary in 1975, Audrey, assisted by her friend and exceptional chef, Louise Woodworth, made plans for the event to be held at the Miller Ranch headquarters.

Hundreds of people attended the fiesta that Audrey and Louise prepared. It was to be the last great gathering of family and friends. Within a year, Ralph Morrow had spent too many cold mornings around the campfire. A few short years later, Juanita Morrow was also gone. Although many of the family still remain, in 1995 Audrey's daughter Elizabeth (Custie) Miller Mauzy left us, and in the spring of 2010 Audrey herself joined her parents and Custie.

The last of the real "old timers" are all gone now, as are many of the good old cattle ranches, divided into parcels and sold off.

Progress, some would argue. Others would disagree.

As A.R. Mooney was fond of saying, "A difference of opinion makes both horse races and missionaries."

Ralph and Juanita Morrow, with Audrey and Wayne Morrow, 1936

EPILOGUE

If you pause about five miles west of the town of Portal on the narrow two-lane "42B Forest Road" that winds up Silver Creek to Paradise, you'll see the entrance to the Paradise Cemetery just south of the road. Within its boundaries, there is a modest granite military-style marker inscribed with these words:

RALPH WAYNE MORROW
1ST LT US AIR FORCE KOREA
OCTOBER 27, 1930 – NOVEMBER 19, 2011
BELOVED HUSBAND FATHER PATRIOT

In the obituary I wrote on November 20th, I tried to expand this simple marker's terse summary. But the paragraphs below were not enough to do justice to a life as full as my father's—even the book you're holding barely scratches the surface:

After graduating from Douglas High School in 1948 and studying at the University of Arizona, Wayne joined the United States Air Force in 1952, where his top-gun flying skills and expert marksman abilities moved him rapidly up the ranks as a fighter-pilot: soloing before his 22nd birthday; receiving an officer's commission by the age of 23; and—as a 24-year-old First Lieutenant flying the F-86 Sabre Jet—becoming one of the youngest flight leaders and alert-team captains in the USAF.

Switching gears in 1960, Wayne returned to the University of Arizona, obtaining a Bachelor of Science Degree in Mining Engineering in 1964. As an engineer, he designed high-tension power lines in California, explored for oil in Texas, and supervised copper mines in Arizona.

In the 1970s, Wayne became a licensed real-estate broker and successfully sold land and ranch properties throughout southern Arizona for more than 30 years, along the way earning a reputation for hard work, honest dealing, and an ability to close difficult property sales. He was that all-too-rare real-estate professional who always left all parties to a transaction feeling they had gotten a great deal, as evidenced by his many repeat customers and clients.

In a life where he consistently proved that he could excel in whatever he turned his hand to, Wayne also worked as a fire-fighting "smoke chaser," a Deputy in the Cochise County Sheriff's department, and a fearless cowboy who roped buffalo when they ran free on the hills of Fort Huachuca (between WWII and the Korean War).

He chronicled all of these adventures (and more) in a published book entitled *The Chiricahua Journals*, demonstrating what may have been the greatest of all his talents—namely, as a storyteller with a playwright's ear for wit and a journalist's eye for detail.

Wayne truly merited the title of "Renaissance Man"—but more than that, he was a big-hearted, generous person who left an unforgettable impression on all who met him. He loved all animals, and was a gifted horseman. At the end, he was walking with two of his beloved dogs.

We remaining Morrows still miss him very much—as does anyone who ever knew him. People we barely know still come up to us on the street, just to tell us that.

§   §   §

If you look around the Paradise Cemetery, you'll see the nearby graves and headstones of other Morrows: Carson, Ralph, Juanita, William King and his wife, Eva Corn—and Audrey, with her husband Aubrey Guy Miller, their daughter Custie at their side. This is also the final resting place for many other pioneers and residents of the Chiricahuas, many of whose stories are included in this very book.

I don't believe it's just my imagination, this feeling that those who have lived in "The Mountains" still have a presence there, something that reaches far beyond the Paradise Cemetery's granite, marble, and iron markers. At such times, I believe there must exist a place very much like the one chronicled in these pages.

And in that place, you can find a beaming Juanita Morrow happily tending to her garden, already planning which of her County-Fair prize-winning vegetables will grace that evening's dinner table. Just down the road, a weary, dusty, but happy Alden Ray Mooney, his body unscarred by any bullets in a far-off land, is almost home from a day's hard work "cow-punching" with his buddies at the McClintock Ranch. Nacho Flores pauses for a moment next to the tree he's chopping down, wiping his brow and looking ahead to swapping some stories later that evening with Ray. Carson Morrow reads what he's typed for the next issue of his "Chiricahua Bullsheet," and chuckles with glee at a particularly barbed turn of phrase. On a bluff overlooking the Cave Creek Basin, Ralph Morrow takes a moment on a long mountain ride to savor the view and reflect on how good life is, to be able to spend it doing the thing you love most. At his horse's feet, his Cow Dogs—joined by Patricia Morrow's "Special Boys"—look up and silently agree.

And above them all, up Sulphur Canyon, down Cave Creek, and over Whitetail Canyon, R.W. Morrow roars in his F-86 Sabre Jet—yet still close enough that those on the ground can see his plane's insignia, and even the wide grin on his face.

He'll be home for dinner. Those of us who remember such gatherings know it will be a convivial, lively occasion, full of much laughter and good conversation.

And I know there's a place at that happy table, waiting for all of us.

MICHAEL MORROW,
AUGUST 2014

54th Fighter Intercept Squadron: F86-D Sabre Jets Over Mount Rushmore, 1954
From Left to Right: Lt. R.W. Morrow (676), Lt. D.S. Jones (658, back),
Lt. G. Brannon (644), Capt. W.C. Norris (673)

THE PILOT'S PRAYER

Aloft in solitudes of space

Uphold me with Thy saving grace

O God protect me as I fly

Through lonely ways beneath the sky.

Amen.

CPSIA information can be obtained at www.ICGtesting.com
Printed in the USA
LVOW03s1154050814

397601LV00002B/3/P